COUNTRY MUSIC FOREVER

First published in Great Britain in 2026 by Greenfinch
An imprint of Quercus
Part of John Murray Group

A CIP catalogue record for this book is available from the British Library

HB ISBN 978-1-52945-012-5
EBOOK ISBN 978-1-52945-011-8

10 9 8 7 6 5 4 3 2 1

Design by Hannah Valentine
Illustrations by Travis Knight
Printed and bound in China by C&C Offset Printing Co., Ltd.

MIX
Paper | Supporting responsible forestry
FSC® C008047
FSC
www.fsc.org

Papers used by Quercus are from well-managed forests and other responsible sources.

Quercus
Carmelite House
50 Victoria Embankment
London EC4Y 0DZ

John Murray Group
Part of Hodder & Stoughton Limited
An Hachette UK company

The authorized representative in the EEA is Hachette Ireland,
8 Castlecourt Centre, Dublin 15, D15 XTP3, Ireland (email: info@hbgi.ie)

COUNTRY MUSIC FOREVER

An A-to-Z Celebration of Icons, Songs, and Stories

LAUREN BLACK

ILLUSTRATIONS BY
TRAVIS KNIGHT

greenfinch

CONTENTS

HOW I FELL IN LOVE WITH COUNTRY MUSIC

Country music has been a part of my life for as long as I can remember. Some of my earliest memories are tied to listening to country radio in my parents' car, falling in love with the story of Trisha Yearwood's "She's in Love with the Boy," counting along to the number sequence in Mark Chesnutt's "Too Cold at Home," and watching Alan Jackson command a packed arena at my first concert. In my teenage years, I would act out mock interviews inspired by the ones I watched on CMT and GAC, dreaming that one day I'd be the one asking the questions.

I've always turned to my favorite records to find songs that reflected what was happening in my life, whether it was a song for my first love or my first heartbreak, country music was always there. But the moment that changed everything for me came in 2004 at Kenny Chesney's "Guitars, Tiki Bars, and a Whole Lotta Love" tour. I found my escape in live music that night, and nothing has been the same since. Miraculously, I've turned my love for country music into a career, and it's something I'm thankful for every single day.

Country music has deep roots. As you'll read in the entry on the Bristol Sessions, the genre was built on what was once called "hillbilly music," blending folk, blues, and Appalachian traditions with African American influences (banjo) and Celtic influences (fiddle). Today's country music may sound quite different, often leaning more toward pop, but at its core, what makes country truly country, at least in my opinion, is the storytelling. It has always been about real stories and real people.

On the pages that follow you'll find some of country music's most legendary artists, iconic places, and rising stars shaping the future of the genre. Writing the book brought me so much joy and allowed me to rediscover some of country music's best stories while learning new fascinating facts along the way.

The book is structured in an A to Z format—you can read it front to back, but it's also designed to be fluid, with entries leading to each other through the "see also" sections. The illustrations bring many of the stories to life, and I hope they make you smile as you thumb through the pages.

One of the greatest stories told on these pages is that of resilience. Many of the artists faced repeated rejection, and for most, success didn't happen overnight. Learning that some of the greatest country music stars, such as Lainey Wilson and Luke Combs, had doors slammed in their faces before making it inspired me to keep going, and I hope it does the same for you.

This book is for longtime fans who want to rediscover the stories behind the music, and for new enthusiasts hoping to learn more about the genre. My hope is that it encourages you to revisit old favorites, discover new songs, experience the magic of seeing your favorite artists play, and maybe even take a trip to Nashville.

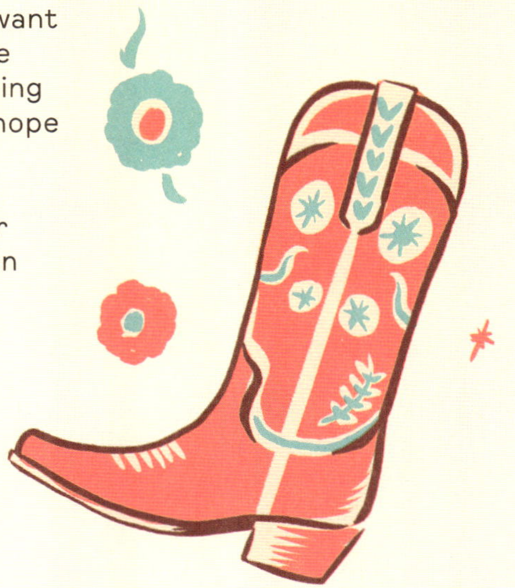

Lauren Black

AN A TO Z OF COUNTRY MUSIC

ACTORS

A

Some country stars don't just sing, they act, too, and not just in music videos. Over the years, many country artists have proved themselves to be as talented on screen as they are on stage.

The crossover goes back to 1929 when Jimmie Rodgers appeared in the 15-minute movie short *The Singing Brakeman*. By the 1930s, Gene Autry had become one of Hollywood's biggest box office draws, starring in countless Westerns. He was followed by Kris Kristofferson, best known for his role in *A Star Is Born*, and of course Dolly Parton, who made her mark in *9 to 5* and *Steel Magnolias*. Then came Kenny Rogers who turned his iconic 1978 hit "The Gambler" into a series of successful TV movies.

In 1990 Reba McEntire made her film debut in the horror movie *Tremors* and went on to star in *The Little Rascals* (1994). Several TV movies followed, as well as her own hit sitcom, *Reba*, which ran for six seasons from 2001. I remember watching *Reba* with my family growing up—we never missed an episode. McEntire continues to be a force on screen with her comedy *Happy's Place* and a string of voice-acting roles.

When watching screen natural Dwight Yoakam act, it's easy to forget that he is first and foremost a country music star. Over the years, Yoakam has appeared in more than 40 films with Hollywood heavyweights, including Matthew McConaughey (*The Newton Boys*, 1998), Jodie Foster (*Panic Room*, 2002), and Daniel Craig and Channing Tatum (*Logan Lucky*, 2017).

Tim McGraw proved that country superstars can hold their own in Hollywood when he appeared in *Friday Night Lights* in 2004, and went on to star alongside Sandra Bullock in *The Blind Side* in 2009. McGraw again made waves in Taylor Sheridan's 2021 Western TV series *1883*, playing husband to his real-life partner and fellow country star, Faith Hill. Many other artists have had dual careers

"Many country artists have proved themselves to be as talented on screen as they are on stage."

SEE ALSO:

MCENTIRE, REBA

MCGRAW, TIM

YOAKAM, DWIGHT

A

as actors, including Randy Travis, Billy Ray Cyrus, and Trace Adkins. Today, country music stars including Lainey Wilson and Kane Brown are keeping that tradition alive for a whole new generation, landing roles on television and in feature films.

ACUFF, ROY

"Acuff was so attached to Opry House that for the final decade of his life he lived next door in what is now called Acuff House."

SEE ALSO:

FIDDLE

GRAND OLE OPRY

The original "King of Country Music," Roy Acuff was country's first true superstar. A longtime member and ambassador of the Grand Ole Opry, he was the first living person inducted into the Country Music Hall of Fame, although he could have easily taken a different path.

As a child growing up in Maynardville, Tennessee, Acuff's early years revolved around sports. He was a gifted baseball player but suffered sunstroke at a major league training camp and, while recovering, began playing the fiddle to pass the time—he never looked back.

In his late twenties Acuff joined a traveling medicine show as a fiddler and singer, touring Tennessee and Virginia in 1932. Soon after, he could be heard playing on radio with his band, the Crazy Tennesseans (later renamed the Smoky Mountain Boys). Their recordings with the American Record Company led to his first hit, "The Great Speckled Bird."

The Grand Ole Opry was a huge part of Acuff's life. He debuted in 1937 and became an official member the following year. Aside from a brief salary dispute in 1946—47, he remained a fixture on the Opry stage until his death in 1992. He was so attached to Opry House that for the final decade of his life he lived next door in what is now called Acuff House.

Prior to Acuff landing on the music scene, country music centered around string bands. The shift to the star-singer-with-band format is credited to Acuff, who not only created great songs but also had a hand in the business of country music. In 1942 he co-founded the first

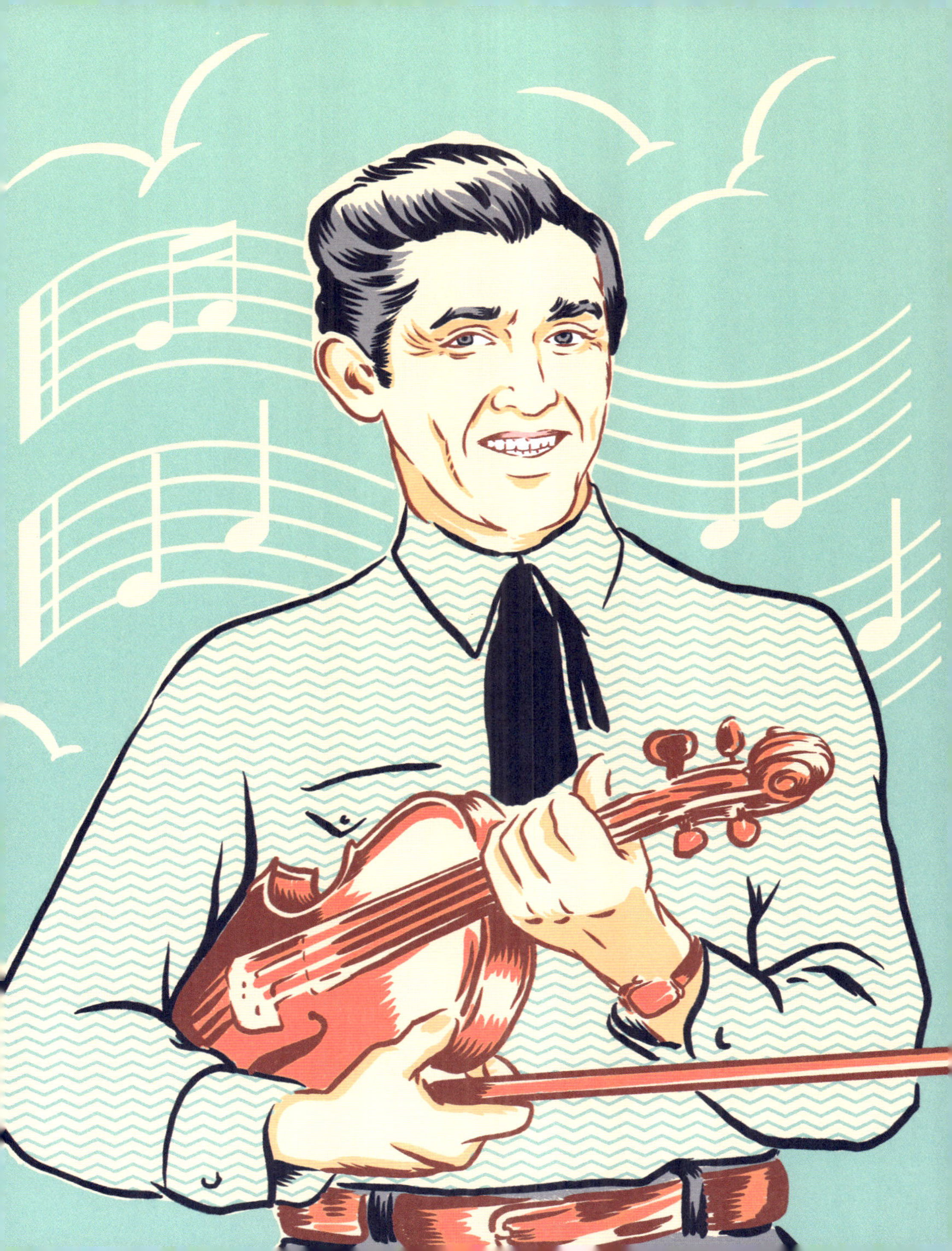

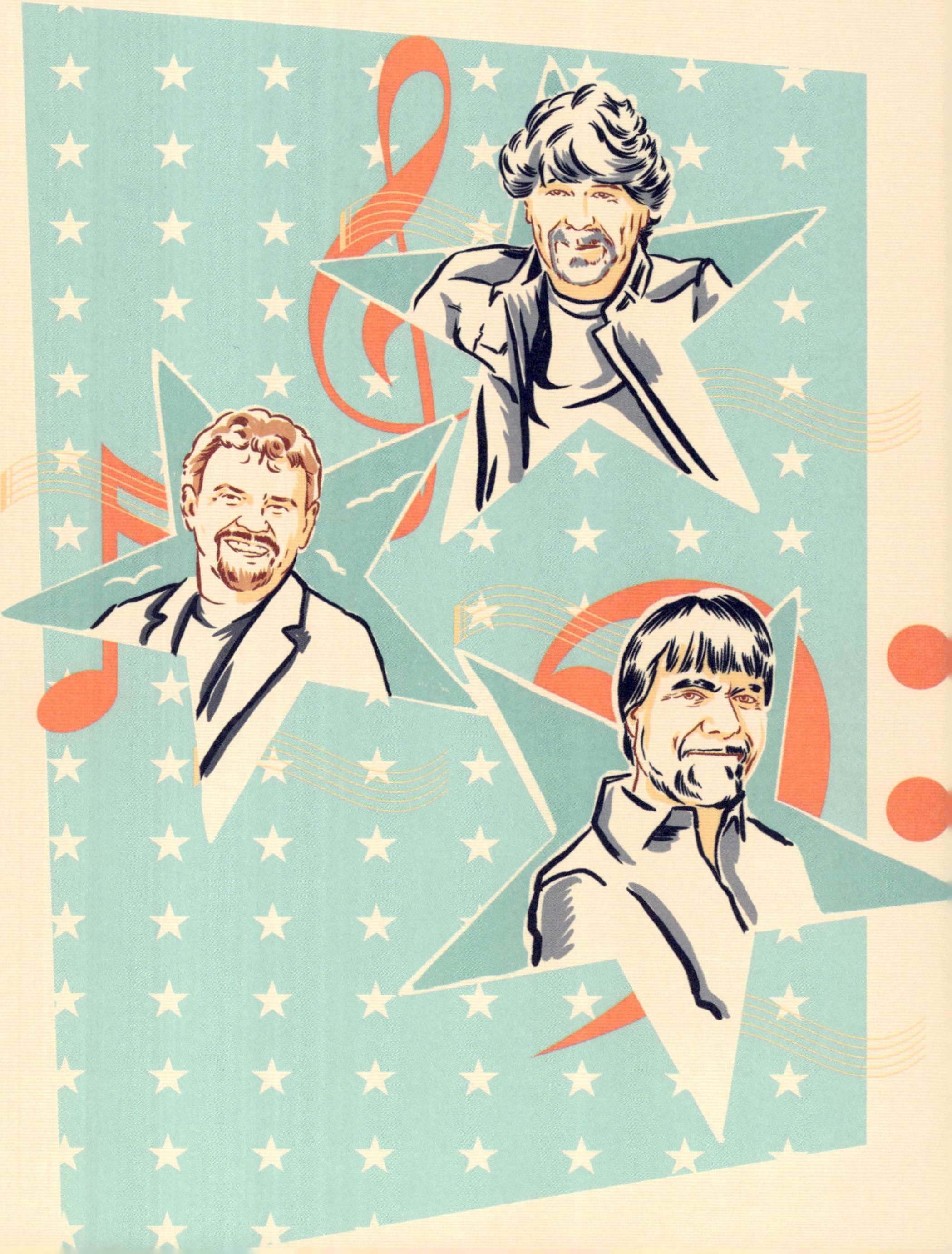

Nashville-based music publishing company, Acuff-Rose Music Publishing, with songwriter Fred Rose. Acuff-Rose went on to sign legends such as Hank Williams and the Everly Brothers, becoming one of the most successful publishing companies in the music business.

Roy Acuff passed away in November 1992 at the age of 89. His many accolades include a Kennedy Center Honors Lifetime Achievement Award as well as a Recording Academy Lifetime Achievement Award. His legacy lives on through a timeless catalog of hits, such as "Wabash Cannon Ball," "Wreck on the Highway," and "Night Train to Memphis."

ALABAMA

It's fair to say that Alabama defined an era of country music. Not only were they the first country band to achieve major commercial success, but they also played a huge part in widening the genre's appeal to reach a global audience. With sales of more than 80 million albums to date and an outstanding 43 number one hits championing the perfect blend of Southern rock and country, it's easy to understand why.

Back in 1973 cousins Jeff Cook, Teddy Gentry, and Randy Owen left their hometown of Fort Payne, Alabama, to chase their music dreams. They soon landed a gig at the Bowery in Myrtle Beach, South Carolina, where they played six nights a week for tips. They remained gigging at the Bowery for the next seven summers with Mark Herndon joining on drums, and before long they were signed to RCA Records—the same record label that made Elvis a star.

Alabama's chart domination began in 1980 with their number one single "Tennessee River" kicking off a monumental streak of 21 consecutive chart-toppers. They're known for hits like "Mountain Music," "Roll On (Eighteen Wheeler)," "Dixieland Delight," and "If You're

"With sales of more than 80 million albums and 43 number one hits, Alabama defined an era of country music."

SEE ALSO:

COUNTRY MUSIC HALL OF FAME AND MUSEUM

FIDDLE

PHILANTHROPY

Gonna Play in Texas (You Gotta Have a Fiddle in the Band)." It's testament to their legacy that these songs continue to be covered by superstars and emerging artists alike.

On tour the band drew unprecedented crowds, including their charitable June Jam which began in 1982 and attracted over 30,000 fans. By 1991, the event was drawing a crowd of 67,000 to their native Fort Payne. To date, the June Jam has raised more than $15 million for various causes. It therefore seems fitting that in 2005, Alabama was inducted into the Country Music Hall of Fame.

Drummer Mark Herndon later parted ways with the group, but Teddy Gentry, Jeff Cook, and Randy Owen continued making music. Cook, a multi-instrumentalist and award-winning guitarist, passed away in November 2022 following a long battle with Parkinson's disease. With his prior blessing, Alabama continued to perform, with a limited schedule.

Alabama remains the only band to win the CMA Entertainer of the Year award, doing so consecutively from 1981 to 1983. As the most successful band in country music, with over 250 industry awards to their name, Alabama paved the way for groups such as Shenandoah, Old Dominion, and Zac Brown Band, and continue to inspire up-and-coming artists.

ALDEAN, JASON

A

As a kid, Jason Aldean dreamed of a career in baseball, until his dad gave him a guitar for his thirteenth birthday. A year later, he played his first gig at a Veterans of Foreign Wars (VFW) post in his hometown of Macon, Georgia.

He performed anywhere that would have him, often getting home at 3a.m. and waking up for school just hours later. After graduating in 1995, Aldean continued playing gigs around Georgia until producer Michael Knox discovered him at an Atlanta nightclub. Although Aldean didn't consider himself a songwriter, Knox, with whom he still collaborates today, offered him a publishing deal to get him to Nashville. By 1998, Aldean was in Music City chasing his dream, but after two record deals fell through, he nearly moved back home. A last chance "Hail Mary" signing with Broken Bow Records kept him in Nashville.

His 2005 debut single "Hicktown" gave fans a taste of his country and rock influences and became his first top ten record. The follow-up, "Why," climbed to number one, while "Amarillo Sky" reached the top five. Powered by these hit singles, his self-titled debut album is now certified four times platinum.

Aldean hit a bit of a sophomore slump with *Relentless*, but things quickly turned around and *Wide Open*, released in 2009, proved his staying power with "She's Country," his second number one. This kicked off a streak of hits, like "Big Green Tractor," "The Truth," and "Crazy Town." Later, he shook things up with the rap-infused "Dirt Road Anthem," opening the door for new sounds on country radio.

"Jason Aldean changed the game, building unparalleled success on songs that deeply connected with his fans."

SEE ALSO:

UNDERWOOD, CARRIE

Duets with Kelly Clarkson ("Don't You Wanna Stay," 2010) and Carrie Underwood ("If I Didn't Love You," 2021) showcased his soaring vocals, and "Try That in a Small Town" (2023) became his first career Billboard Hot 100 chart-topper.

The country-rocker has built an impressive touring career, selling out arenas, amphitheaters, and even stadiums. Named ACM Artist of the Decade and a three-time ACM Entertainer of the Year, he had 30 number one singles by the time he was 48.

Jason Aldean changed the game, building unparalleled success on songs that deeply connected with his fans. When he hit the radio in 2005, no one sounded like him. He capitalized on that, carving out a lane of his own—a lane he very much still dominates.

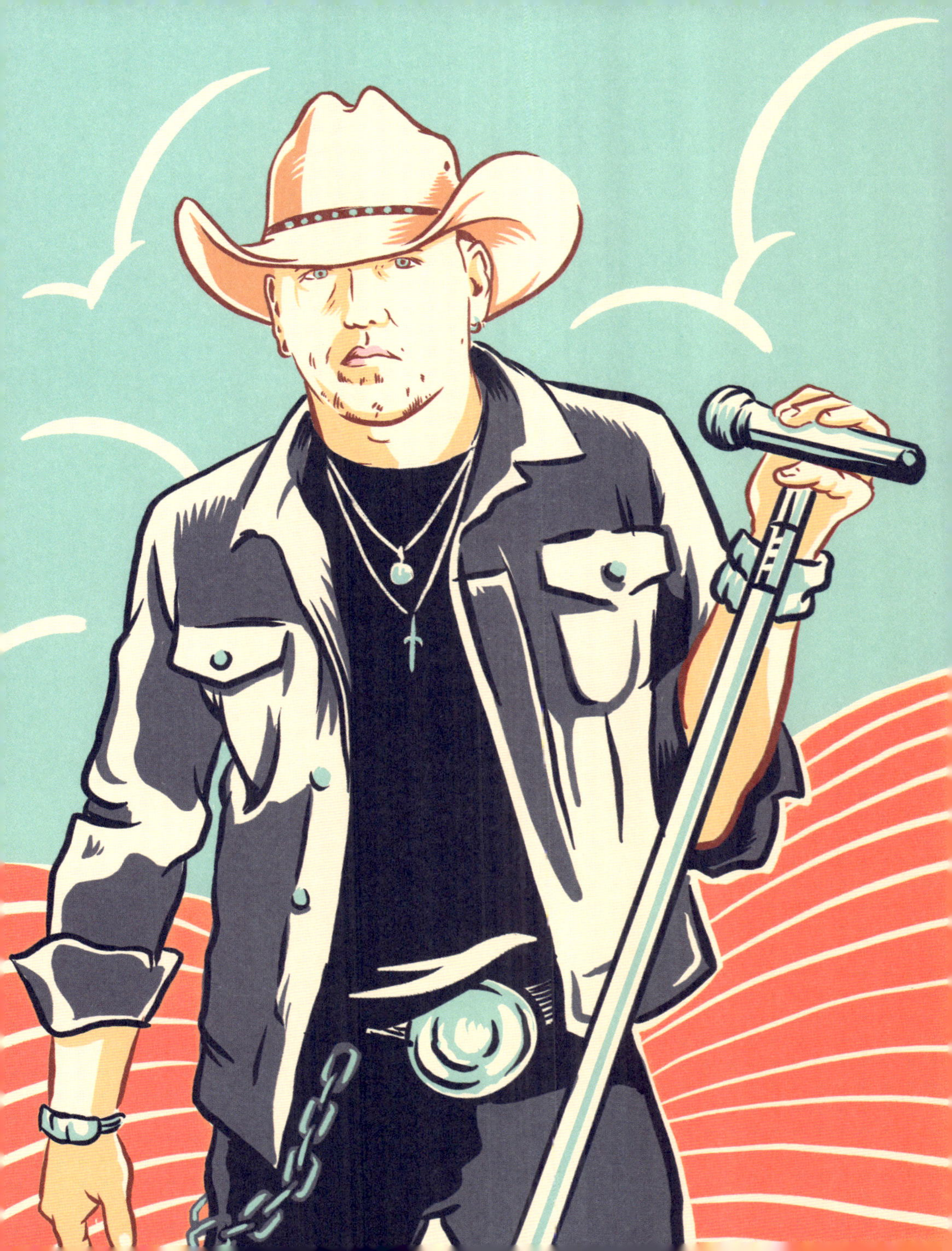

BARITONE

"The deep tones are instantly recognizable, commanding your attention from the first note."

SEE ALSO:

BROWN, KANE
OUTLAW COUNTRY
PRIDE, CHARLEY
TRAVIS, RANDY

When I think about country music's most iconic voices, my mind instantly goes to the baritones and bass singers. The deep tones are instantly recognizable, commanding your attention from the first note. Without getting too technical, baritones sit in the middle-low range while bass is the lowest, but to me, it doesn't matter whether they are technically baritone or bass—these voices carry a weight that sets them apart.

Some of the earliest country legends set the standard here. Jim Reeves's smooth voice helped shape the Nashville Sound, while Waylon Jennings and Merle Haggard's gritty tones defined Outlaw Country. Charley Pride was part of that legacy too, his voice so full and rich that you knew it was him the second he sang a note. And then there's Johnny Cash, whose booming voice may be the most famous in country music history.

By the 1980s, Randy Travis carried the torch with his distinctive low voice on classics like "Diggin' Up Bones," forever changing the sound of country music. Today, artists like Josh Turner and Trace Adkins keep that tradition alive. Turner's unmistakable voice shines on hits like "Long Black Train." Adkins's voice is so deep it almost doesn't seem real, and when you see him live, the crowd goes wild every time he hits those low notes.

Kane Brown and Scotty McCreery are also part of this new generation of baritones. Brown first caught fans' attention online with covers of Randy Travis and George Strait hits, before becoming a star in his own right. McCreery rose to fame as a teenager on *American Idol*, impressing audiences with his surprisingly low range, even covering Josh Turner's "Your Man" on the show. Years later, his story came full circle when he was inducted into the Grand Ole Opry, standing on stage with both Turner and Randy Travis by his side, a reminder that country's deep voices are still going strong.

BELMONT UNIVERSITY

Just a block from Nashville's Music Row sits Belmont University, a private Christian college with deep ties to the city's music scene. Founded in 1890 to educate female students, Belmont became co-ed in 1951 and launched its music business program in 1973, right as Music Row was booming with new record labels, publishers, and studios. The program was built in collaboration with industry professionals, giving students a direct connection to Nashville's creative community.

Over the years, Belmont has become a launchpad for artists, songwriters, producers, executives, and more. Country stars including Brad Paisley, Trisha Yearwood, Tyler Hubbard, and Russell Dickerson studied at Belmont before making it big, as did hit songwriters Ashley Gorley and Hillary Lindsey, and producer Dann Huff. Countless other alumni now work behind the scenes on Music Row.

Belmont students have the chance to get hands-on experience in recording studios, at live concerts, and even at award shows like the Grammys, all while learning directly from leaders in the industry.

While New York University made headlines for offering a course on Taylor Swift, Belmont recently introduced Dolly U, a set of classes dedicated to studying Dolly Parton. Now those are courses I'd sign up for!

"Over the years, Belmont has become a launchpad for artists, songwriters, producers, executives, and more."

SEE ALSO:

MUSIC ROW

NASHVILLE

PAISLEY, BRAD

SONGWRITERS

YEARWOOD, TRISHA

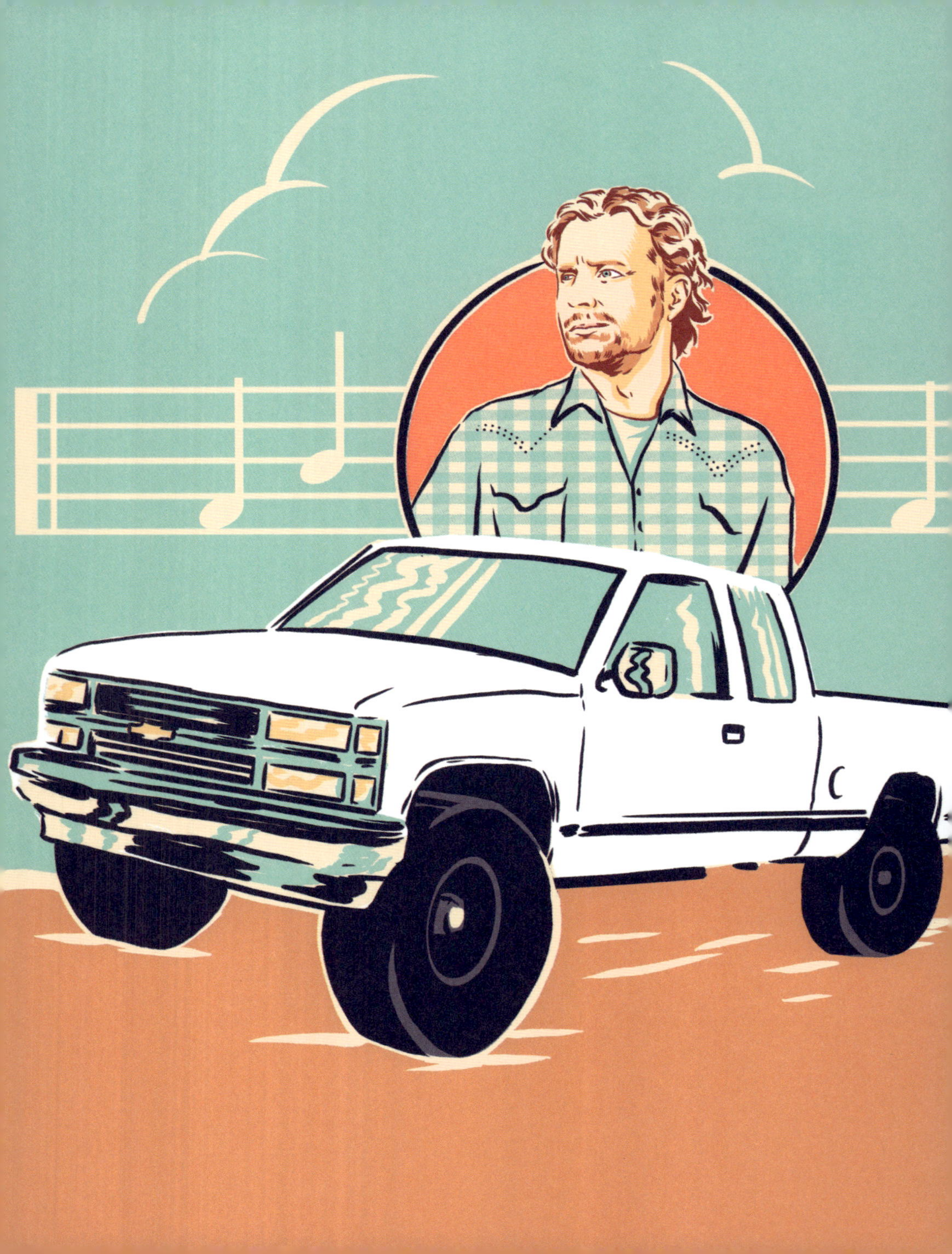

BIG WHITE

In 1994, 19-year-old Dierks Bentley packed his bags, hopped into his new 1994 Chevrolet Silverado, and set off from Arizona to Nashville (a journey of approximately 1,636 miles/2,633km) with his father by his side. Little did he know that this road trip would change his life forever. One day he would become a Grammy-nominated country superstar, but at that moment, it was just him, his dad, the open road, and his truck. Nicknamed Big White, Bentley's beloved Silverado has been with him from the very beginning, a constant companion through the highs and lows of his career.

Bentley was inspired to move to Nashville after falling in love with the music of Hank Williams Jr. and Marty Stuart as a teenager. "Eaten up" with the dream of becoming a country singer, he made the move and quickly discovered the Station Inn and the world of bluegrass music, which would later influence his career. But success didn't come overnight. He graduated from Vanderbilt University in 1997, spent years playing in bars with Big White parked outside, and worked tirelessly on demos to pay the bills. In 2003, he signed with Capitol Records and almost immediately earned a hit with "What Was I Thinkin'."

Big White was by his side for every step of Bentley's journey, from opening act to headliner, and "Every Mile a Memory," as he sings in his 2006 chart-topper. She saw him consistently topping the charts with his signature blend of country, classic country, bluegrass, and rock, and even witnessed the surprise release of his full-on bluegrass album. Big White was there when he welcomed his three children with his wife, Cassidy; said goodbye to his father and hero who had made that road trip to Nashville with him so long ago; and stood by his side as he became a member of the Grand Ole Opry and earned 15 Grammy nominations.

In his 2013 release "I Hold On," Bentley paid tribute to his "old beat-up truck" Big White, and the things that matter most to him. She has been by his side for over 30 years

"For Bentley, Big White is more than just a truck; she's a reminder of where it all began for him."

SEE ALSO:

GRAND OLE OPRY
STATION INN

B

and more than 215,000 miles (346,000km). Big White even appeared in some of his music videos, including "5-1-5-0" and "Living." For Bentley, Big White is more than just a truck; she's a reminder of where it all began for him.

BILLY BOB'S TEXAS

"Over the decades the walls of Billy Bob's have seen countless iconic moments."

SEE ALSO:

FILM & TV
BROOKS, GARTH
HAGGARD, MERLE
STRAIT, GEORGE

At the height of the Urban Cowboy movement, Texas businessman Billy Bob Barnett set out to create the ultimate honky-tonk in Fort Worth, Texas—and he did just that with Billy Bob's Texas. The world's largest honky-tonk boasts 100,000 square feet (9,290 square meters) of entertainment space, complete with a massive dance floor and bull riding. And no, not a mechanical bull… Billy Bob's has real bull riding inside the venue every weekend.

The history of what is now Billy Bob's dates back to the early 1900s when the site housed cattle. It later transformed into an airplane factory during World War II before becoming a giant department store in the 1950s. Billy Bob's Texas as we know it opened its doors on April 1, 1981, kicking things off with a concert from Larry Gatlin and the Gatlin Brothers followed by a week of performances from Waylon Jennings, Willie Nelson, and more.

Over the decades the walls of Billy Bob's have seen countless iconic moments. In 1983, Merle Haggard set a Guinness World Record when he bought the largest round of drinks ever: 5,095 made with 40 gallons (150 liters) of Canadian Club whiskey. The tab came to a whopping $12,737.50. Hank Williams Jr. also left his mark by setting a record for the most bottles of beer sold during a single show: 16,000, a record that stood strong for 30 years. And in 1989, a then-budding star named Garth Brooks made his Billy Bob's debut, with tickets priced at just $5.

In 1989, the venue started a unique tradition where artists leave their mark by pressing their hands in concrete for the now-famous Celebrity Wall of Fame.

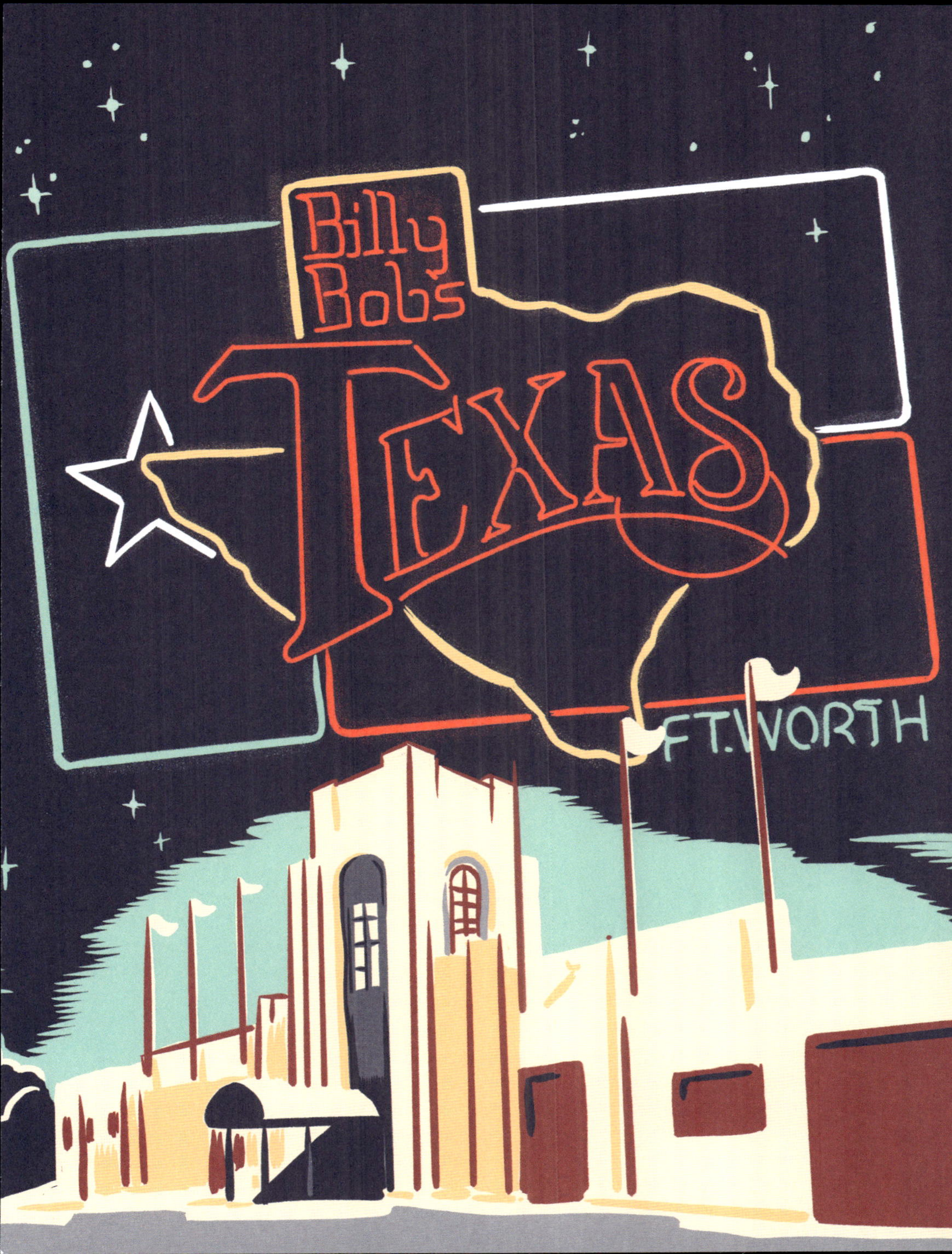
Billy Bob's
TEXAS
FT. WORTH

B

Visitors to Billy Bob's can see the handprints of more than 200 artists as well as over 75 guitars autographed by an array of performers.

The award-winning venue has welcomed more than 17 million visitors and hosted performances by country icons like George Strait, Alan Jackson, and Randy Travis, as well as modern stars such as Luke Combs, Parker McCollum, and Lainey Wilson. During its 40-plus years of business, Billy Bob's Texas has been featured in a variety of TV shows and movies, including *Walker, Texas Ranger*, *Dallas*, and *Pure Country* starring George Strait. They say "everything's bigger in Texas," and Billy Bob's sure proves it.

BLUEBIRD CAFE

"The Bluebird evolved into a true listening room, where the songs (and the people who write them) take center stage."

SEE ALSO:

BROOKS, GARTH
HILL, FAITH
MUSIC CITY
NASHVILLE
SONGWRITERS
SWIFT, TAYLOR

One of Nashville's most cherished venues, The Bluebird Cafe, sits in an unassuming strip mall in the Green Hills area, just outside downtown. From the outside, it doesn't look like much, but inside, visitors experience the true heart of Music City: the songs. It's become both a must-see stop for fans and one of Nashville's most coveted stages, with performances that helped launch the careers of Garth Brooks, Faith Hill, and Taylor Swift after talent scouts spotted them from the crowd.

Amy Kurland opened the now-famous venue in June 1982, originally envisioning it as a small restaurant with a stage for local talent. It quickly became a late-night hangout, but complaints about the noise led Kurland to try something different: a writers' night. With just 90 seats, the intimate space was perfect for this kind of setting. In 1985, a group of songwriters suggested performing in a circle in the middle of the room to discourage the audience from talking during the performance. From that moment, The Bluebird evolved into a true listening room, where the songs (and the people who write them) take center stage. And so the tradition of "in the round" performances were born, along with the venue's

"SSHHHH! policy," reminding audiences to stay quiet and soak up the music.

Each night, three or four songwriters share their songs and the stories behind them. Here you might see brand new songwriters alongside those behind some of the biggest country music hits, and there's always a possibility of surprise guests. My first time at The Bluebird Cafe, Aerosmith's Steven Tyler showed up to perform. Seeing him in a room of just 90 people was quite the experience! Though always a Music City staple, The Bluebird's popularity skyrocketed in 2012 when it was featured in the hit ABC series *Nashville*. The "accidental landmark" was also celebrated in the 2019 documentary *Bluebird*.

Kurland eventually sold the venue to the non-profit Nashville Songwriters Association International (NSAI), an organization that works to protect songwriters' rights. Today, The Bluebird draws more than 70,000 visitors a year. Reservations are required most nights, and getting one can be a challenge, making it one of the most sought-after tickets in town.

BRISTOL SESSIONS

When most people think of the home of country music, they think of Nashville, Tennessee. But its birthplace is actually about four and a half hours east in the city of Bristol—an Appalachian Mountain area with distinct musical traditions—which sits directly on the Tennessee-Virginia state line.

Bristol's role in country music began in 1927 with the historic Bristol Sessions, at a time when "hillbilly music" was gaining popularity. Hillbilly music was shaped by instruments like the banjo (brought to America by enslaved people from Africa) and the fiddle, with its Celtic roots. Looking to capitalize on this rise in popularity, the Victor Talking Machine Company sent producer Ralph Peer to Bristol.

B

"Bristol's role in country music began in 1927 with the historic Bristol Sessions, at a time when 'hillbilly music' was gaining popularity."

SEE ALSO:

COUNTRY MUSIC HALL OF FAME AND MUSEUM

"WILL THE CIRCLE BE UNBROKEN"

With the latest recording technology in hand, Peer and his team set up a temporary studio and launched a marathon of sessions from July 25 to August 5. The event was advertised in newspapers and spread by word of mouth, drawing performers from far and wide. Over the course of those 12 days, 19 acts recorded 76 songs, sparking the beginning of the commercialization of country music.

Among those songs were six by The Carter Family, made up of husband-and-wife team A.P. and Sara Carter, along with Sara's cousin Maybelle. Now remembered as "The First Family of Country Music," their influence would continue through generations of the Carter family, including June Carter Cash.

Another star discovered during the sessions was Jimmie Rodgers. Originally planning to record with a band, he decided at the last minute to go solo, performing with just his voice and guitar. Though he only recorded two songs in Bristol, his talent impressed Peer. Soon, Rodgers landed his first hit, "Blue Yodel (T for Texas)," and quickly rose to fame, earning the title "The Father of Country Music."

Rodgers became the first inductee into the Country Music Hall of Fame in 1961, with The Carter Family following in 1970. And in 1998, Congress officially designated Bristol, Tennessee-Virginia, as the Birthplace of country music. Johnny Cash once called the Bristol Sessions "the most important event in the history of country music," and he was right—the genre wouldn't be what it is today without them.

BROOKS & DUNN

Brooks & Dunn are the undisputed best-selling country duo of all time. The unprecedented career of Kix Brooks and Ronnie Dunn boasts 20 number one hits and a catalog that blends country, rock, and honky-tonk swagger.

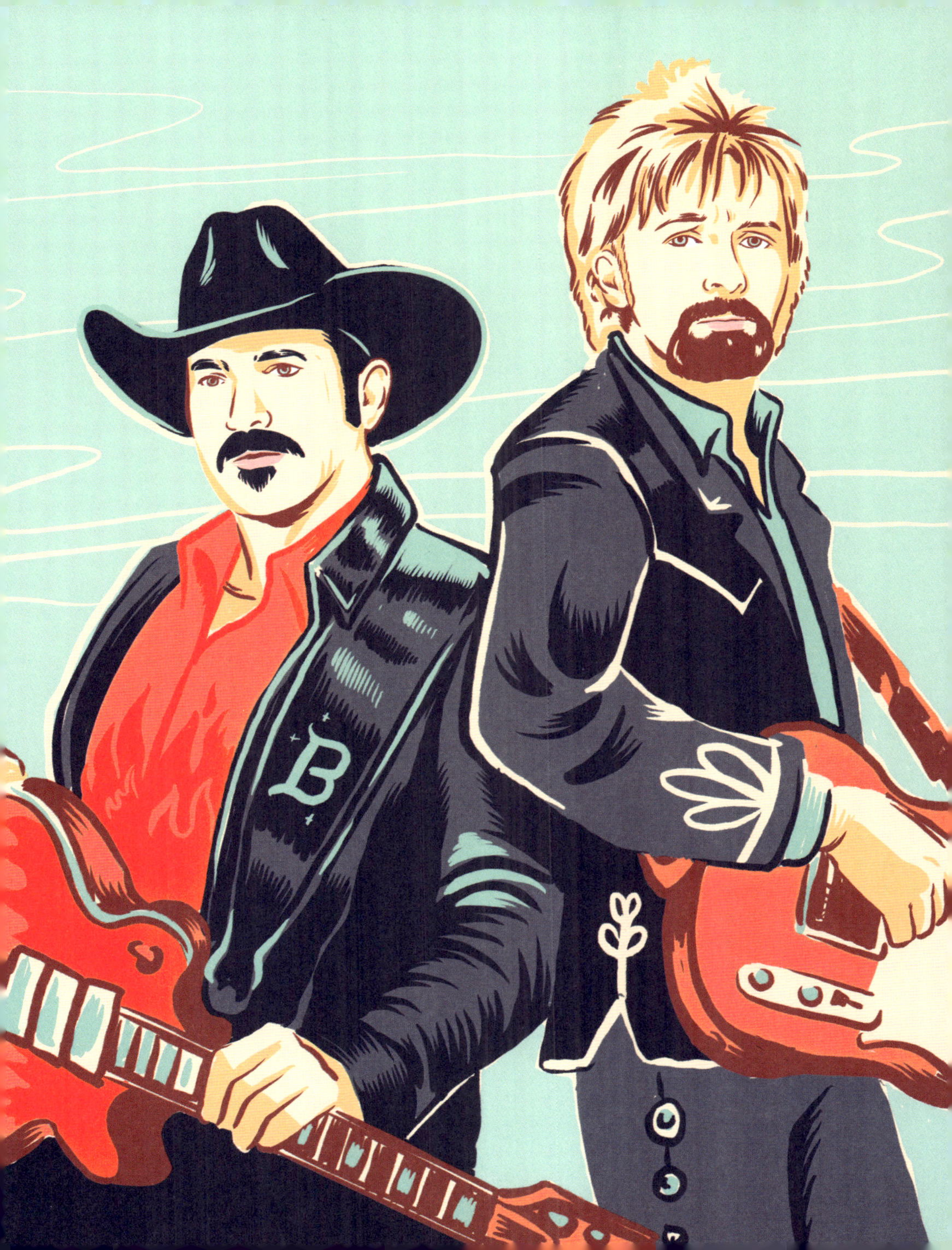

B

"Brooks & Dunn are the undisputed best-selling country duo of all time."

SEE ALSO:

COUNTRY MUSIC HALL OF FAME AND MUSEUM

NINETIES COUNTRY

It may come as a surprise to some, but Brooks & Dunn are an industry-formed duo. They came together after record executive Tim DuBois suggested they stop pursuing solo careers and join forces. While it wasn't necessarily what either of them had in mind, they agreed, formed Brooks & Dunn, and signed with Arista Nashville in 1991.

Fans soon saw what DuBois intended with the release of their chart-topping debut single "Brand New Man" in 1991, and the hits didn't stop there. Their debut album spawned subsequent number ones like the toe-tapping "My Next Broken Heart," the sorrow-soaked "Neon Moon," and the fiddle-laced "Boot Scootin' Boogie," which helped ignite a nationwide line-dancing craze. Their career certainly has its share of ups and downs, including a breakup in 2009 and a farewell tour in 2010. During their hiatus, both Brooks and Dunn explored solo efforts.

The duo reunited in 2015 for a Las Vegas residency that became the longest-running country music residency in Vegas history, running until 2021. In 2019, amid their Sin City run, the duo was inducted into the Country Music Hall of Fame. They later returned to the touring circuit and continue to tour to this day.

Brooks & Dunn introduced their music to a new generation of country fans with the 2019 release of *Reboot*, an album featuring remakes of 12 of their biggest hits alongside rising country artists. Thanks to the success of that project, the duo revisited the idea in 2024 with *Reboot II*, this time allowing their collaborators full creative control of their songs.

Brooks & Dunn remained a staple in country music for decades, which is certainly something to be proud of. The secret to their success is that they each bring their own strengths to the table: Ronnie Dunn is known for his dynamic vocals, while Kix Brooks injects an undeniable energy to the stage. Together, they created a kind of musical magic that cannot be replicated.

B

BROOKS, GARTH

Garth Brooks is one of the best-selling solo artists in history, having sold an impressive 162 million albums. And if that wasn't enough, he's also received almost every accolade imaginable, including seven CMA Entertainer of the Year awards and an induction into the Country Music Hall of Fame. He is, without doubt, one of the most influential country artists of all time.

Born in Tulsa, Oklahoma, in 1962, Brooks grew up in a musical family. His dad loved traditional country, while his mother was a talented singer who was once signed to Capitol Records. Brooks learned to play guitar and banjo as a teen and began performing regularly in college.

However, at first Brooks didn't have an easy route to stardom. Having moved to Nashville in 1987, he was initially turned down by every major label and resorted to selling boots and singing demos on the side. His big break came a year later at The Bluebird Cafe when he filled in for a performer who hadn't shown up. A Capitol Records executive was in the crowd and, despite having previously rejected him, was so impressed that Brooks was offered a deal the following day. His self-titled debut album arrived in 1989, and he was inducted into the Grand Ole Opry the following year.

By the early 1990s, Brooks was country music's biggest star and dominated the charts with hits including "The Dance," "Friends in Low Places," "The River," and "If Tomorrow Never Comes." His live shows, which saw Brooks leaping across the stage while wearing a wireless headset microphone, climbing the rafters, and even smashing guitars, set a whole new standard and brought an energy never seen before in country music.

The 1990s also brought world tours, multimillion-selling albums, and countless chart-topping hits. His landmark 1997 concert in New York's Central Park drew an estimated one million people. Broadcast as an HBO special, it became the most-watched cable event of the year, with 14.6 million viewers, proving just how massive his career had become.

"By the early 1990s, Brooks was country music's biggest star and dominated the charts."

SEE ALSO:

BLUEBIRD CAFE

COUNTRY MUSIC HALL OF FAME AND MUSEUM

GRAND OLE OPRY

LOWER BROADWAY

YEARWOOD, TRISHA

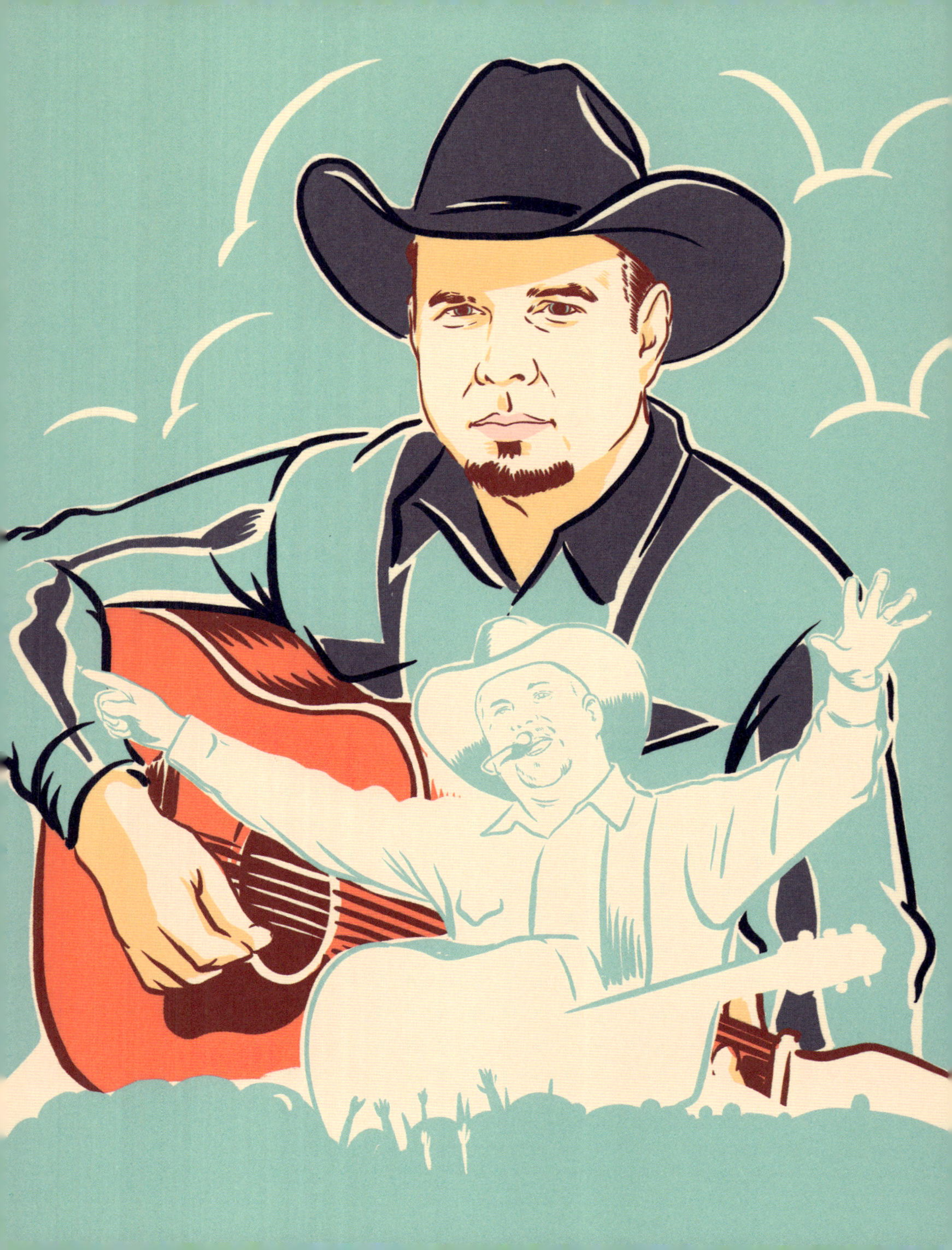

Brooks's hold on the country music world was going from strength to strength, but in 2000 fans were stunned by the announcement of his retirement. Following his divorce from college sweetheart Sandy Mahl, he decided to step away from the spotlight and returned to Oklahoma to help raise his three daughters. Brooks later married Trisha Yearwood in 2005 but remained out of the spotlight until 2007, when he released a surprise new single, "More Than a Memory."

Over the next few years, Brooks played only a handful of shows. By 2014, he officially came out of retirement, releasing new music and launching a record-breaking stadium tour with Yearwood. In 2023, Brooks joined the Broadway bar scene with Friends in Low Places Bar & Honky-Tonk. Garth Brooks' music has stood the test of time, still sounding just as fresh on the radio today as it did in the 1990s. New fans, though, may have a harder time finding it—he hasn't fully embraced streaming, so his songs are only available on Amazon Music or the old-school way: on CDs.

B

"Despite his international fame, Brown has never forgotten where he came from."

SEE ALSO:
BARITONE

BROWN, KANE

Kane Brown's story is nothing short of inspiring. As a child growing up in Georgia and Tennessee, he faced racism and periods of homelessness as well as abuse at the hands of a stepfather. While the odds may have been stacked against him, music became his escape and Brown built a solid career from the bottom up, making history along the way.

After a rejection from *American Idol* and a stint in a boy band on *The X Factor*, Brown turned to Facebook to share his voice and built up a massive online following. Between shifts at Lowe's Home Improvement and FedEx, he recorded country covers in his bathroom, singing songs by Lee Brice, Randy Travis, and George Strait.

Brown soon began writing his own songs and, following a move to Nashville, successfully crowd funded his first EP. In 2016, he signed with Sony Nashville and released his self-titled debut album, immediately making history as the first artist to top all five of Billboard's main country charts at once. The album produced two Diamond-certified hits, "Heaven" and "What Ifs," the latter featuring Lauren Alaina, which remain among the most-streamed country songs of all time.

Brown's second release, *Experiment*, continued his record-breaking run, making him the first country artist in more than 24 years to debut at number one on the Billboard 200 with a sophomore album. *Different Man* and *The High Road* followed, delivering fan favorites like "Bury Me in Georgia" and "One Mississippi." His duet with his wife Katelyn, "Thank God," marked another career high point.

His unique blend of country, pop, and R&B coupled with cross-genre collaborations have introduced country music to new audiences around the globe, and his live shows bring an unmatched energy to the stage. Fans love him not just for his music, but for his down-to-earth

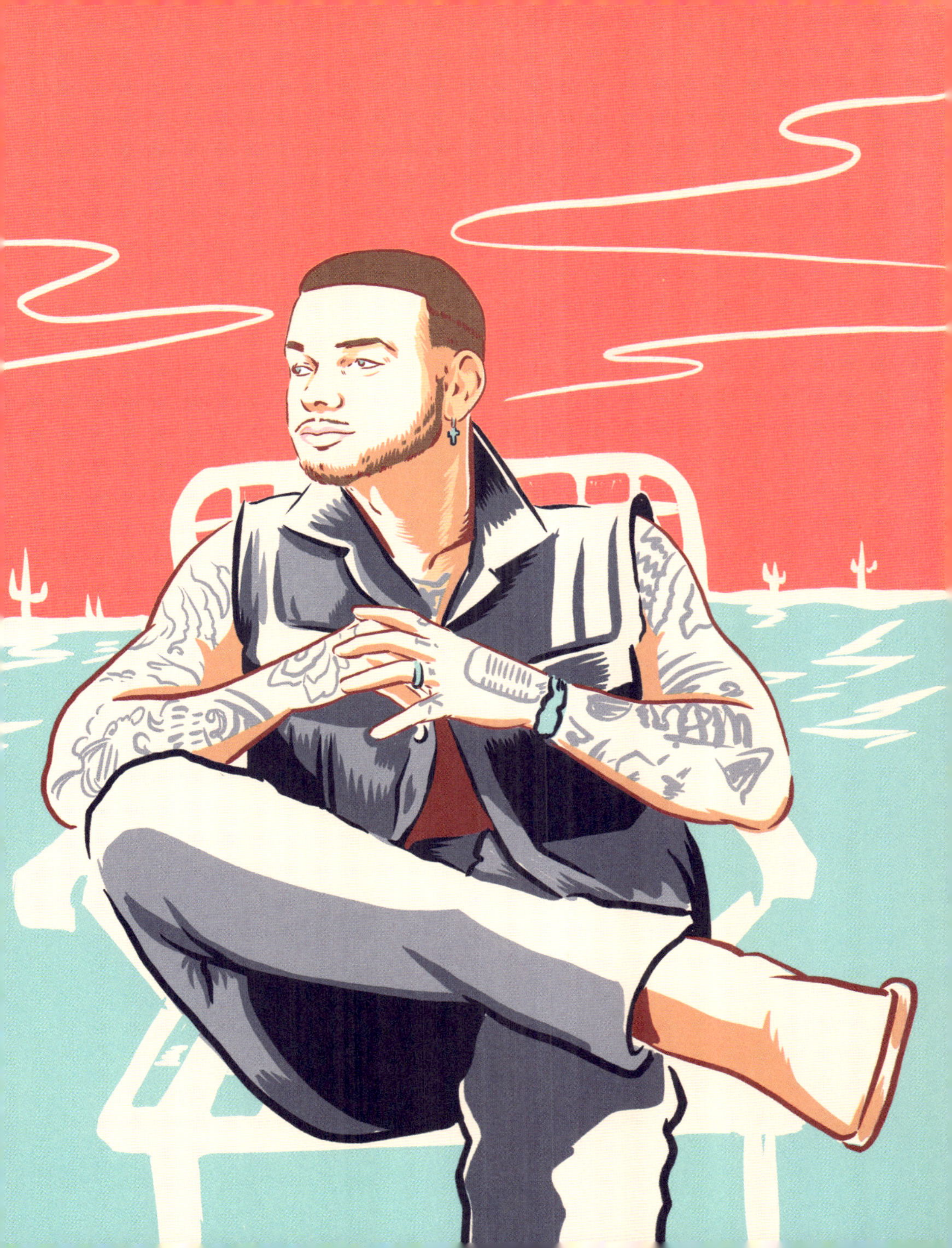

B

nature and devotion to his family. He and Katelyn often share glimpses of their private lives on social media, inviting fans to get to know them at home as well as onstage.

With a heart of gold, Brown supports causes close to him, including the Boys & Girls Club of America, which honored him with the Champion of Youth Award. Despite his international fame, Brown has never forgotten where he came from, and that's part of what makes his story so special.

BRYAN, LUKE

"Known for his high-energy shows, charming personality, and hip-shaking dance moves, Bryan is also a five-time Entertainer of the Year."

SEE ALSO:
PHILANTHROPY

One of the greatest joys of my career has been watching Luke Bryan grow from a budding singer-songwriter into a bona fide superstar. He worked tirelessly for his success, starting from small gigs where no one knew his name to headlining stadiums. Along the way, he's faced unimaginable personal tragedy, yet through it all, Bryan has remained one of this generation's greatest entertainers and most consistent hitmakers, with more than 30 number one singles, several of which he co-wrote.

Born in July 1976, Bryan was raised on a peanut farm in Leesburg, Georgia. He grew up singing in church and got his first guitar at age 14. Five years later, Bryan planned to move to Nashville, but just before leaving, his older brother Chris died in a car accident. He put his dreams on hold and enrolled at Georgia Southern University to stay close to his family. In college, he formed a band and played local gigs, then finally made the move to Nashville after graduating.

Bryan arrived on the country music scene in 2001 when he began writing songs, landing cuts with artists like Travis Tritt and Billy Currington. In 2007, he signed with Capitol Nashville and released his top five debut single, "All My Friends Say." That same year, he made his Grand Ole Opry debut, a bittersweet night as it was the last time he saw his sister Kelly before her unexpected passing. Bryan honored his siblings by pressing forward, earning his first

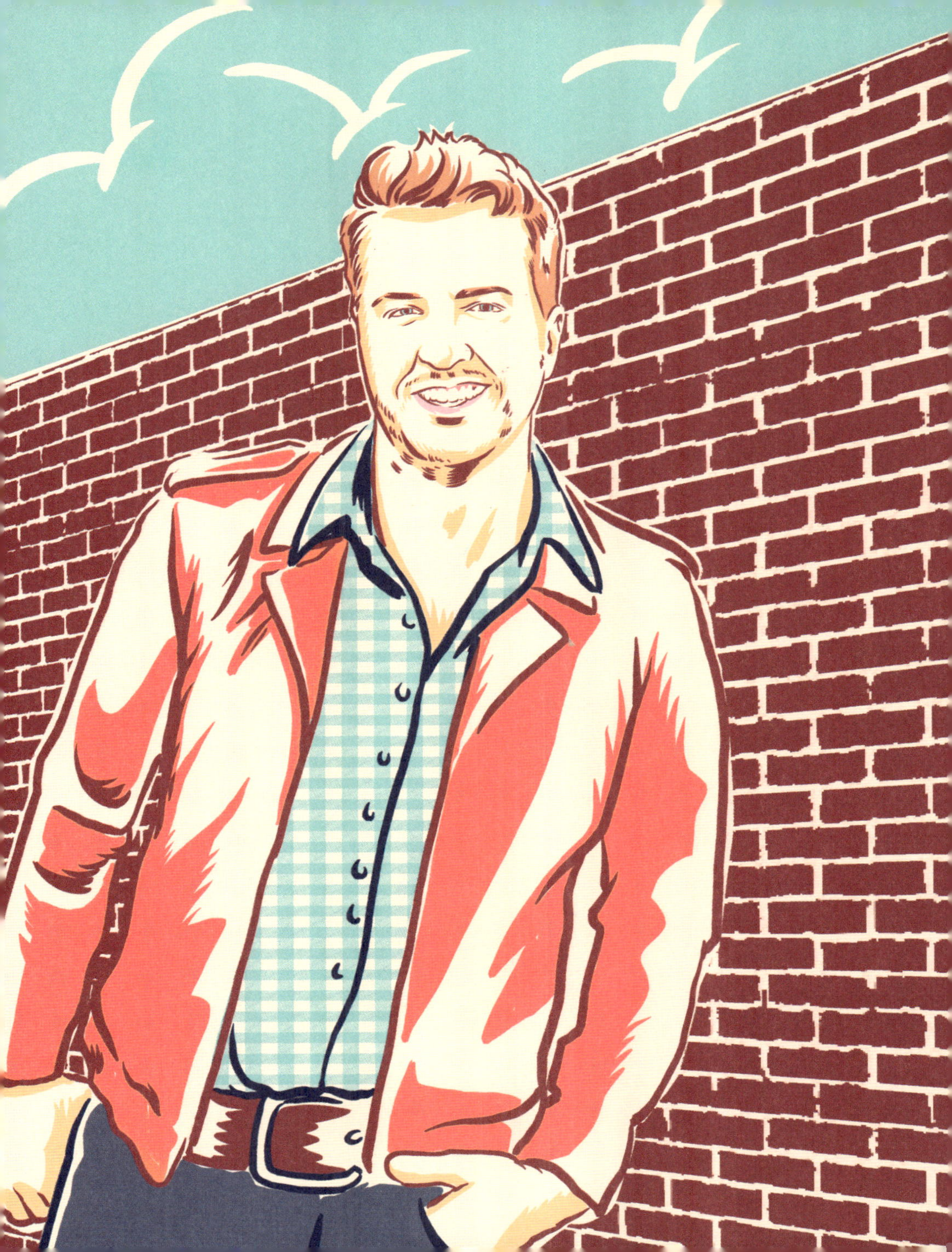

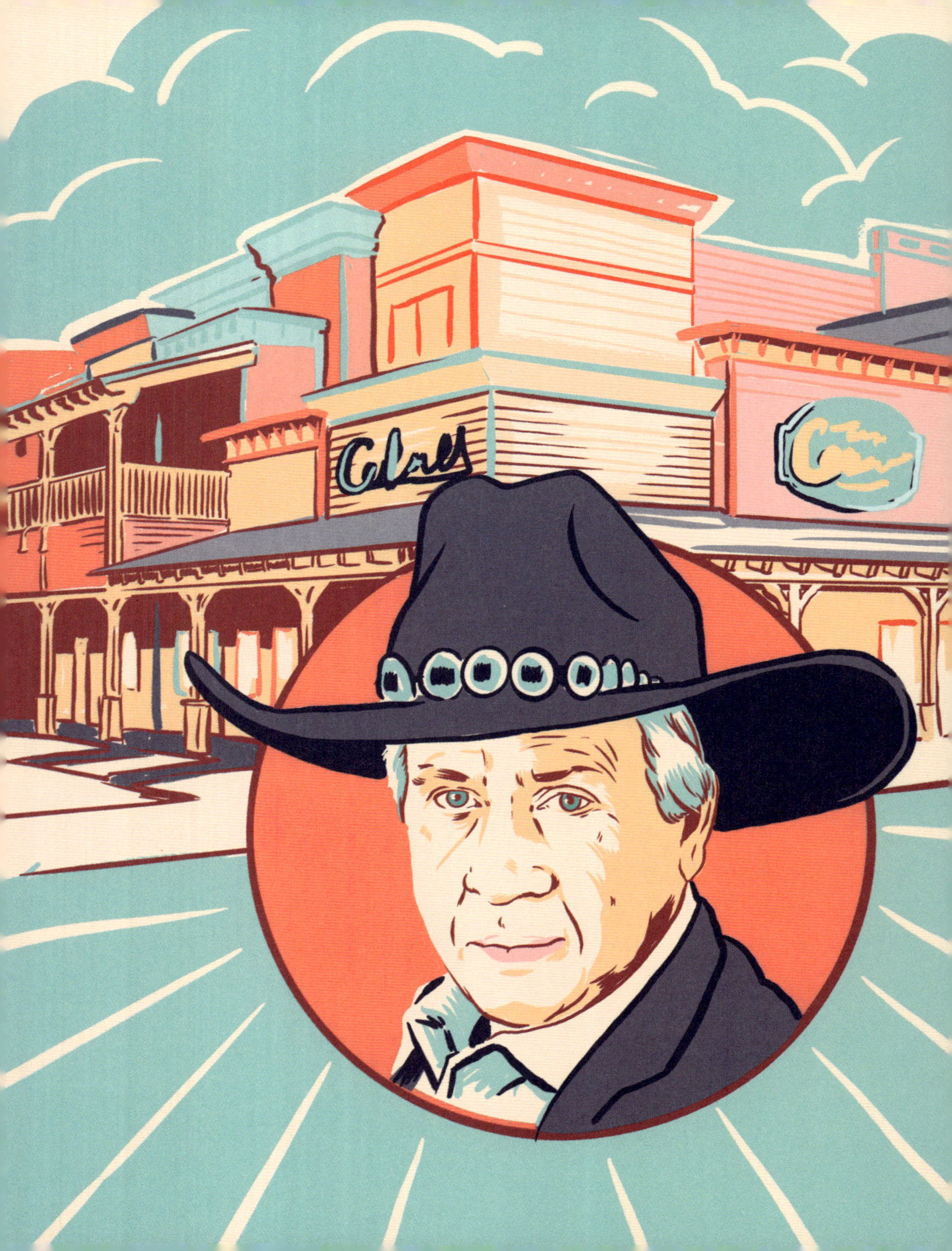

number one in 2009 with "Do I," which would signal the beginning of his chart dominance.

His 2011 release "Country Girl (Shake it for Me)" marked a major turning point. Though it didn't hit number one, it catapulted him to a new level of superstardom. More arena-ready anthems followed, as did heartfelt hits like "Drink a Beer" and "Most People Are Good." By the end of the decade, Bryan was named Billboard's Top Country Artist of the 2010s, Country Aircheck's Most-Heard Artist of the Decade, and his album *Crash My Party* was crowned the first-ever ACM Album of the Decade.

Known for his high-energy shows, charming personality, and hip-shaking dance moves, Bryan is also a five-time Entertainer of the Year. Now a household name, he's hosted both the ACM and CMA Awards multiple times, and serves as a judge on *American Idol*. But despite his success, Bryan honors his roots with his annual Farm Tour, launched in 2009, providing college scholarships to children from farming families. Witnessing Bryan's journey in country music is something I will never forget.

BUCK OWENS' CRYSTAL PALACE

Approximately 100 miles (160km) north of Los Angeles lies Bakersfield, California, the birthplace of the country music subgenre known as Bakersfield Sound. This raw, rock-influenced style, popularized by Buck Owens and Merle Haggard, was a direct response to the polished, pop-leaning Nashville Sound.

In October 1996 country music star Buck Owens, best known for his stint as a *Hee Haw* co-host, fulfilled a longtime dream when he opened Buck Owens' Crystal Palace. Built in the city he called home for many years,

"The Crystal Palace quickly became the top country music venue on the West Coast."

SEE ALSO:
HEE HAW

C

the 18,000-square-foot (1,670-square-meter) tribute to Bakersfield Sound included a music hall, restaurant, and museum. Inside, visitors were transported to an Old West-style downtown scene, like something out of a movie set.

The Crystal Palace quickly became the top country music venue on the West Coast, hosting performances by artists including Willie Nelson, Brad Paisley, and George Strait. What's more, Garth Brooks famously proposed to Trisha Yearwood at the venue in 2005, creating one of country music's most-loved power couples.

Owens and his band, the Buckaroos, played at the legendary venue every Friday and Saturday night until March 24, 2006. That evening, Owens wasn't feeling well and asked the Buckaroos to perform without him. On his way to his car, he ran into a couple who had traveled 700 miles (1,120km) to see him on stage. Not wanting to disappoint them, Owens went back inside to perform his typical 90-minute set. Afterward, he returned home to his nearby ranch, fell asleep, and peacefully passed away.

With the construction of Buck Owens' Crystal Palace, Owens helped put Bakersfield on the map and cemented its rightful place in country music history. It remained the top tourist destination in the area until its closure in 2025.

CAMPBELL, GLEN

Glen Campbell escaped poverty, and even death, to become an internationally known artist, gifted guitarist, and Country Music Hall of Fame inductee. Born the seventh of 12 children in rural Arkansas in 1936, Campbell almost drowned near his family's home when he was a toddler, but thanks to his brother's heroic action he was resuscitated and went on to earn his rightful place in country music history.

Campbell's father recognized his musical talent early on and bought him a $5 guitar when he was just four. His uncle Boo taught him to play, and by the age of ten the

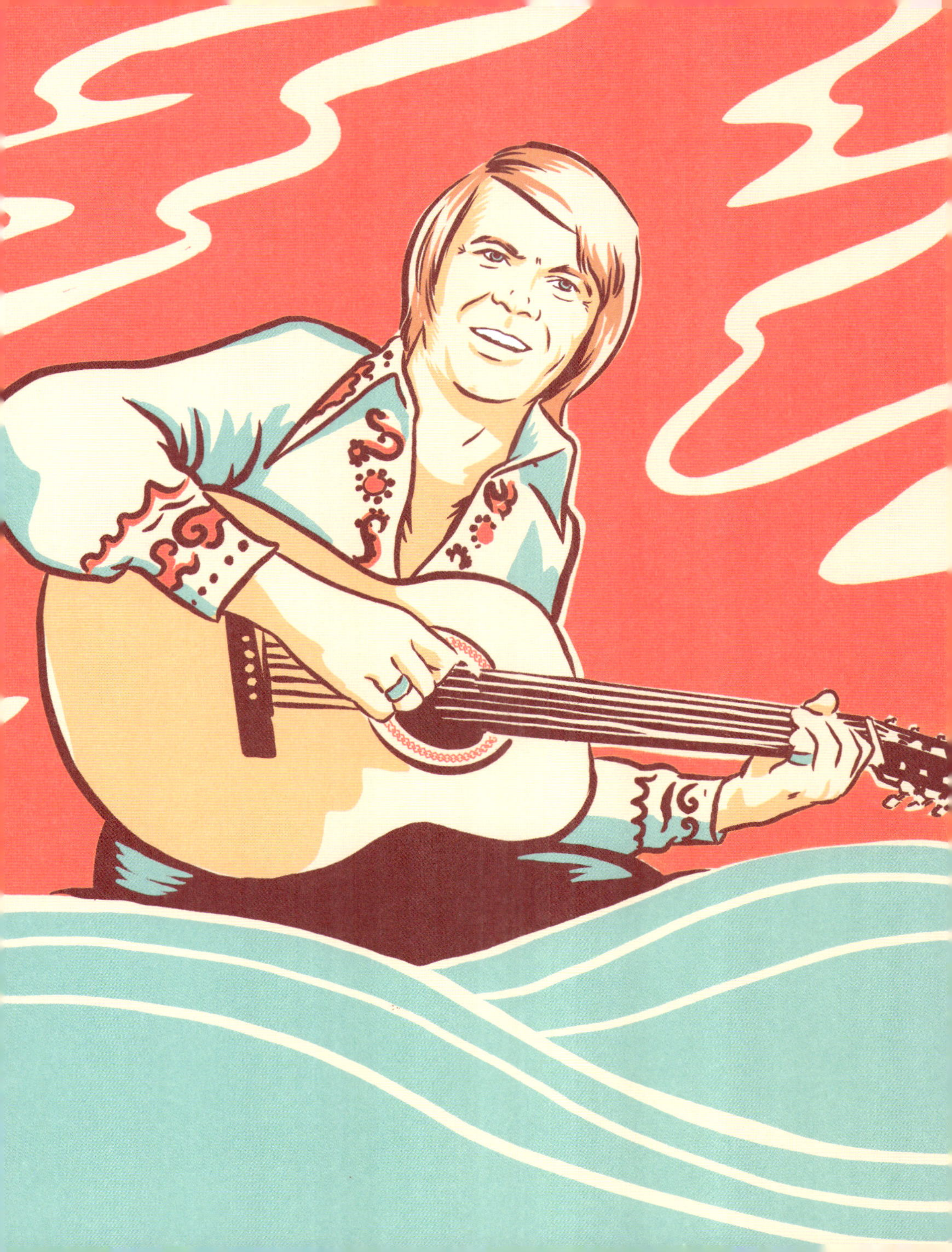

C

"Campbell's legacy lives on, and he's lovingly remembered as The Rhinestone Cowboy."

SEE ALSO:

COUNTRY MUSIC HALL OF FAME AND MUSEUM

FILM & TV

JACKSON, ALAN

two were opening for none other than Hank Williams. The duo later moved to New Mexico, where Campbell appeared on local radio and TV. He formed a band and eventually relocated to Los Angeles, landing work as a studio musician. His guitar skills can be heard on records by The Beach Boys, Frank Sinatra, Elvis Presley, and many more. He even toured with The Beach Boys in 1964.

While working as a sought-after studio musician, Campbell pursued a solo career and signed with Capitol Records in 1962. Radio success didn't come right away, and he had to wait until 1967 for his first real breakthrough with the release of "Gentle on My Mind," which landed on both the pop and country charts. The follow-up, "By the Time I Get to Phoenix," soared into the top five.

Hits like "Wichita Lineman," "Galveston," and "Southern Nights" followed in the 1970s and as Campbell's fame grew, so did his reach. He hosted *The Glen Campbell Good Time Hour* from 1969 to 1972, bringing country music into homes worldwide. In 1969, he also starred alongside John Wayne in *True Grit*, leading to more roles on the big screen.

During his career, Campbell struggled with and overcame addiction, continuing to release music into the 2000s. In 2011, he revealed he had been privately battling Alzheimer's disease. He launched a farewell tour and performed his final show on November 30, 2012. Campbell passed away in August 2017, aged 81. That year he said goodbye to fans with his 64th and final album, fittingly titled *Adiós*. Campbell's legacy lives on, and he's lovingly remembered as The Rhinestone Cowboy after his chart-topping 1975 hit.

CHESNEY, KENNY

At just 12 years old, Kenny Chesney stood in a Tennessee field and watched the band Alabama headline a concert in his hometown, an experience that ignited a fire in him that never went out. Born in March 1968 in the small East Tennessee town of Luttrell, Chesney grew up loving music and sports. In college, he played in his school's bluegrass band, and after graduation he set his sights on Nashville.

By 1990, Chesney had arrived in Music City and within just three years had secured both a publishing and a record deal. In 1994 his debut album, *In My Wildest Dreams*, was released via Capricorn Records, however the label's country division soon folded and he signed with BNA Records the following year. Over the next few years he released three more albums and a steady stream of number one hits, including "She's Got It All," "How Forever Feels," and "She Thinks My Tractor's Sexy."

Chesney hit a turning point in the early 2000s when he realized that fans knew his songs but didn't truly know him. Instead of "trying to be George Strait," he dug deeper into his songwriting and spent more time in the Virgin Islands, where he found creative inspiration. In 2002, he released the career-changing *No Shoes, No Shirt, No Problems*, the album that introduced fans to his island lifestyle.

On June 7, 2003, Chesney headlined his first stadium concert, drawing more than 61,000 fans to Neyland Stadium in Knoxville, near his hometown. That night marked the beginning of an unrivalled touring career. Sold-out arenas, amphitheaters, and NFL stadiums followed, and his high-energy live shows became synonymous with summer. Few artists have managed to connect with their audience the way he does, creating a feeling of pure joy, freedom, and an escape from reality night after night. Now, Chesney is an eight-time Entertainer of the Year who has played to over a million fans on every full-scale tour since 2002. He's also built a dedicated fan base known as No Shoes Nation.

"Few artists have managed to connect with their audience the way he does, creating a feeling of pure joy, freedom, and an escape from reality."

C

SEE ALSO:

ALABAMA

COUNTRY MUSIC HALL OF FAME AND MUSEUM

FANDOMS

STRAIT, GEORGE

TOUR BUS

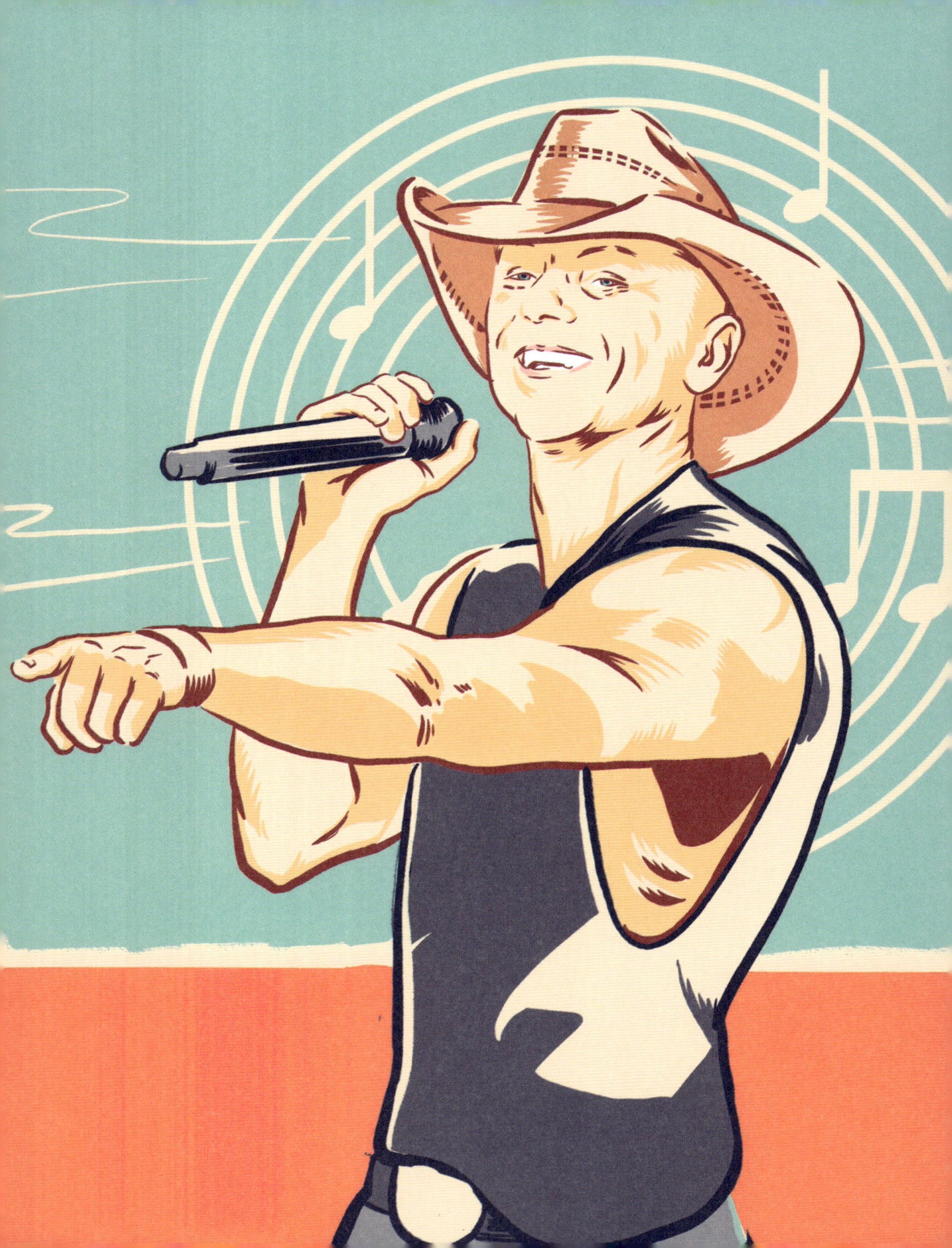

There's no denying that Kenny Chesney is one of the greatest entertainers of all time. His career spans four decades and he's still going strong, most recently becoming the first country artist to headline Sphere Vegas. With 36 number one singles—from the heartfelt "The Good Stuff" to the carefree "Summertime" and the anthemic "American Kids"—and 105 million units certified by the RIAA, that young boy who once dreamed of performing on stage like his idols in Alabama is now a member of the Country Music Hall of Fame, standing proudly alongside his heroes.

CHURCH, ERIC

From the start of his career, Eric Church has been unapologetically himself. He records the music he wants, plays by his own rules, and refuses to compromise his art. Often described as an "outlaw" or "rebel," Church shrugs off those titles, letting his signature blend of country and rock speak for itself.

Born in May 1977, Church was given his first guitar at age 13 and began writing songs soon after. He cut his teeth playing local gigs, including a steady slot performing at a barbecue joint. He later joined a band while attending Appalachian State University, although music wasn't yet his focus.

In 2001, with his degree in hand, he moved to Nashville with dreams of becoming a songwriter. After signing a publishing deal and writing songs for other artists for over a year, he set his sights on a solo career. By 2004 he'd signed with Capitol Nashville and connected with rock producer Jay Joyce, who has produced every one of his albums. His debut, *Sinners Like Me*, pushed boundaries with songs like "Lightning," detailing a man's final moments before facing the death penalty, and "Two Pink Lines" about teen pregnancy. His sophomore album, *Carolina*, even included a pro-marijuana track.

His third album, *Chief*, was a career-defining project, delivering his first two number one singles—"Drink in My Hand" and "Springsteen"—and earning both ACM and CMA Album of the Year honors. His live shows are legendary, often running three hours or more, with ever-changing set lists that make every night unique.

Never one to play by the rules, Church was famously fired from a Rascal Flatts tour in 2006 for playing too long and once mailed an album directly to fans and retailers without telling his label. His rebellious spirit has never faded.

In 2024, when his home state of North Carolina was ravaged by a hurricane, Church stepped up without

"Eric Church is living proof that doing things your own way can truly change the game."

SEE ALSO:

FANDOMS

LOWER BROADWAY

OUTLAW COUNTRY

PHILANTHROPY

SIGNATURE STYLE

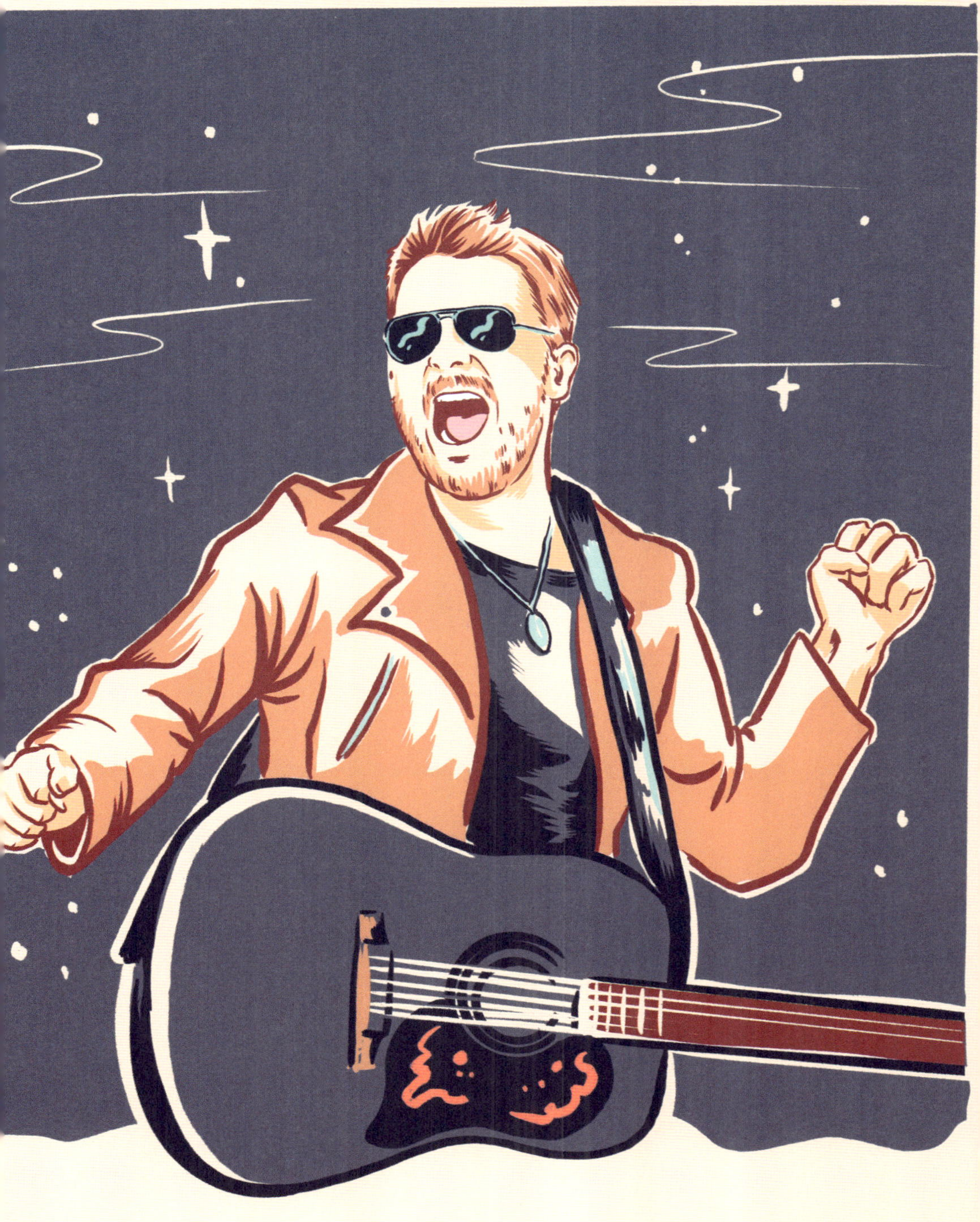

C

hesitation, donating proceeds from his song "Darkest Hour" to recovery efforts and pledging housing for those displaced by the storm. Outside of music, Church welcomes fans to his six-story Nashville bar, Chief's, on Lower Broadway, and is a minority owner of the Charlotte Hornets and co-owner of the Field & Stream brand alongside Morgan Wallen. To me, Eric Church is living proof that doing things your own way can truly change the game.

CLINE, PATSY

"A true pioneer, she broke down barriers for women and became the first female country artist to achieve many major milestones."

SEE ALSO:

COUNTRY MUSIC HALL OF FAME AND MUSEUM

GRAND OLE OPRY

LYNN, LORETTA

NELSON, WILLIE

Although she tragically died at just 30, Patsy Cline left an indelible mark on country music. A true pioneer, she broke down barriers for women and became the first female country artist to achieve many major milestones, including the first solo female to be inducted into the Country Music Hall of Fame.

Virginia Patterson Hensley, as she was then known, was born in 1932 in Winchester, Virginia. Growing up in a working-class family with a single mother as the head of the household, education took a backseat while she worked various jobs to help support the family. Later, a career in music beckoned and she began performing at venues along the East Coast and built a regional following.

She married Gerald Cline in 1953 and adopted her stage name. While the name stuck, her marriage didn't, and they divorced in 1957. This proved to be an eventful year for the singer with her first big break performing "Walking After Midnight" on the variety show *Arthur Godfrey's Talent Scouts*—the track which also earned her first hit on both the country and pop charts—and her marriage to Charlie Dick.

Her following releases didn't have the same impact, and it wasn't until 1961 when "I Fall to Pieces" climbed to the top of the charts that Cline thrived on the radio again. That same year, she was involved in a head-on collision that left

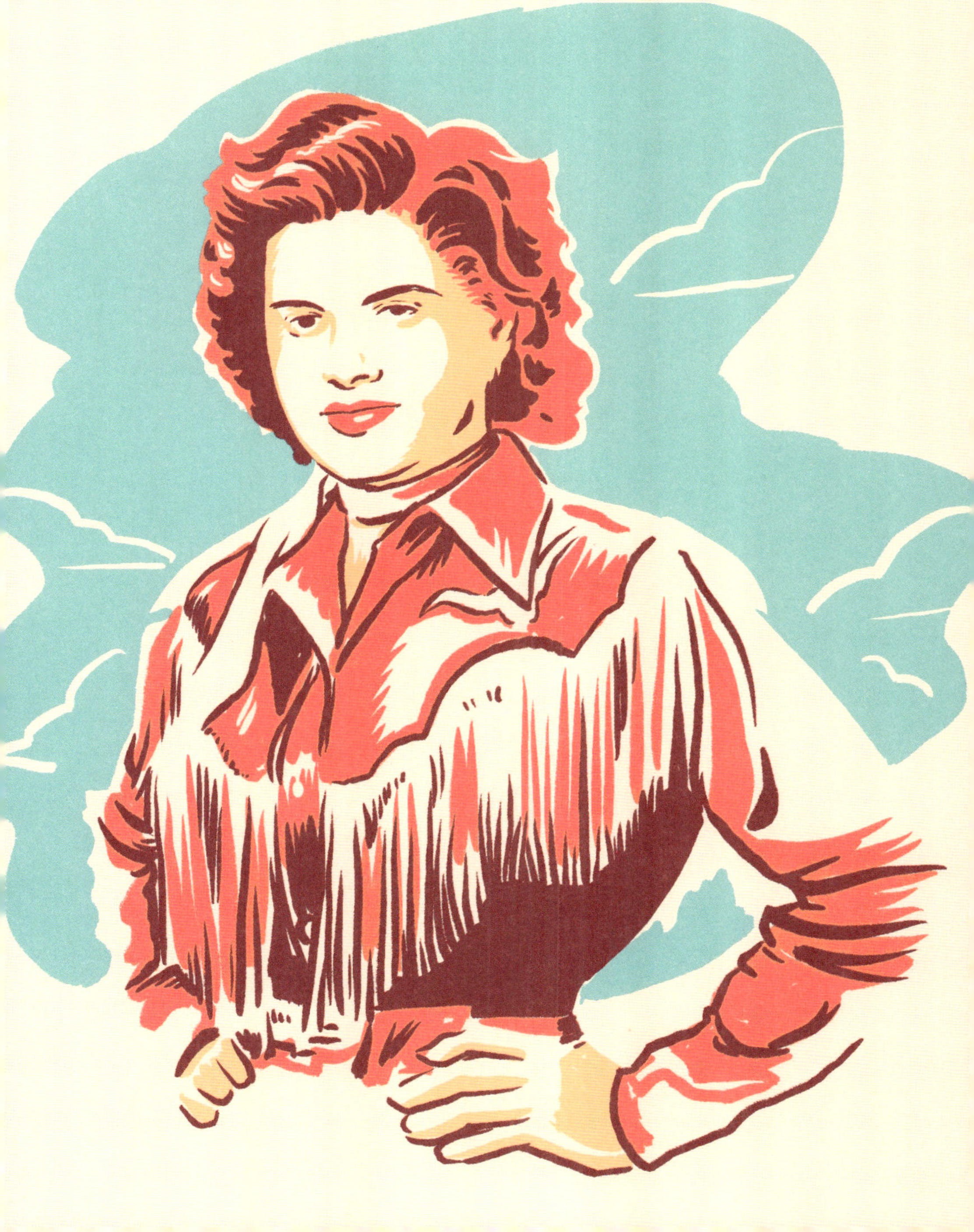

her hospitalized for a month. She returned to the stage despite serious injuries and during her recovery recorded "Crazy," written by a young Willie Nelson. It would go on to become her signature hit and the most-played jukebox song of all time.

Cline made history as the first person to ask to join the Grand Ole Opry (rather than wait to be invited) and was the first female country star to headline a Las Vegas residency. She was also a devoted mother of two, balancing her career with family life until her unexpected passing in March 1963 when she died in a plane crash returning home from a show in Kansas City.

Her career inspired generations of artists, including Loretta Lynn, Trisha Yearwood, and Reba McEnitre. It's impossible not to wonder how much incredible music the world missed out on because of her untimely death.

CMA FEST

"Its success is a testament to the unique bond between country artists and fans, which CMA Fest continues to celebrate."

SEE ALSO:

BROOKS, GARTH
NASHVILLE
SWIFT, TAYLOR

The idea for CMA Fest, the world's longest-running country music festival, stemmed from a desire to bring artists and fans closer together. Planning began in 1970, and two years later 5,000 people attended the first event, then called Fan Fair, at Nashville's Municipal Auditorium. For just $20 attendees enjoyed four days of performances, autograph signings, and two meals. The lineup included country music legends George Jones, Roy Acuff, and Tammy Wynette, along with over 100 exhibit booths for photos and autographs.

In 1973, the festival moved to June for better weather, a tradition that continues today. The 1974 event featured a surprise visit from Paul McCartney and an unforgettable performance from Porter Wagoner and Dolly Parton, who wouldn't perform together for another ten years. Fan Fair relocated to the Tennessee State Fairgrounds in 1982 to handle growing crowds. By 1993 artist booths had become major attractions, with Alan Jackson's "Chattahoochee" booth winning first prize. In 1996, Garth Brooks famously signed autographs for a staggering 23 hours.

A major shift came in 2001 when Fan Fair returned to downtown Nashville, expanding to multiple venues, including nightly concerts at The Coliseum (now Nissan Stadium). That year, 115 artists performed, 175 participated in the exhibit hall, and the Country Music Association donated $100,000 to artist-selected charities. Fan Fair was rebranded as CMA Music Festival in 2003, and the following year CBS documented the event in a two-hour television special. By 2005, the festival expanded to include a kick-off parade, running through downtown Nashville.

Following the devastating Nashville flood in 2010, CMA pledged to donate half of the net proceeds from the festival to flood relief efforts. The other half was donated to Keep the Music Playing, an initiative supporting music education in local public schools. That year, Taylor Swift signed autographs at the festival for 13 hours straight.

What has now become known as The Ultimate Country Music Fan Experience once again had a name change in 2018, becoming CMA Fest. The festival continued to grow and thrive, even broadcasting a four-hour virtual variety show when the pandemic postponed the 2020 event. CMA Fest celebrated its 50th anniversary in 2023 and continues to expand. By 2025, the festival was drawing 95,000 fans from around the world, with more than 300 performances and 475 meet and greets. All artists appear and perform for free in support of the CMA Foundation, which funds music education programs across the US. Its success is a testament to the unique bond between country artists and fans, which CMA Fest continues to celebrate.

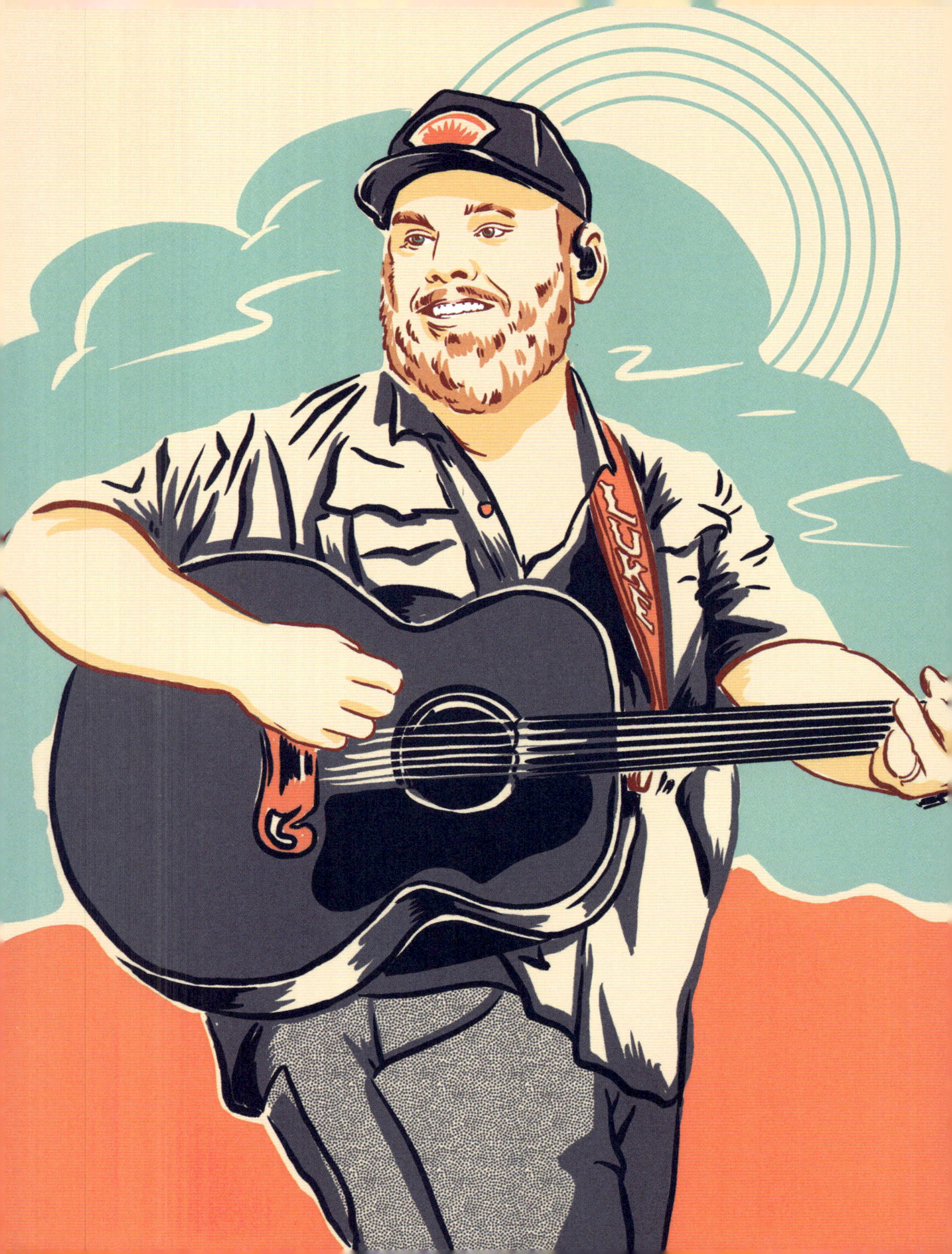
LUKE

COMBS, LUKE

Long before he was a country music superstar selling out stadiums around the world, Luke Combs was just a kid with a dream of becoming a homicide detective, until everything changed when he picked up a guitar in college.

Born in March 1990 in Asheville, North Carolina, Combs enjoyed a typical childhood. He played football, sang in church, and was a member of his school chorus. His first concert was a Vince Gill show when he was just six years old. Little did he know that Gill would be the one to induct him into the Grand Ole Opry decades later. Talk about a full-circle moment! Although he received a guitar from his parents in seventh grade, he didn't learn to play until his time at Appalachian State University. After his mother pointed out that Kenny Chesney and Tim McGraw hadn't picked up the guitar until they were around his age, Combs began teaching himself.

Soon, he began performing at local spots around North Carolina. He auditioned for *The Voice* but was turned down because producers didn't think his story was "interesting enough" for television. He used that rejection as motivation to keep going, sharing covers and original songs on YouTube and the now-defunct Vine app.

In 2014, Combs took a trip to Nashville to record an EP and later relocated to Music City. He started building a regional following across the Southeast as fans discovered his music online. He kept releasing EPs and playing shows, even as he faced rejection. Managers told him he was better suited writing songs than performing them, and labels passed on him because he didn't have the right "look" for country music. But Combs never gave up.

In 2016, he signed with River House Artists/Columbia Nashville and released his debut single "Hurricane," which skyrocketed to number one. Fan favorites like "When It Rains It Pours," "Beautiful Crazy," and "Beer Never Broke My Heart" followed. One of his biggest musical inspirations was fellow North Carolina native Eric Church

"Combs has proven to be one of the greatest country singers and songwriters of his generation."

SEE ALSO:

CHURCH, ERIC
GILL, VINCE
GRAND OLE OPRY
PHILANTHROPY

C

and, in 2020, things came full circle when they released their chart-topping duet, "Does to Me."

His live shows grew from clubs to theaters, arenas, and eventually stadiums, and his global reach expanded with sold-out tours overseas. Now an Opry member, two-time CMA Entertainer of the Year, and among the best-selling country artists in history with over 168 million units, Combs has proven to be one of the greatest country singers and songwriters of his generation.

Fun fact: Luke Combs' song "Doin' This" was inspired by a question I asked him during an interview in 2018. The song goes, "Someone asked me once in an interview: What was growing up like, where'd you go to school? And what would you do if you weren't doin' this?" That someone was me. It's still one of the coolest moments of my career.

COUNTRY MUSIC HALL OF FAME AND MUSEUM

This homage to country music is a fan must-see. First opening its doors on Music Row, Nashville, in 1967, the operation would later relocate to its current home on Rep. John Lewis Way in 2001. Often referred to as "The Smithsonian of country music," the museum aims to preserve and interpret the rich history of country music for future generations.

The site boasts an impressive 350,000 square feet (32,500 square meters) of galleries, exhibits, and archives, and houses thousands of iconic artifacts dedicated to country music. A tour around the museum takes visitors on a journey from country music's humble

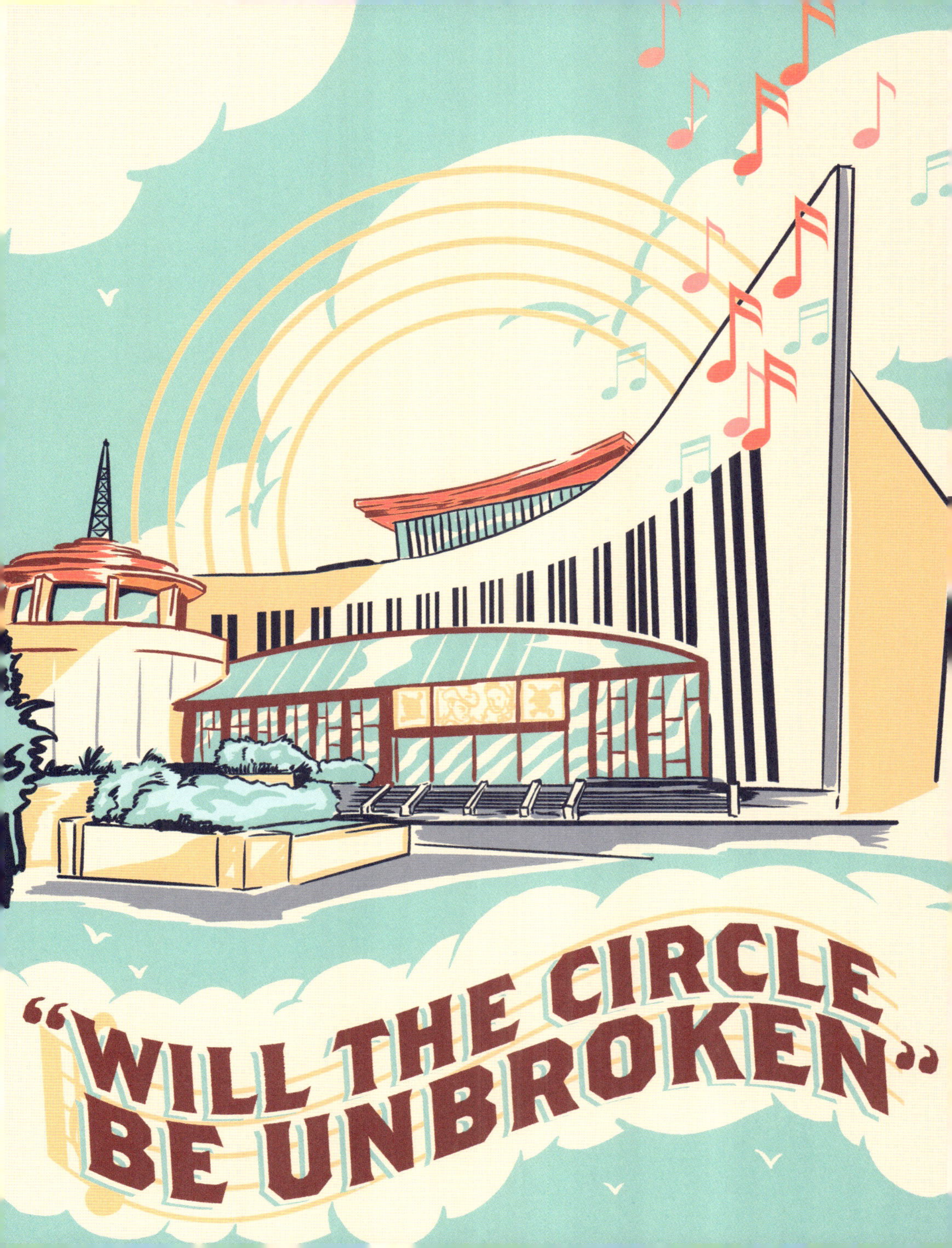
"WILL THE CIRCLE
BE UNBROKEN"

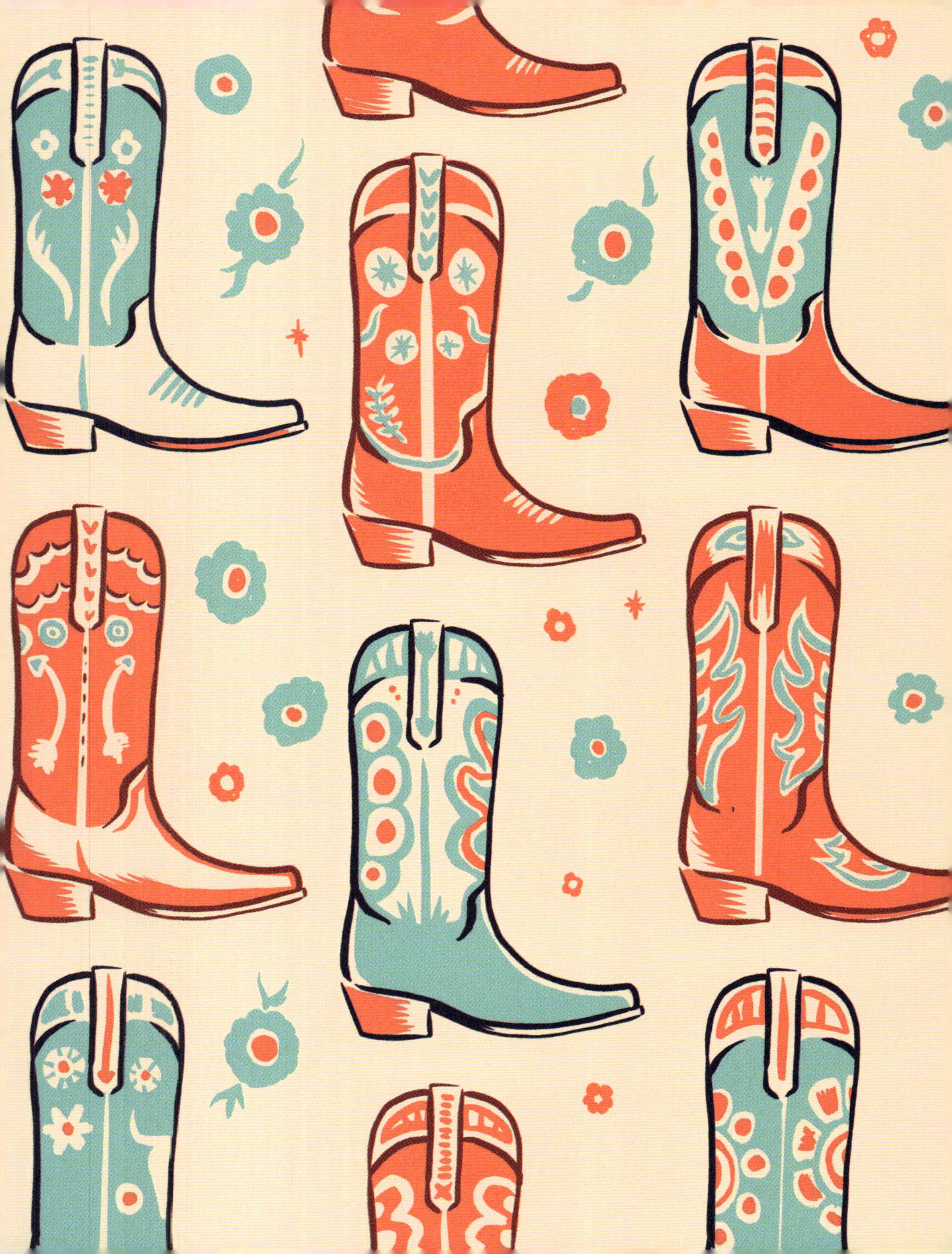

beginnings to those who shaped the genre and the making of today's stars.

The priceless pieces on display include Alan Jackson's father's radio (referenced in his song "Chasin' That Neon Rainbow"), Johnny Cash's all-black stage wear, Little Jimmy Dickens's cowboy hat, and Patsy Cline's famous cowgirl costume. It's also home to nearly 500 musical instruments that once belonged to renowned musicians and artists.

In 2012, Taylor Swift made a generous $4 million donation to the museum, which lead to the creation of the Taylor Swift Education Center. Here, guests of all ages can experience the video-conference lab and interactive galleries as well as viewing outfits and instruments belonging to Swift herself.

Members of the prestigious Country Music Hall of Fame are honored in the hallowed Rotunda with bronze plaques lining the walls. "Will the Circle Be Unbroken," lyrics from the song made famous by the Carter Family, encircles the room, and the tower was created to resemble the WSM radio tower, the station that is home to the *Grand Ole Opry*. The museum was awarded the National Medal of Arts in 2024 and welcomes more than one million guests each year, making it one of the US's most-visited museums. It really is the ultimate tribute to country music.

C

"Members of the prestigious Country Music Hall of Fame are honored in the hallowed Rotunda with bronze plaques lining the walls."

SEE ALSO:

NASHVILLE

SWIFT, TAYLOR

"WILL THE CIRCLE BE UNBROKEN"

COWBOY BOOTS

Originally designed for function rather than fashion, it's thought that the first true cowboy boots were crafted in Texas or Kansas. Their rise to popularity in the 1800s was thanks to the increase in cattle ranching across North America, but it would be a few decades before they entered the mainstream. Made from cowhide, the boots featured high shafts to protect ranchers' legs from snakes and stirrup rub, while also shielding ankles from bruising. Originally each pair was handmade by a cobbler and custom-fitted for its owner, and the signature high heels were to prevent feet from slipping through the stirrups.

C

"Cowboy boots may have been designed for function, but today they stand as a lasting symbol of country music style."

SEE ALSO:

LOWER BROADWAY

STAPLETON, CHRIS

STYLE

WILSON, LAINEY

By the early 1900s, cowboy boots were showing up as more than just ranch wear. Hollywood Westerns brought the boots onto the big screen and, as country music began to take shape, artists leaned into the iconic cowboy look which, of course, included cowboy boots.

What started as functional footwear quickly became a fashion statement. Designers began adding colorful stitching and experimenting with more exotic materials like snakeskin, ostrich, bison, and alligator. Nudie Cohn, creator of the famous Nudie suits, designed boots that were just as flashy as his clothing, complete with rhinestones, inlays, overlays, and intricate patterns.

Even as country music's style evolved, the boots never went away. To this day, they remain a staple. Walk down Nashville's Lower Broadway or attend a country concert or festival, and you're bound to see them everywhere.

Cowboy boots are so tied to country music that they've inspired plenty of songs, from Eric Church's "These Boots" and Morgan Wallen's "Sand in My Boots," to Shania Twain's "Whose Bed Have Your Boots Been Under," and, of course, Nancy Sinatra's "These Boots Are Made for Walkin'."

Some artists have even gone as far as launching their own boot brands or teaming up with designers to create curated lines: Lainey Wilson has Golden West Boots, while Chris Stapleton partnered with Lucchese on a men's collection. Cowboy boots may have been designed for function, but today they stand as a lasting symbol of country music style.

COWBOY CARTER

In 2024, Beyoncé took the world by storm with her eighth studio album, *Act II: Cowboy Carter*. Five years in the making, the project drew from the Texas native's influences—including blues, soul, and folk—creating a far-reaching album that is rooted in country while also pushing genre boundaries.

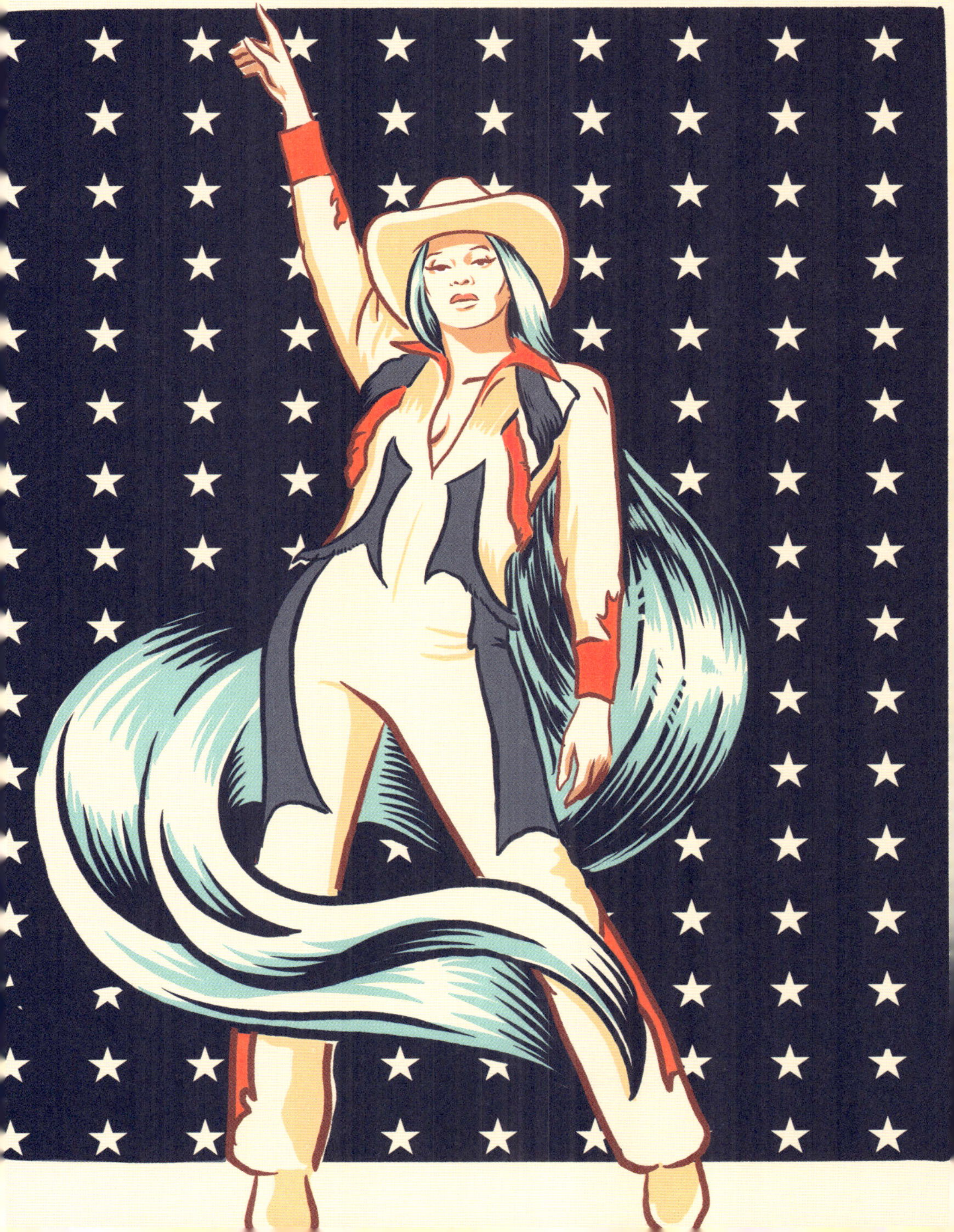

C

"A far-reaching album that is rooted in country while also pushing genre boundaries."

SEE ALSO:

NELSON, WILLIE

PARTON, DOLLY

Beyoncé took a "no rules" approach when recording *Cowboy Carter*, allowing the music to lead the way without category limitations. She used a plethora of instruments, including harmonica, acoustic guitar, pedal steel, banjo, mandolin, and fiddle, throughout the album and even used her own nails as percussion.

On the 27-track project, Beyoncé shines a light on Linda Martell, the first Black woman to perform at the Grand Ole Opry, and also shares the spotlight with contemporary Black country artists Willie Jones, Brittney Spencer, Shaboozey, Reyna Roberts, Tanner Adell, and Tiera Kennedy.

Country icons Willie Nelson and Dolly Parton lend their voices to a few of the album's spoken-word tracks, while Miley Cyrus and Post Malone join Beyoncé on standout tracks "II Most Wanted" and "Levii's Jeans," respectively.

With the release of *Cowboy Carter*, Beyoncé challenged stereotypes and sparked important conversations about race and inclusion in country music. She also made history as the first Black woman to top Billboard's Top Country Albums chart and Hot Country Songs chart.

At the 67th Annual Grammy Awards, *Cowboy Carter* was crowned Best Country Album and Album of the Year. In a surprising turn of events, the Recording Academy later announced a major change to the ballot, adding a brand-new category for Best Traditional Country Album and changing the existing Best Country Album category to Best Contemporary Country Album. With these changes, Beyoncé's *Cowboy Carter* will go down as the last album to ever receive the title of Best Country Album.

DEMOS

In the inner workings of the music industry, demos are used to showcase songs rather than performers. They're typically recorded with stripped-back instrumentation, often just a guitar or keyboard, so the lyrics and melody can be clearly heard and interpreted. While not fully produced, demos convey the songwriter's vision for the song.

Demos are an essential tool for pitching songs to publishers, producers, artists, and record labels, giving a song the chance to be noticed with the ultimate goal of being recorded professionally.

Many artists started out singing on demos, including legends like Loretta Lynn and Garth Brooks. Songwriters and publishing companies often hire talented vocalists to bring their songs to life, recording demos that can then be pitched to established performers. In many cases, this work helped launch these artists' own careers.

Before signing her record deal, Trisha Yearwood earned $10–$30 per song singing demos. The experience proved invaluable, teaching her to recognize a great song and helping her develop her own voice along the way.

Demos have also been crucial for artists in discovering songs. Many performers who follow a "best song wins" approach are constantly searching for their next hit, whether or not they wrote it themselves. Blake Shelton discovered "God's Country" while listening to a demo, and Tim McGraw was inspired to record "Humble and Kind" after hearing songwriter Lori McKenna's stunning demo of the song.

Though technology has evolved and demos are no longer passed around on tapes, they remain a vital tool for getting songs discovered.

"Many artists started out singing on demos, including legends like Loretta Lynn and Garth Brooks."

SEE ALSO:

BROOKS, GARTH
LYNN, LORETTA
MCGRAW, TIM
SHELTON, BLAKE
SONGWRITERS
YEARWOOD, TRISHA

D

DOLLYWOOD

"Dollywood is unlike any other theme park in the world because only Dolly could dream it up."

SEE ALSO:

PARTON, DOLLY
PHILANTHROPY

As well as her timeless songs and generous philanthropy, part of Dolly Parton's enduring legacy is Dollywood, a 160-acre (65-hectare) theme park located in Pigeon Forge, Tennessee. Nestled in the foothills of the Great Smoky Mountains near her hometown of Sevierville, Dollywood is the state's most-visited tourist attraction, welcoming more than two million guests each year.

Parton partnered with Herschend Family Enterprises in 1986 to transform the park—which was formerly known as Rebel Railroad, Goldrush Junction, and, later, Silver Dollar City—into Dollywood. Since then, the park has undergone several expansions and earned its place as one of the top theme parks in the country.

Every visit is packed with fun—from roller coasters like the winding Tennessee Tornado for the thrill seekers, to the charming Black Bear Trail, a sweet nod to the Smoky Mountains' famous inhabitants, where guests young and old can ride on smiling bears. There's plenty of live entertainment and seasonal events, like the I Will Always Love You Music Festival and Smoky Mountain Christmas. Honoring her Appalachian roots, the park even features a replica of Dolly's childhood home and showcases East Tennessee artisans and master craftsmen demonstrating traditional skills. One of the most iconic attractions is the Dollywood Express, a 110-ton coal-fired steam engine that takes guests on a scenic 5-mile (8-km) ride through the mountains.

But Dollywood is far more than a theme park. The resort also hosts performances by country and bluegrass artists—notably, Grand Ole Opry member Carly Pearce started out singing at Dollywood when she was just 16 years old. The Dolly Parton Experience is a must-see. This museum-like attraction spans her life and career with sections dedicated to her humble beginnings, iconic fashion, songwriting, and more. Nearby is Dollywood's DreamMore Resort, where Parton stores her Dream Box:

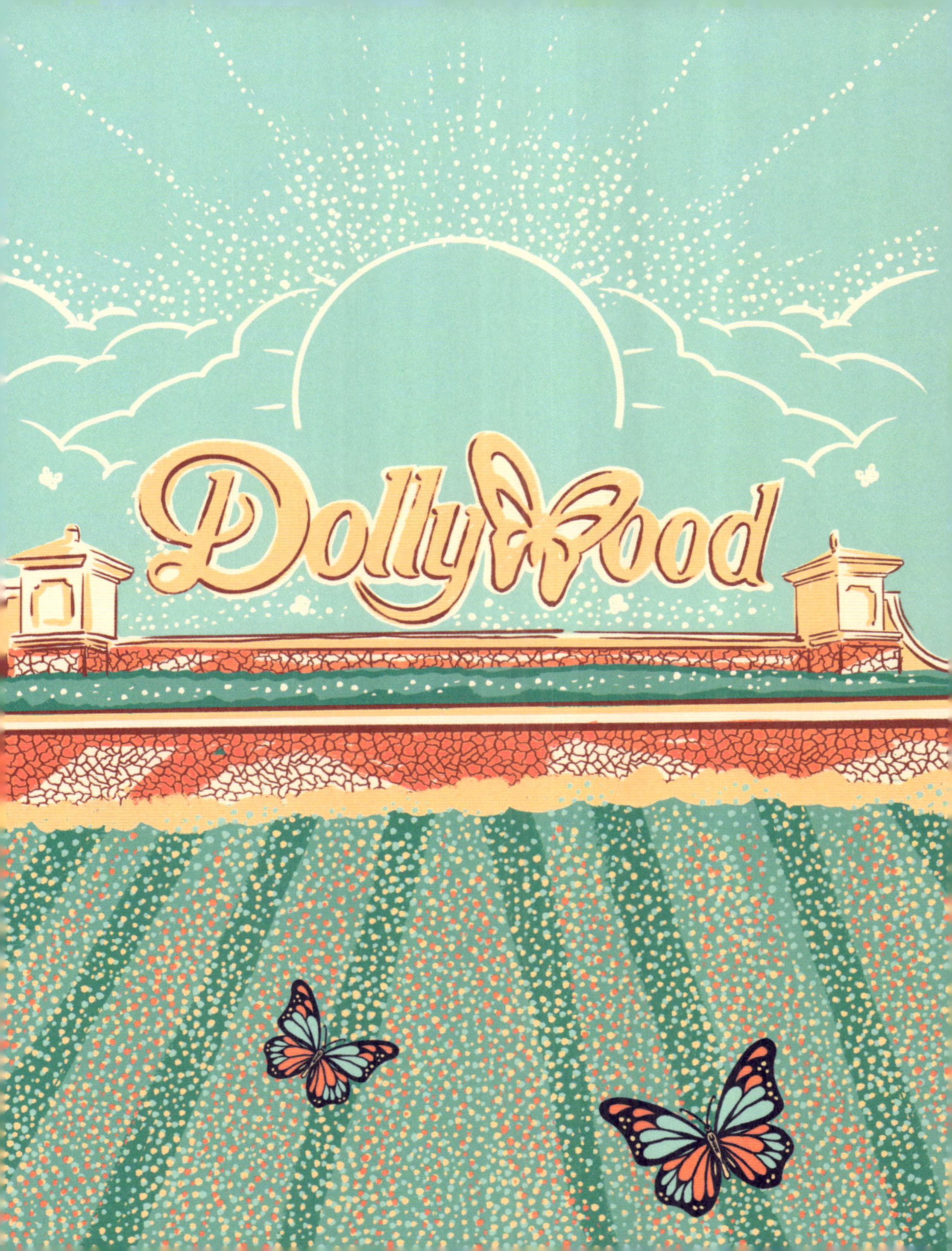
Dollywood

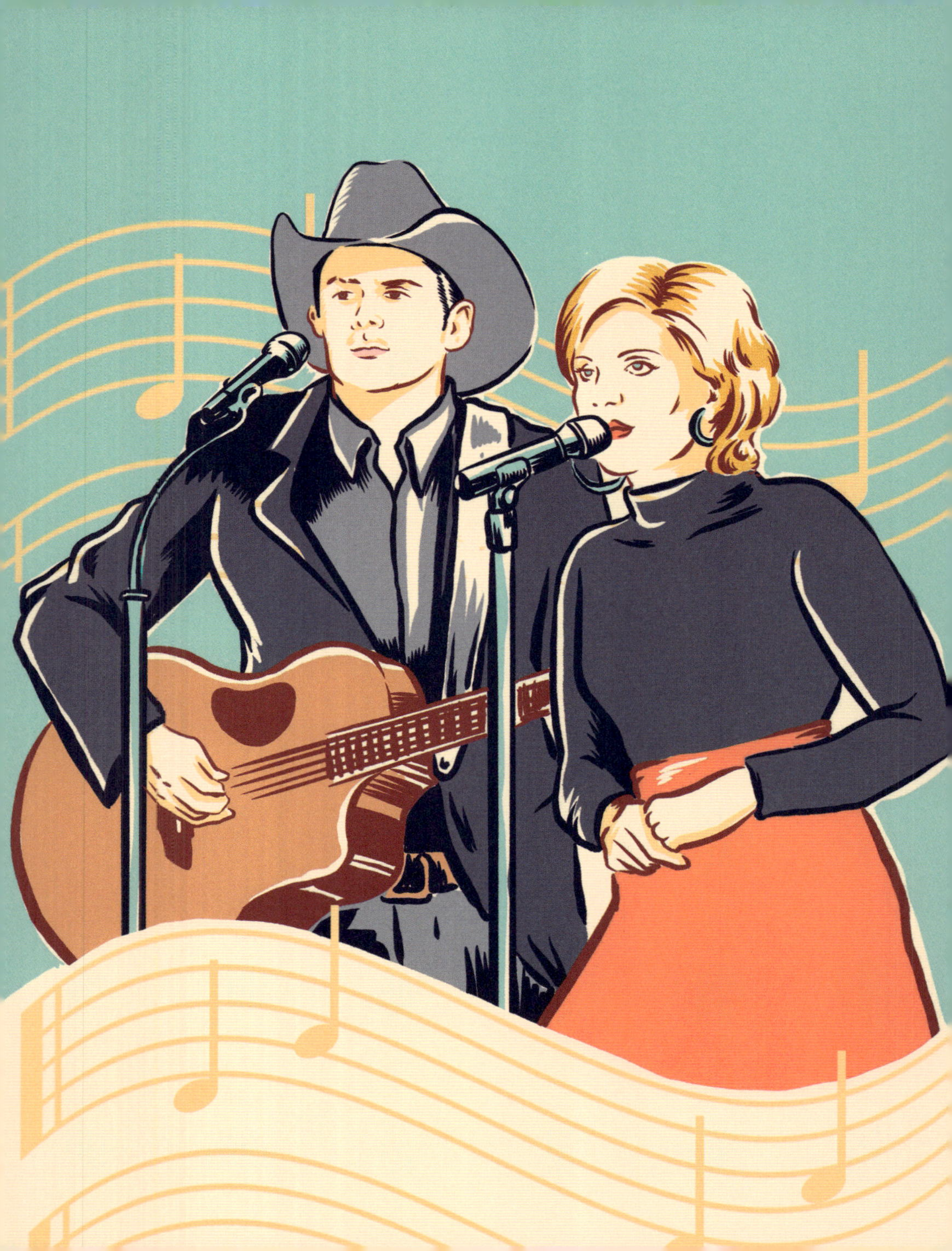

a time capsule that is not to be opened until 2045. Among other items, it holds an unreleased song Dolly wrote in 2015, detailing her hopes and dreams for the future.

Dolly Parton serves as the park's "Dreamer-in-Chief" and her magical touches are felt throughout. Dollywood is unlike any other theme park in the world because only Dolly could dream it up. Tip: If you go, don't miss the famous cinnamon bread at the Grist Mill.

DUETS

Something special happens when country artists come together for a duet. There's nothing quite like hearing two voices blend to tell a story, and maybe it's just me, but there's something especially magical about a male-female pairing.

"There's nothing quite like hearing two voices blend to tell a story."

Country music is full of unforgettable duets, many of which have stood the test of time and sound just as good today as they did 50 years ago. Songs like "Jackson" by Johnny Cash and June Carter Cash, "Louisiana Woman, Mississippi Man" by Loretta Lynn and Conway Twitty, and "Mamas Don't Let Your Babies Grow Up to Be Cowboys" by Willie Nelson and Waylon Jennings all prove that two voices really are better than one.

The late 1960s through to the early 1980s felt like the golden era of country duets. Artists like Dolly Parton and Porter Wagoner, and George Jones and Tammy Wynette made duet albums that became a big part of their careers, setting the bar for what a country duet should be.

And then came "Islands in the Stream." When Dolly teamed up with Kenny Rogers in 1983, they created what might be the most iconic duet of all time. Even if you're not a country fan, chances are you know that song, and that says a lot.

The 1990s brought us two of my personal favorites, both tied to Reba McEntire: "Does He Love You" recorded

SEE ALSO:

ALDEAN, JASON
BROOKS & DUNN
BROOKS, GARTH
BROWN, KANE
HILL, FAITH
JOHNNY & JUNE
JONES, GEORGE
LYNN, LORETTA
MCENTIRE, REBA
MCGRAW, TIM
NELSON, WILLIE
PAISLEY, BRAD
PARTON, DOLLY
ROGERS, KENNY
TWITTY, CONWAY

E

UNDERWOOD, CARRIE

WAGONER, PORTER

WYNETTE, TAMMY

YEARWOOD, TRISHA

with Linda Davis, and "If You See Him/If You See Her," her unforgettable collaboration with Brooks & Dunn. If you don't know them, drop everything and go listen.

When it comes to the cream of the crop of duets, though, my mind goes straight to "Whiskey Lullaby" by Brad Paisley and Alison Krauss. It's one of the most heartbreaking songs ever recorded, and the way they bring the emotional story to life is nothing short of perfect.

Power couples like Trisha Yearwood and Garth Brooks, and Faith Hill and Tim McGraw kept the tradition of duet albums alive in more recent years, but these days the duet record feels like a thing of the past.

But don't worry, there's no shortage of stand-alone duet singles. From Jason Aldean and Carrie Underwood's "If I Didn't Love You" and Kane and Katelyn Brown's "Thank God," to Ella Langley and Riley Green's "You Look Like You Love Me," the magic of the country duet is still very much alive.

EMO COWGIRL

"Moroney has become the embodiment of the emo cowgirl—embracing the term through her music, her aesthetic, and her live shows."

Not to be confused with the punk-rooted genre, "emo cowgirl" is short for emotional cowgirl and was popularized by singer-songwriter Megan Moroney.

For Moroney, "emo" reflects her ability to wear her heart on her sleeve through raw and honest songs inspired by her experiences with love. Her unique, raspy tone helps convey the emotion behind her heartbreak anthems, and emo cowgirl really is the perfect way to sum up both her sound and her songs.

She first introduced fans to her one-of-a-kind brand of country music through her independently released EP, *Pistol Made of Roses*, but her breakout moment came with the release of "Tennessee Orange" in 2022. The track, which tells the story of a girl from Georgia falling head over heels for a boy from rival state Tennessee, had fans

SEE ALSO:

SWIFT, TAYLOR

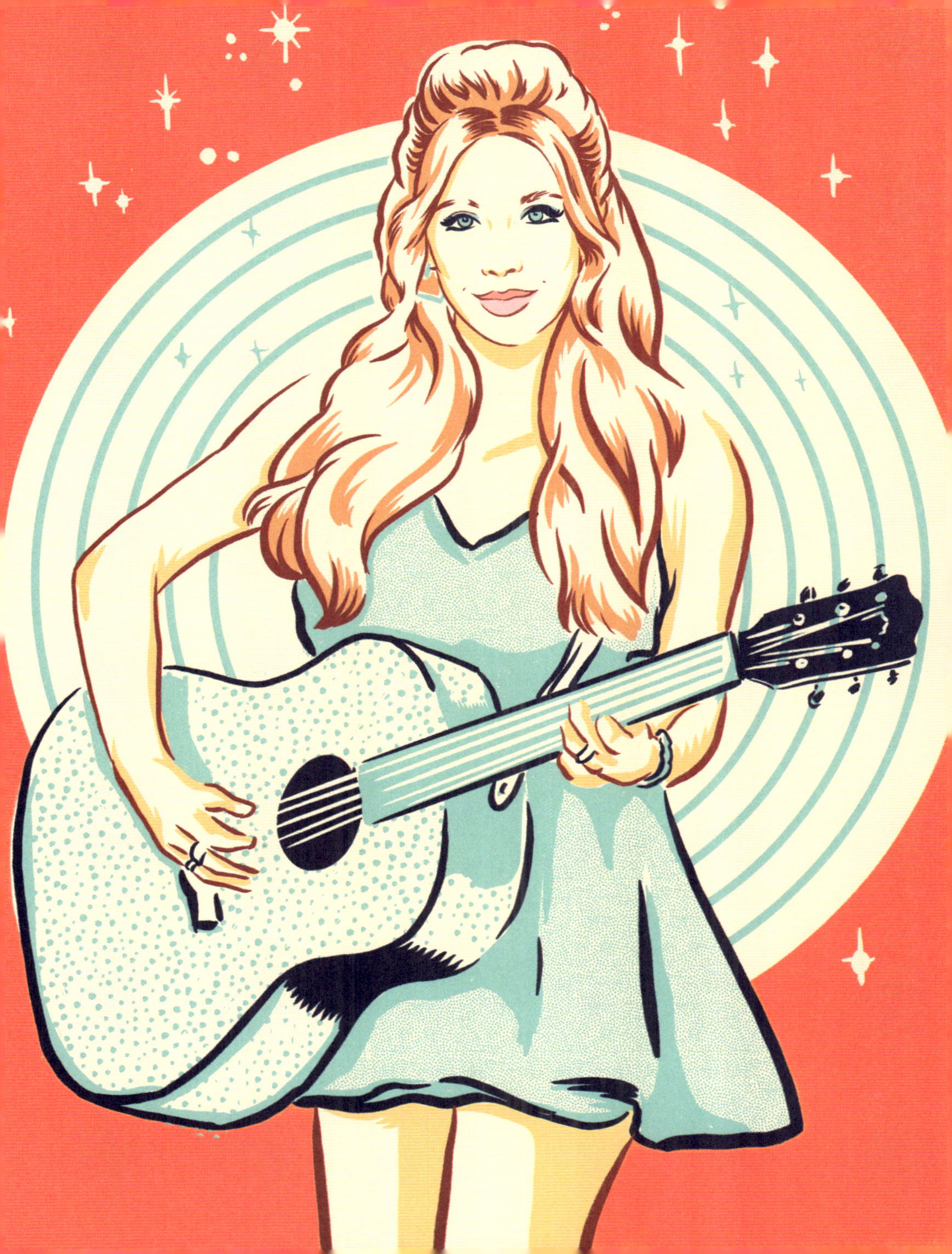

E

dissecting every lyric in hopes of uncovering the true story behind the song.

Moroney solidified her emo cowgirl status with her albums *Lucky* and *Am I Okay?*, both of which showcase her ability to deliver vulnerable, deeply relatable stories about love, heartbreak, and the messy emotions in between.

Much like Taylor Swift, whom Moroney often cites as a major influence, she channels real stories of love gone wrong into her music. She's admitted it sometimes feels like she's oversharing, but says she's inspired to keep writing by the messages she receives from fans thanking her for helping them navigate their own breakups. Songs like "Girl in the Mirror," "28th of June," "Mama I Lied," and "Hell of a Show" are quintessential emo cowgirl anthems.

Over time, Moroney has become the embodiment of the emo cowgirl—embracing the term through her music, her aesthetic, and her live shows. She even sports a guitar strap with "emo cowgirl" emblazoned on it. What started as a simple way to describe her music has since become her identity. There's something to be said for writing songs about real-life experiences and the ups and downs of love—the kind that leave fans guessing who each one is about. It worked for Taylor Swift, and Moroney is carrying on the tradition.

END OF TOUR GIFTS

At some point, it became customary for headlining artists to show their gratitude to their tour openers with parting gifts. I'm not exactly sure when this tradition started, but it's been a staple in Nashville for at least the past decade. The gesture serves as a way to say thank you for joining the run. Not only do these rising stars leave the tours with valuable experience and the chance to learn from some of the best in the business, they also often head home with a memorable keepsake.

Some artists get creative and personal with their thank-yous. For example, Luke Combs once surprised Ashley McBryde with a custom tour bar cart, complete with her logo, lights, and more. Morgan Wallen gifted his One Night at a Time tourmates with diamond "One Night" necklaces, while Lainey Wilson thanked HARDY for joining her on the road with a custom guitar engraved with his album title and name.

Others lean toward luxury items. Kane Brown has gifted several of his tourmates, including Jordan Davis, a Rolex watch, which is also a favorite gift for Jason Aldean to give to his tour openers.

Some gifts are all about practicality. Kenny Chesney arranged for a custom-built sauna to be installed at Megan Moroney's home while she was out on the road, and Miranda Lambert gifted Dierks Bentley an ATV (all-terrain vehicle). Then there's Luke Bryan, who kept it simple (and straight to the point) by giving rising star Ashley Cooke an envelope filled with cash.

No matter how big or small, these end-of-tour gifts demonstrate how country artists really show up for one another and that's what makes the country music community feel like family.

"No matter how big or small, these end-of-tour gifts demonstrate how country artists really show up for one another."

SEE ALSO:

ALDEAN, JASON
BROWN, KANE
BRYAN, LUKE
CHESNEY, KENNY
COMBS, LUKE
LAMBERT, MIRANDA

&

"The Ernest Tubb Record Shop became a landmark when it opened its doors in May 1947 as the first all-country record store."

SEE ALSO:

GRAND OLE OPRY
LOWER BROADWAY
NASHVILLE
RYMAN AUDITORIUM

ERNEST TUBB RECORD SHOP

Located at 417 Broadway, Nashville, nestled among the honky-tonks and glowing neon signs, the Ernest Tubb Record Shop became a landmark when it opened its doors in May 1947 as the first all-country record store.

The store was founded by the "Texas Troubadour" himself, Ernest Tubb, who helped popularize honky-tonk music with his hit "Walking the Floor Over You." A member of the Country Music Hall of Fame and a true road warrior, Tubb was the first artist to play electric guitar on the Grand Ole Opry stage and the first to take the iconic show to Carnegie Hall in New York City.

Originally located at 720 Commerce Street, the store moved to its longtime home on Broadway in 1951. Tubb chose the spot for its proximity to the Ryman Auditorium, then home to the *Grand Ole Opry*. By day, it was a bustling record shop selling vinyl, eight-tracks, and more. By night, it came alive as a gathering place for artists, musicians, and fans.

On Saturday evenings, the shop hosted the *Midnite Jamboree*, a post-*Opry* concert radio show that welcomed legends like Johnny Cash, Loretta Lynn, and Marty Stuart. It also offered a stage to rising stars, including Randy Travis before his big break. Broadcast weekly on WSM radio, the *Jamboree* became the second-longest-running radio show in history, right behind the *Opry* itself. Artists often stuck around after shows to sign records, CDs, and memorabilia, sometimes into the early morning hours.

The record shop officially closed in spring 2022, sparking heartbreak and outrage among country fans. Soon after, Ernest Tubb's family, together with hospitality group Tusk Brothers, announced plans to restore the beloved establishment at its original Broadway location. It officially reopened in the fall of 2025.

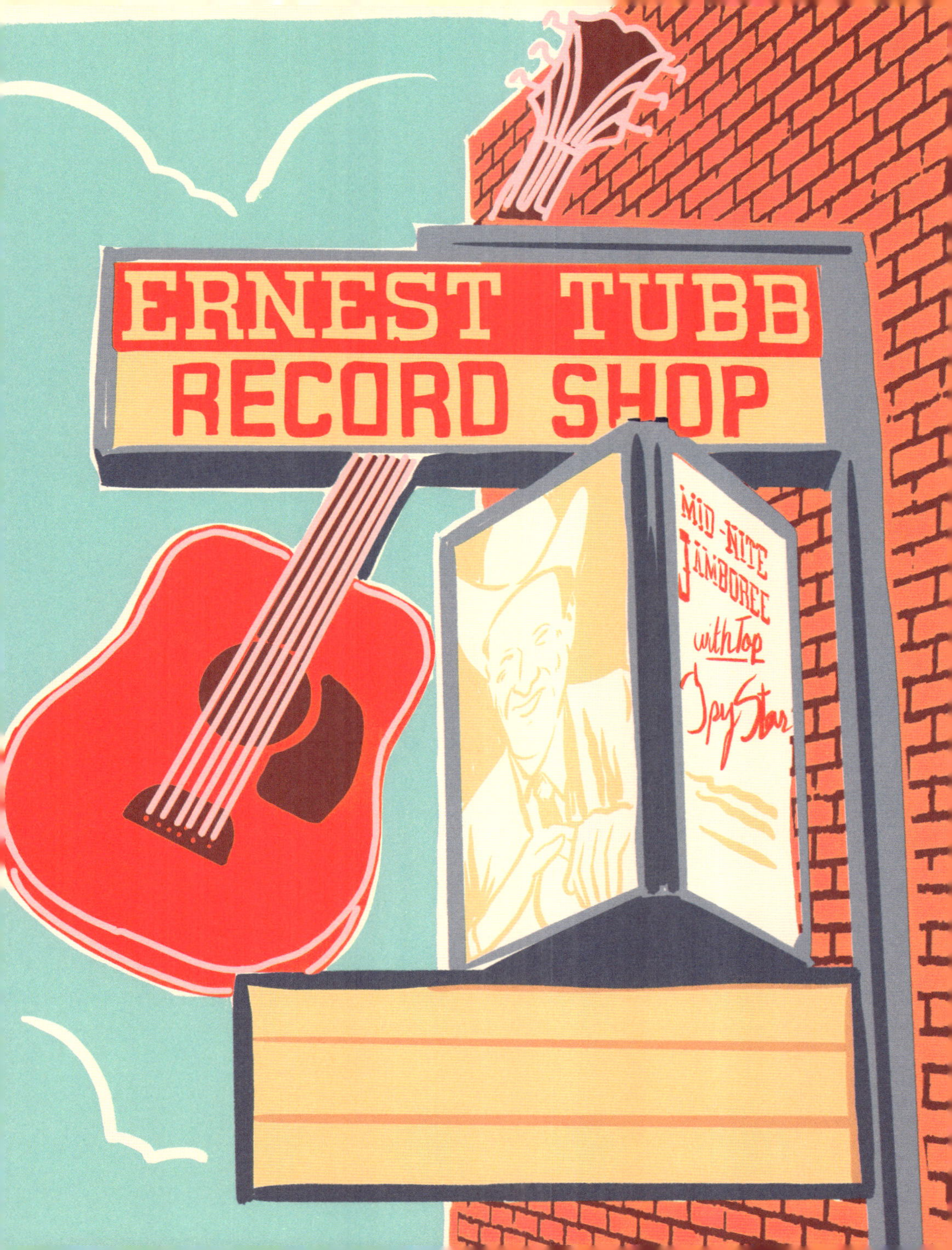
ERNEST TUBB
RECORD SHOP
MID-NITE
JAMBOREE
with Top

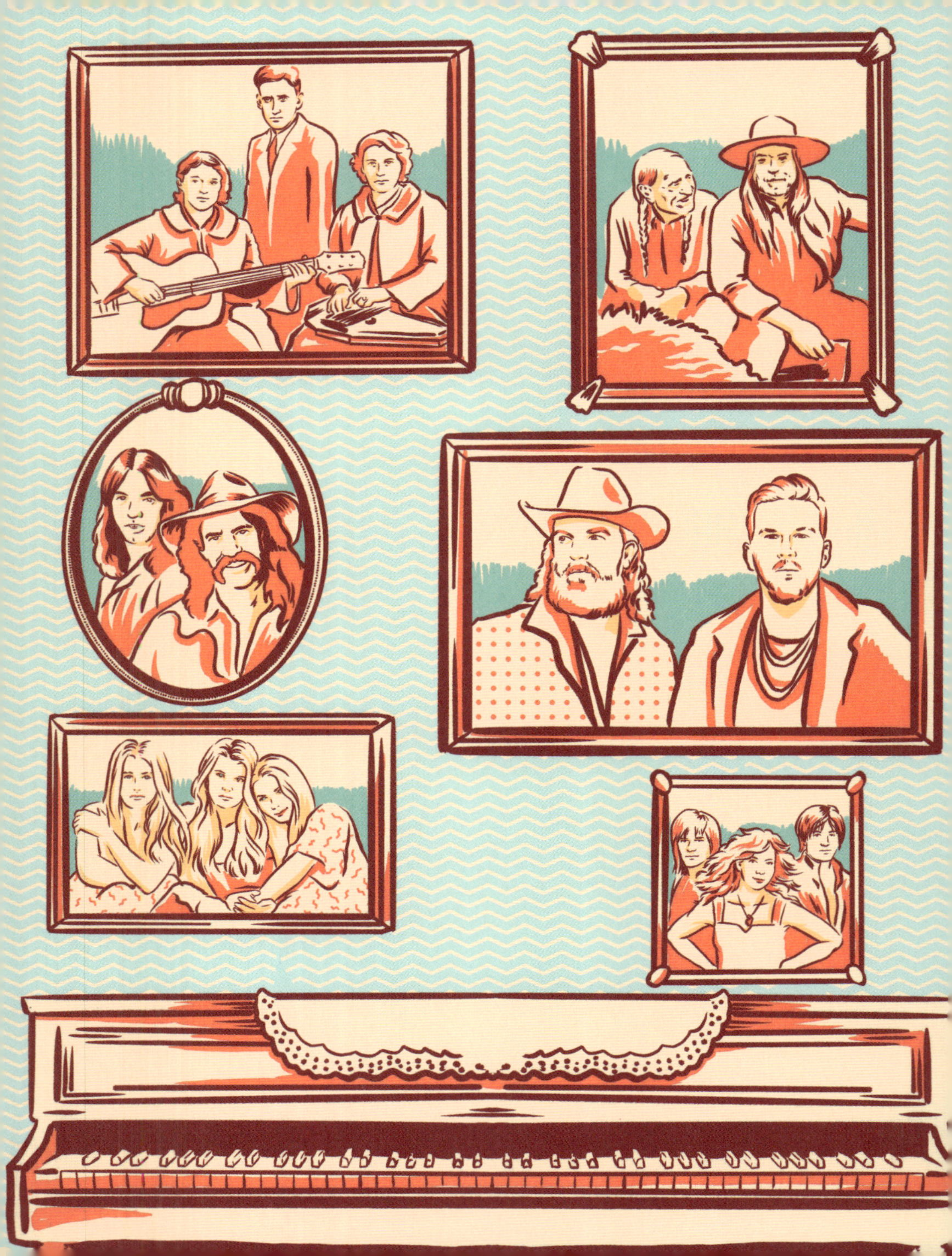

FAMILY TIES

In some families, country music becomes the family business. Whether it's a mother-daughter duo, a father-son bond, or a sibling connection, these artists have proven that music is in their blood.

Family bands date back to the early days of country music, with The Carter Family, often referred to as "The First Family of Country Music." Discovered during the Bristol Sessions, the group originally included A.P. Carter, his wife Sara Dougherty Carter, and Sara's cousin, Maybelle Addington Carter. Over time, they began incorporating their children, including Maybelle's daughter June, who later found success as a solo artist.

Other family bands and duos that rose to fame include The Bellamy Brothers (David and Howard Bellamy), The Band Perry (siblings Kimberly, Reid, and Neil Perry), Brothers Osborne (John and T.J. Osborne) and, more recently, The Castellows (sisters Eleanor, Lily, and Powell Balkcom).

You may have heard of iconic mother-daughter duo The Judds, but Wynonna Judd isn't the only one who inherited a love for music from a parent. Hillary Scott of the Grammy-winning trio Lady A is the daughter of Linda Davis, who rose to fame as Reba McEntire's "Does He Love You" duet partner, and 1990s hitmaker Pam Tillis followed in the footsteps of her father, country legend Mel Tillis.

Country superstar Thomas Rhett is the son of Rhett Akins, who is best known for his 1995 hit "That Ain't My Truck." Rhett Akins is a hit-making songwriter with more than 35 number one songs, some of which he co-wrote with his son. That's an impressive father-son connection! Other notable family ties include Lukas Nelson, who has been playing music with his father, the great Willie Nelson,

"Whether it's a mother-daughter duo, a father-son bond, or a sibling connection, these artists have proven that music is in their blood."

SEE ALSO:

BRISTOL SESSIONS

LADY A

THE JUDDS

WILLIAMS FAMILY

F

for as long as he can remember, and Lorrie Morgan, the daughter of George Morgan, a Grand Ole Opry member and Country Music Hall of Famer.

While they didn't perform together, Eddie Montgomery of the award-winning duo Montgomery Gentry and 1990s country music star John Michael Montgomery are brothers. Loretta Lynn and her sister, Crystal Gayle, also made names for themselves as solo artists. Hank Williams' family is full of talented artists—flip to to the Williams Family entry for more.

FANDOMS

"For many, it's more than just being a fan; it's a way of life."

SEE ALSO:

CHESNEY, KENNY
CHURCH, ERIC
UNDERWOOD, CARRIE

Fandoms are crucial to an artist's career and create a sense of community among their followers. While Taylor Swift's Swifties and Justin Bieber's Beliebers often get the spotlight, country music is home to its own passionate and uniquely loyal fan bases.

Blake Shelton has his BSers, Lainey Wilson is supported by her Wild Horses, Dierks Bentley's fans are collectively known as the DB Risers, and Luke Combs's Bootleggers have quickly become sone of the most dedicated supporters in country music.

When I think about fandoms in country music, one of the most passionate that comes to mind is Carrie Underwood's Care Bears. They rallied behind her during her *American Idol* journey, calling in to vote each week, and they've stood by her side every step of her career. When the ACM Awards shifted to a fan-voted model for Entertainer of the Year, the Care Bears showed up in full force, voting her to the top in 2008 and 2009 (she later earned the trophy again in 2019 when it returned to member voting). And when her beloved dog Ace passed away, the Care Bears joined together to donate thousands of dollars to her foundation in his honor.

Another standout fan base is Eric Church's devoted Church Choir. They've been with him from the days of smoky bar shows all the way to sold-out arenas. What sets them apart is their heartfelt appreciation for his music—not just the radio singles but the deep cuts on every album. And Church has always given that love back. He's been known to send new music directly to fans before releasing it publicly, and when he opened his Nashville bar, Chief's, he gave Church Choir members deeds to individual bricks in the building. "You've helped me build my career brick by brick, and I want the whole world to know that the building is yours," he told them.

Kenny Chesney dubbed his fans No Shoes Nation in 2012, during a sold-out show at Gillette Stadium in Foxborough, Massachusetts. A nod to his 2002 hit "No Shoes, No Shirt, No Problems," No Shoes Nation embodies everything his fans are all about. They live for the music and the escape Chesney's shows give them from reality. But for many, it's more than just being a fan; it's a way of life, something Chesney captured perfectly in his 2020 release "We Do."

FIDDLE

As the band Alabama taught us, "You gotta have a fiddle in the band," and that rings true: the fiddle has played an integral role in country music since the very beginning. It became a staple in folk, bluegrass, and country, adding an exciting layer to live performances and inspiring listeners to dance and clap along.

When you think of iconic fiddle moments, The Charlie Daniels Band's "The Devil Went Down to Georgia" is likely the first that comes to mind. Not only does it feature an unforgettable fiddle solo, but it also tells an epic story of a boy named Johnny facing off against the devil in a fiddle showdown. Released in 1979, the song remains a country classic and is often covered by artists during their live shows. It even earned the Charlie Daniels Band their first (and only) Grammy Award.

"No matter how much country music changes, one thing's for sure: it just wouldn't sound the same without that signature fiddle sound."

SEE ALSO:

ALABAMA
BROOKS, GARTH
STRAIT, GEORGE
THE CHICKS

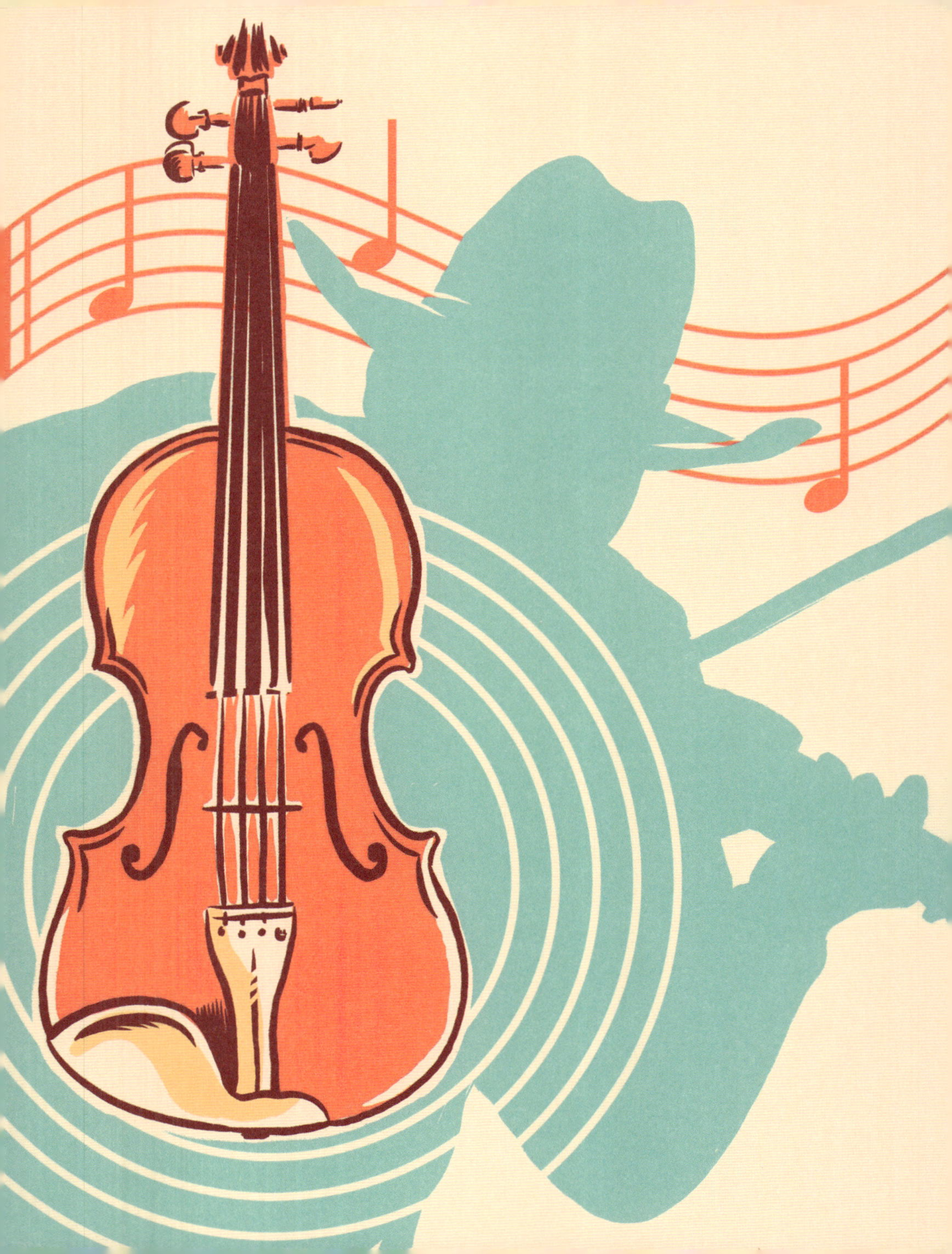

Charlie Daniels was known for his incredible fiddle-playing skills and is joined by other legendary country fiddlers, including the "King of Western Swing" Bob Wills and Johnny Gimble, who recorded with Willie Nelson. Merle Haggard and Conway Twitty were also keen fiddlers, as was the original "King of Country Music" Roy Acuff. More recently, bluegrass icon Alison Krauss has kept the tradition alive.

Today, multi-CMA Musician of the Year winner Jenee Fleenor is one of modern country's most in-demand fiddlers, having recorded with Blake Shelton, Cody Johnson, Rascal Flatts, and Reba McEntire.

If you're looking for other famous fiddle songs, look no further than Garth Brooks' "Callin' Baton Rouge," George Strait's "Amarillo by Morning," John Denver's "Thank God I'm a Country Boy," Mel McDaniel's "Louisiana Saturday Night," and The Chicks' "Cowboy Take Me Away."

No matter how much country music changes, one thing's for sure: it just wouldn't sound the same without that signature fiddle sound.

F

FILM & TV

"Any exposure to national or international audiences through film and television continues to be a win for country music."

SEE ALSO:

- BLUEBIRD CAFE
- CAMPBELL, GLEN
- GRAND OLE OPRY
- HEE HAW
- JOHNNY & JUNE
- NASHVILLE
- SHELTON, BLAKE
- UNDERWOOD, CARRIE
- WAGONER, PORTER

Over the years, film and television have played a huge role in bringing country music to a wider audience. Before TV became widespread, many discovered the genre on the radio, thanks in part to the Grand Ole Opry's broadcasts on WSM Radio. As televisions became more common, shows like *Hee Haw* brought the country lifestyle and music into living rooms, alongside other variety programs such as *The Porter Wagoner Show, The Glen Campbell Goodtime Hour, and The Glen Campbell Music Show*, which aired from the 1960s to the early 1980s.

In 1980, *Urban Cowboy* starring John Travolta brought country music into the mainstream, sparking a national craze. The movie influenced fashion, shaped the sound of the genre to lean a bit more into pop, and even prompted conversations about what is and what isn't country music.

Walk the Line, the biopic about Johnny Cash and June Carter Cash starring Joaquin Phoenix and Reese Witherspoon, became a major box office success and earned the Golden Globe for Best Motion Picture (Musical or Comedy), introducing Cash's story to a new generation.

The TV drama *Nashville*, which debuted in 2012, gave viewers a fairly accurate look at the inner workings of the music business. Over its six seasons, the show highlighted the city's songwriting community, boosted careers for stars including Charles Esten, and brought audiences to venues like The Bluebird Cafe. One study found nearly one in five visitors to Nashville cited the show as a motivating factor for their trip.

Yellowstone and other shows in the Taylor Sheridan realm like *Landman* have also impacted the genre by featuring songs in various scenes. This kind of exposure has proven to be invaluable for artists, often boosting streaming and sales.

F

The influence of reality television on country music is undeniable. Shows like *American Idol* introduced audiences to artists like Carrie Underwood, Scotty McCreery, and Lauren Alaina, while *The Voice* helped make coach Blake Shelton a household name.

In my eyes, any exposure to national or international audiences through film and television continues to be a win for country music.

FRIED BOLOGNA SANDWICH

The fried bologna sandwich is a staple in Southern cuisine. It's simple, inexpensive, delicious, and a reminder of simpler times, as Tim McGraw sings in his song "Back When": "A fried bologna sandwich with mayo and tomato." If you're in Nashville and looking to try this Southern classic, the place to grab one is Robert's Western World.

The Lower Broadway jaunt is known as the home of traditional country music, and Robert's happens to serve up the best fried bologna sandwich in Music City. Fans can order one at the Honky Tonk Grill inside Robert's as part of the famous Recession Special. For $6, guests can enjoy a fried bologna sandwich on thick, buttery Texas toast, piled high with fresh bologna and topped with crisp lettuce and tomato. It's served with chips, a MoonPie (similar to a Wagon Wheel), and an ice-cold PBR (Pabst Blue Ribbon beer). Hundreds of these sandwiches are served every night.

The Recession Special was created by owner JesseLee Jones in 2008 while playing on stage at the legendary honky-tonk. His wife and co-owner, Emily, told me that even if they have to go into the red, they'll keep it at an affordable price. The special has become a part of Robert's identity.

"If locals head to Broadway, this is where you'll find them; at Robert's enjoying live music and chowing down on a fried bologna sandwich."

SEE ALSO:

JELLY ROLL

LOWER BROADWAY

MCGRAW, TIM

NASHVILLE

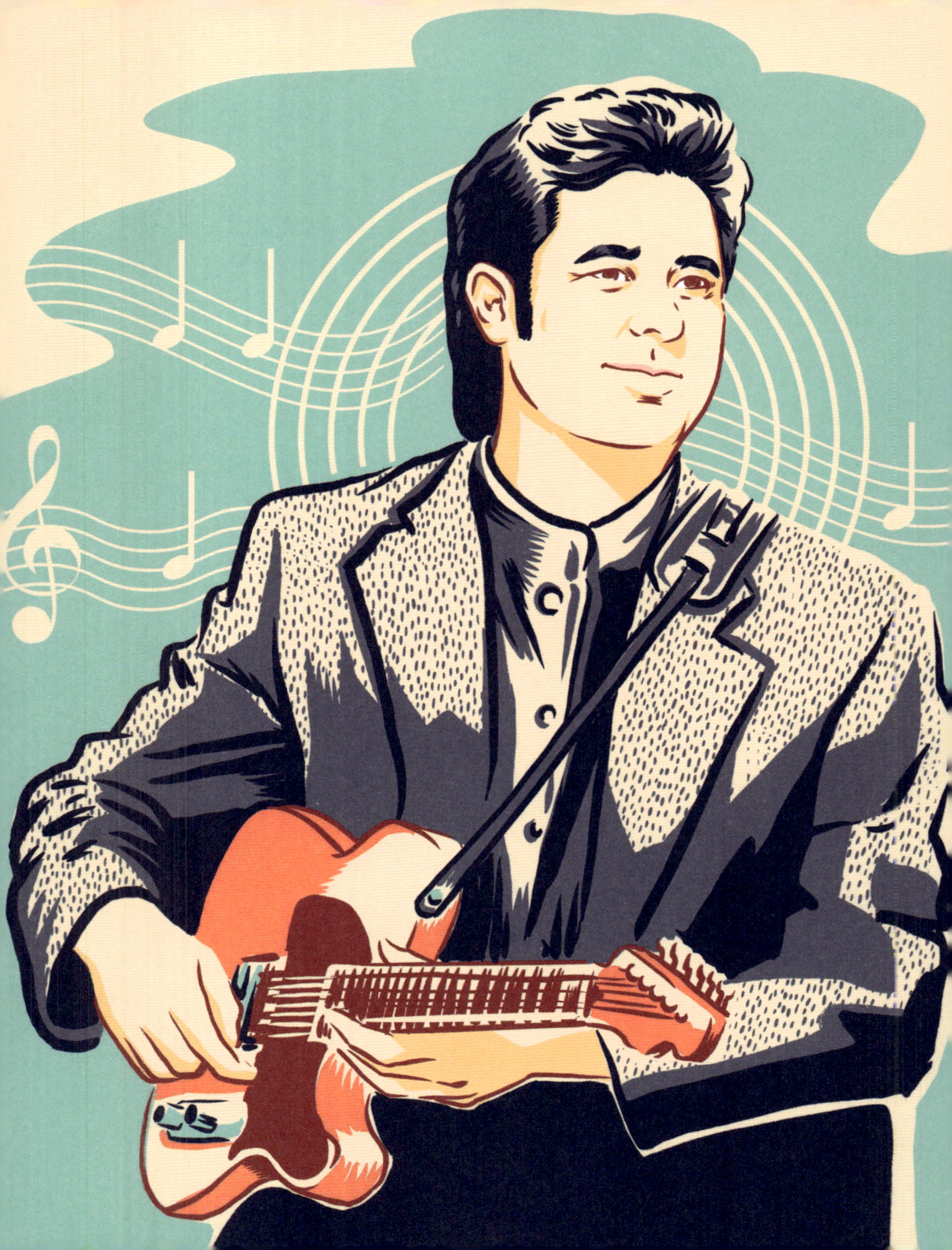

Robert's fried bologna sandwich has become so famous it draws people from all over, including a few well-known faces: country hitmaker Jelly Roll, who likes his with potato chips dumped right on the sandwich instead of on the side, and actor Dennis Quaid, who now calls Nashville home and has proven himself a gifted singer-songwriter.

If locals head to Broadway, this is where you'll find them; at Robert's enjoying live music and chowing down on a fried bologna sandwich.

GILL, VINCE

Vince Gill is best known for his songwriting, musicianship, and unmistakable tenor. He's a 22-time Grammy winner, 18-time CMA Award winner, and a member of both the Nashville Songwriters Hall of Fame and the Country Music Hall of Fame. He's appeared on more than 1,000 albums and is one of Nashville's most beloved and respected musicians. To me, he's the unofficial mayor of country music—always around town, showing up at events, and treating everyone he meets with kindness. He's soft-spoken and easy-going, the kind of person who makes you feel like you're talking to a member of your family rather than a country music icon.

"He's the unofficial mayor of country music—always around town, showing up at events, and treating everyone he meets with kindness."

Born in 1957 in Norman, Oklahoma, Gill credits his family for instilling in him a love and appreciation for music. Impressively, he learned to play not just guitar, but also banjo, fiddle, dobro, mandolin, and bass at a young age. After high school, Gill played in various bands, including Boone Creek with Ricky Skaggs and the Cherry Bombs with Rodney Crowell.

He moved to Nashville in 1983 and launched his solo career with RCA. After a steady stream of chart-climbing singles, he signed with MCA, where he released his breakthrough album *When I Call Your Name* in 1989. Produced by the legendary Tony Brown, the album and its title track marked a major turning point in Gill's career.

SEE ALSO:

COUNTRY MUSIC HALL OF FAME AND MUSEUM

GRAND OLE OPRY

JONES, GEORGE

LOVELESS, PATTY

G

In the 1990s, Gill became a certified country superstar, notching a string of hits including "I Still Believe in You," "Don't Let Our Love Start Slippin' Away," and "Whenever You Come Around." He was named CMA Entertainer of the Year in 1993 and 1994 and served as host of the CMA Awards from 1992 to 2003.

Above all, Gill prides himself on his musicianship. His guitar skills earned him a personal call from Eric Clapton and invitations to perform at Clapton's Crossroads Guitar Festival in 2004 and 2007, where he shared the stage with some of the world's greatest players. He spent a decade with the Western swing band the Time Jumpers and, in 2017, was invited to join the legendary rock band the Eagles, a band he continues to tour with today.

Gill is as kind as he is talented. His gentle nature earned him the nickname "Sweet Pea" from George Jones, a name he says he'll "cherish forever." A longtime member of the Grand Ole Opry, Gill champions the preservation of country music as president of the Board of Officers and Trustees of the Country Music Hall of Fame and Museum. Gill is married to Christian artist Amy Grant, and they often collaborate on stage and in the studio.

GRAND OLE OPRY

"The feeling you get at the Grand Ole Opry is indescribable."

"The show that made country music famous" is like an exclusive club—you must be invited to perform, and only select artists are asked to become members. Having the opportunity to perform on the Opry stage is a rite of passage, and being invited to become an Opry member is one of country music's highest honors.

The Grand Ole Opry is the longest-running live broadcast show in the world. It began on November 28, 1925 as the *WSM Barn Dance* with Uncle Jimmy Thompson. Two years later, after a broadcast of Walter Damrosch's *Music Appreciation Hour*, George D. Day dubbed the show the "Grand Ole Opry" and the name caught on.

SEE ALSO:

NASHVILLE

RYMAN ALLEY

RYMAN AUDITORIUM

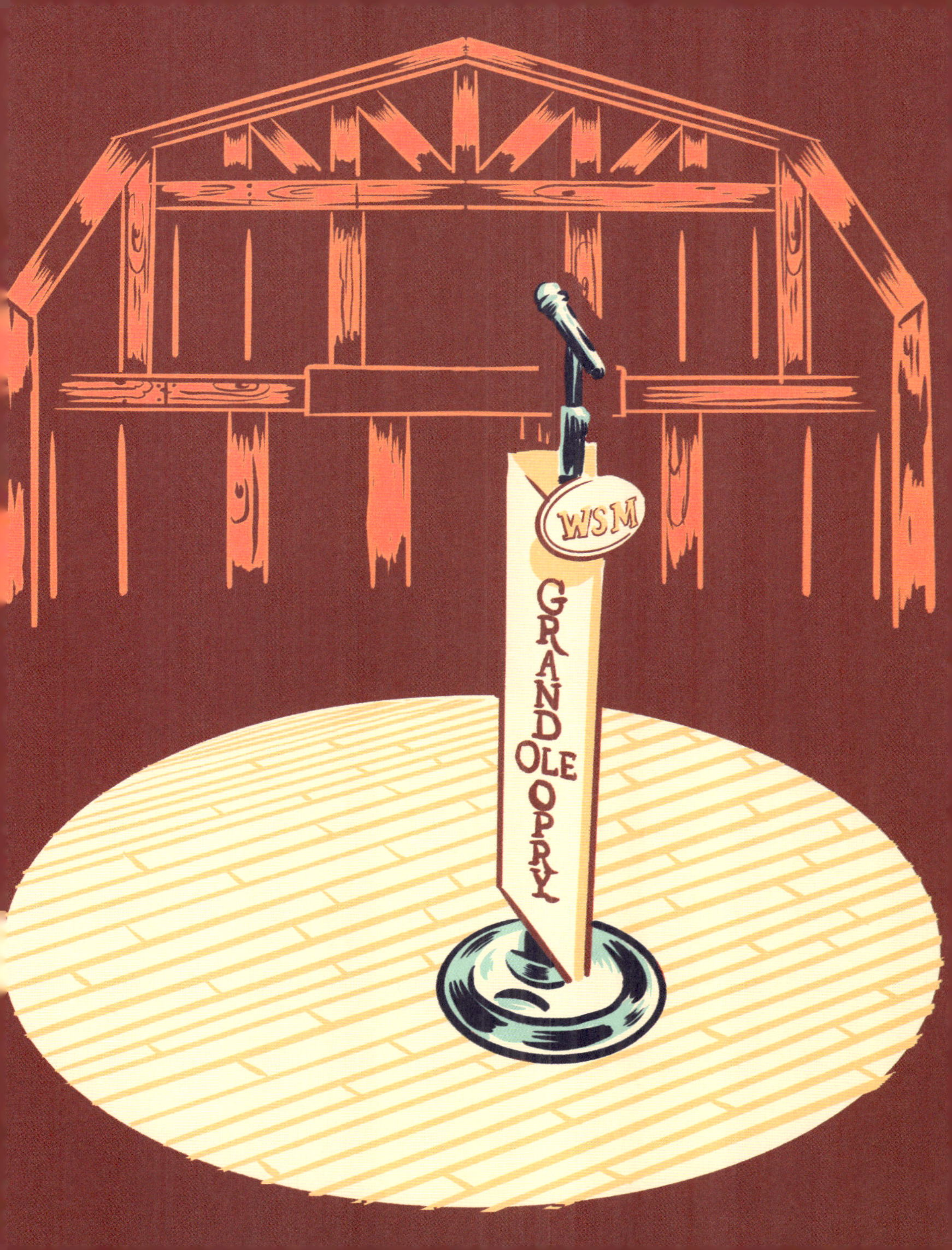
WSM
GRAND OLE OPRY

G

While the *Opry* originally broadcast from several locations around Nashville, it found a home at the Ryman Auditorium in 1943. For over 30 years, the *Opry* hosted performances at the Ryman with icons like Dolly Parton, Johnny Cash, Loretta Lynn, Hank Williams, and Elvis Presley taking to the stage.

As the *Opry*'s popularity grew, so did the need for a larger venue. In March 1974 it relocated to the Grand Ole Opry House, a 4,000-seat venue built specifically for the show. To honor the Opry legacy and its history at the Ryman Auditorium, an 8-foot (2.5-meter) square was cut from the Ryman stage, perfectly carved into a 6-foot (1.8-meter) circle and meticulously placed on the new stage by longtime member Roy Acuff. He became the first artist to step into that circle, which has now become one of the most sacred spots in country music. The wood is worn and marked but holds so much history.

The Opry House remains the home of the *Grand Ole Opry* to this day, despite suffering unimaginable damage during the historic Nashville flooding in May 2010. The venue was forced to close its doors for several months as many areas were submerged under water, including the hallowed Opry circle. Amazingly, the circle remained intact and was able to be saved. Through it all, the music never stopped, because the *Opry* continued at various venues in Nashville. After several months, the Opry House was restored and reopened with a star-studded show.

The feeling that you get at the Grand Ole Opry is indescribable. I am lucky enough to have experienced it many times, and I still get goosebumps when I walk through those doors.

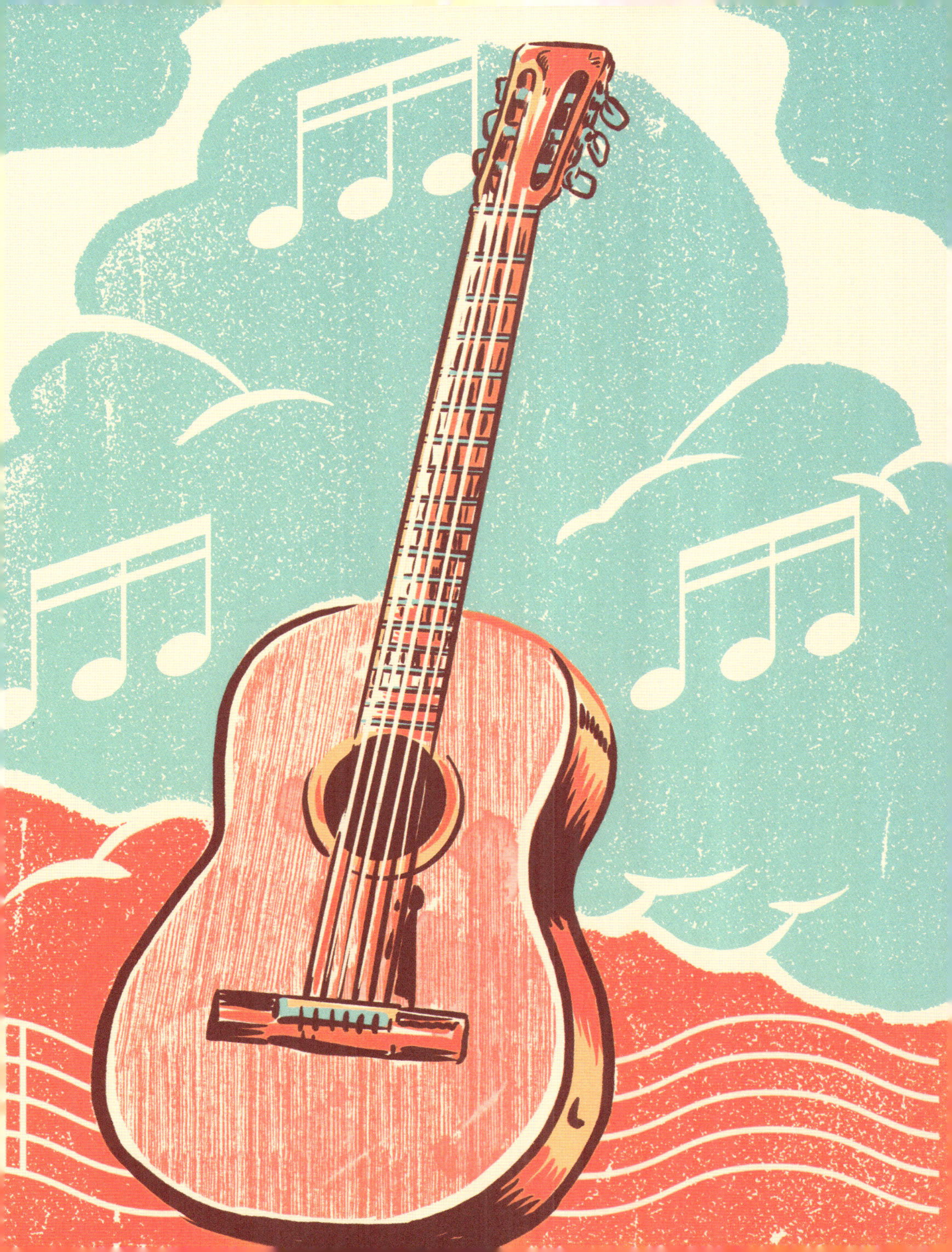

G

GUITAR

"The guitar is always by their side. It's there for the good days and the bad, the happy songs and the sad ones."

SEE ALSO:

NELSON, WILLIE

STAPLETON, CHRIS

URBAN, KEITH

Country Music Hall of Famer Chet Atkins once said, "A guitar's your friend for life, it'll be your best friend," and I like to think he was right. I'm no guitar player—I'm probably the furthest thing from it—but when I think about an artist and their guitar, I imagine a bond like that. The guitar is always by their side. It's there for the good days and the bad, the happy songs and the sad ones. It's with them in their most vulnerable moments, in the writing room as they pour their hearts into lyrics. Many country artists even name their guitars, and for some, that instrument is their most prized possession.

Take Chris Stapleton, for example. When he moved to Nashville from his native Kentucky, he bought a $380 acoustic guitar. It's nothing fancy, but it's the guitar he used to write 90 percent of his songs. It's weathered years of wear and tear, survived a flood, and even has mud inside. Still, among his massive collection of guitars and prized instruments, it's the one he cherishes most.

Known for his guitar skills, Keith Urban found his prized guitar in 1999 during his first trip to the US from Australia. He stumbled upon the 40th Anniversary Telecaster at Manny's Music in New York. It was sitting in a glass case, and he was instantly drawn to it. The salesman let him play it and, luckily, he was able to scrape together enough money to buy it. Urban named the guitar Clarence after the angel in the beloved film *It's a Wonderful Life*. He toured with the guitar extensively and wrote countless songs on it. Reflecting on its role in his life and career, Urban once questioned, "I wonder what life would have been like if I hadn't had this guitar?"

No guitar in country music is more famous than Willie Nelson's Trigger. In 1969, the then-struggling singer-songwriter bought an acoustic Martin guitar and named it after Roy Rogers' horse. That same year, when his home burned down on Christmas Eve, Nelson ran inside to save Trigger. Traveling with him from city to city for decades, Trigger has become as much a part of the band as any player. Worn with a large hole from years of playing and etched with autographs from country icons, this one-of-a-kind guitar is truly legendary.

HAGGARD, MERLE

"Poet of the Common Man" Merle Haggard is widely regarded as one of the most influential country singer-songwriters of all time. His career spanned six decades, during which he released more than 100 albums and earned 38 number one singles.

Born just outside of Bakersfield, California—the birthplace of Bakersfield Sound—in 1937, Haggard had a difficult start in life. His family was poor, and their home was a converted boxcar. When he was just nine, his father died of a stroke, sending his life down a dark path. He spent much of his youth in and out of juvenile detention facilities but, despite his difficulties, Haggard found a love for music. Encouraged by his mother, he first picked up the fiddle and later taught himself guitar.

In 1958, at the age of 20, Haggard was sent to California's San Quentin State Prison. A stint in solitary confinement left him wanting to turn his life around, and witnessing Johnny Cash's famous San Quentin performance gave him the inspiration he needed to make it happen. Following his parole in 1960, he worked in various manual jobs before landing gigs at a local club. Before long, he quit his day job to focus solely on music.

Haggard joined Buck Owens's band briefly and launched his solo career in the early 1960s, influenced by honky-tonk and rock 'n' roll. After a few modest hits, he formed his band The Strangers, and by 1966 earned his first number one with "I'm a Lonesome Fugitive." He wrote

"Merle Haggard's music left a lasting mark, influencing artists from Vince Gill to Eric Church."

SEE ALSO:

CHURCH, ERIC

COUNTRY MUSIC HALL OF FAME AND MUSEUM

GILL, VINCE

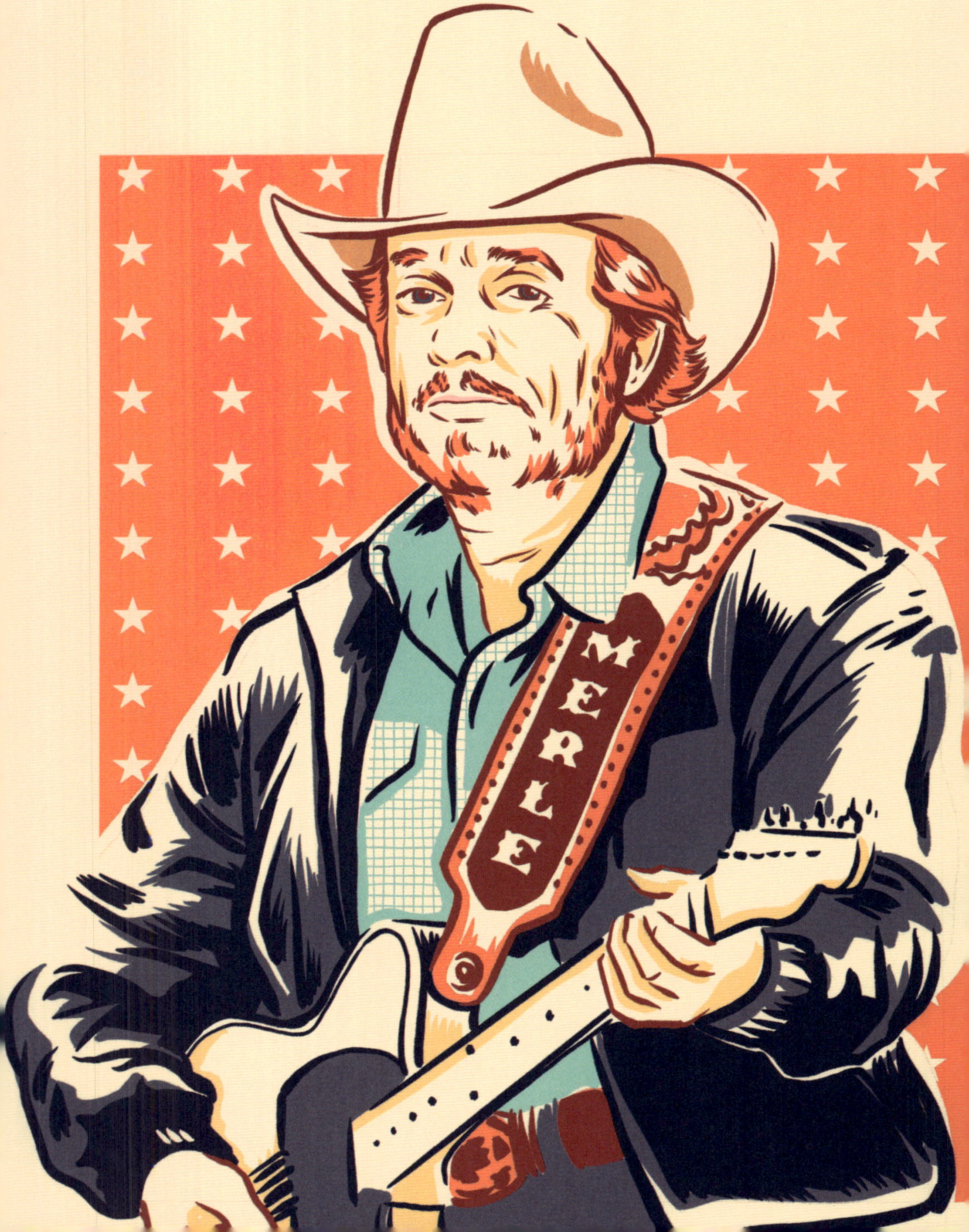
MERLE

about his life experiences: "Mama Tried," inspired by his prison time; "Workin' Man Blues," an anthem for blue-collar workers; and "Hungry Eyes," based on his difficult childhood. One of his signature hits, "Okie from Muskogee," was written in response to Vietnam War protests.

A celebrated artist, Haggard earned 20 ACM Awards, six CMA Awards, two Grammys, a 1994 induction into the Country Music Hall of Fame, a 2006 Grammy Lifetime Achievement Award, and a 2010 Kennedy Center Honor. Yet he considered his greatest accomplishment to be the pardon he received for his crimes in 1972 from then-California governor Ronald Reagan, meaning he no longer needed to declare his legal history.

Haggard was diagnosed with lung cancer in 2008 and was declared cancer-free after surgery. He never stopped writing or touring, even as he approached 80. He passed away on April 6, 2016, his 79th birthday, from complications of pneumonia. Merle Haggard's music left a lasting mark, influencing artists from Vince Gill to Eric Church.

H

HAIR

"These artists prove that hair isn't just hair; it's part of who they are."

SEE ALSO:

JACKSON, ALAN
KEITH, TOBY
MCENTIRE, REBA
NELSON, WILLIE
PARTON, DOLLY
SHELTON, BLAKE
STAPLETON, CHRIS
WALLEN, MORGAN
WHITLEY, KEITH

Many country artists use their hair as a form of self-expression, and often it becomes part of their identity. This rings especially true for artists who choose not to wear hats, letting their hair become a key part of their signature style.

Big hair has been a trend in country music almost since the beginning, with Dolly Parton becoming the epitome of the age-old saying, "The higher the hair, the closer to God." Parton has famously worn wigs throughout her career, and her striking blonde styles have defined her look. Kitty Wells, Tammy Wynette, and Loretta Lynn are also known for their big hair. While Reba McEntire has rocked some iconic hairstyles throughout her career, she is best known for her striking red locks, which reflect her feisty personality.

Grand Ole Opry member Crystal Gayle famously has long, brown hair that almost touches the floor. She's admitted to thinking about cutting it over the years, but says it's become such a big part of who she is that she just can't bring herself to do it.

Surprisingly, the mullet has withstood the test of time, popping up on artists from various generations. Keith Whitley rocked the hairstyle in the 1980s and Billy Ray Cyrus, Alan Jackson, Tracy Lawrence, and Toby Keith all had mullets in the early 1990s. Blake Shelton kept the trend going into the early 2000s then Morgan Wallen famously brought the mullet back in style in 2019—and shocked fans when he completely shaved his head in the summer of 2023.

Willie Nelson has embraced many styles throughout his career. Most notably, he sported a clean-cut look in his early days, and later his trademark two long braids. And when it comes to facial hair, Chris Stapleton immediately comes to mind with his long, rugged beard, while Jamey Johnson is known for a long hair-and-beard combo that is uniquely him. These artists prove that hair isn't just hair; it's part of who they are.

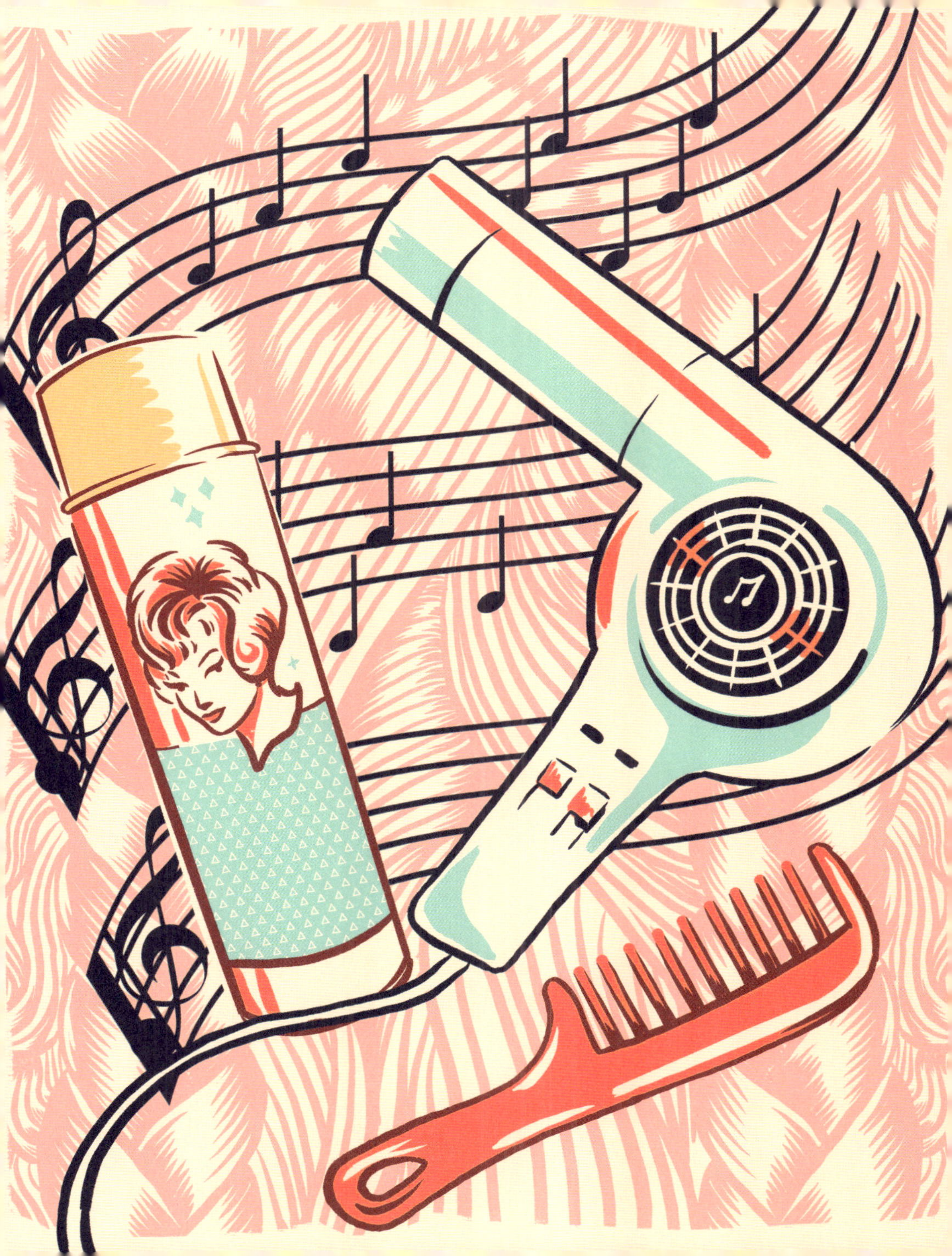

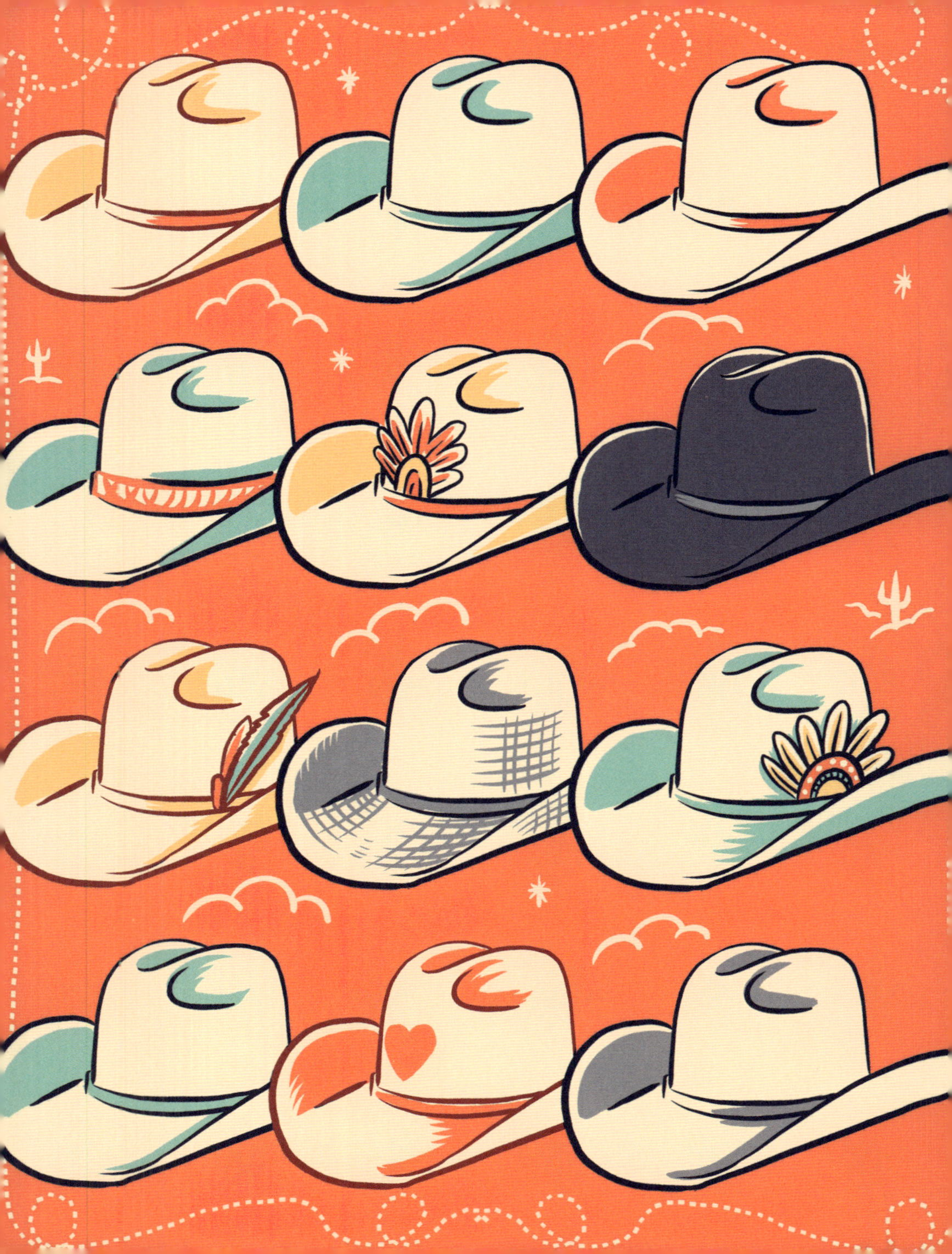

H

HAT ACTS

For many country music artists, wearing a cowboy hat is more than just a fashion statement: it's a nod to country music's roots. Artists who don cowboy hats are called "hat acts" in the industry and are rarely seen without them.

The cowboy hat dates back to 1865 when hatmaker John B. Stetson designed the "Boss of the Plains," a functional hat for real working cowboys in the West. The Stetson arrived in country music in the 1930s, when Gene Autry and Roy Rogers popularized the singing cowboy look. They didn't know it at the time but they were trendsetters.

The cowboy hat remained a popular accessory for decades, yet its presence on stage dwindled in the 1970s and 1980s. Some of the biggest stars of that era, like Charley Pride, Ronnie Milsap, and Glen Campbell, didn't wear cowboy hats, but George Strait was one of the few who kept the tradition alive.

A boom of hat acts arrived in the 1990s with the neo-traditional movement, as artists including Alan Jackson, Toby Keith, and Garth Brooks dominated the scene. This success prompted labels to seek out hat acts—Tim McGraw, Kenny Chesney, and Clint Black all rose to fame during this period and made the cowboy hat a defining feature of their look.

The 2000s brought another wave of hat acts with artists like Brad Paisley and Jason Aldean stepping into the spotlight. While the term "hat act" is typically associated with male artists, Terri Clark is one female artist known for consistently rocking a cowboy hat.

Today, Lainey Wilson has made hats part of her signature style. While she often sports cowboy hats, she's also known to mix in unique Western-inspired styles. Other modern artists like Cody Johnson, Jon Pardi, and Zach Top proudly wear their Stetsons, continuing this timeless country music tradition.

"Wearing a cowboy hat is more than just a fashion statement; it's a nod to country music's traditional roots."

SEE ALSO:

BROOKS, GARTH
JACKSON, ALAN
PAISLEY, BRAD
SIGNATURE STYLE
STRAIT, GEORGE
STYLE
WILSON, LAINEY

HATCH SHOW PRINT

"The shop's distinctive style of hand-crafted posters has played a major role in the history of country music."

SEE ALSO:

COUNTRY MUSIC HALL OF FAME AND MUSEUM

RYMAN AUDITORIUM

Nashville is home to one of America's oldest working letterpress print shops, Hatch Show Print. The shop's distinctive style of hand-crafted posters has played a major role in the history of country music.

Hatch Show Print dates back to 1879, when brothers Charles and Herbert Hatch, who had grown up learning the craft of letterpress printing, founded C.R. & H.H. Hatch, Printers. Their earliest known work was a poster promoting a speech by Henry Ward Beecher in 1883. Over the years, their prints became a popular way to advertise concerts, carnivals, sporting events, and more.

In 1924, the shop moved to Lower Broadway, just steps from the Ryman Auditorium. By the 1940s, Hatch Show Print began producing posters for the *Grand Ole Opry*, held at the Ryman at the time, and eventually creating posters for nearly every performance at the Ryman, a tradition that still continues today.

Over its 140-plus years, Hatch Show Print has crafted custom designs for country legends including Loretta Lynn, Glen Campbell, Garth Brooks, and Wynonna Judd, as well as rock icons from the Foo Fighters to ZZ Top.

Hatch's old-school approach to design and printing is what sets it apart. The shop utilizes thousands of carved wood blocks, traditional metal type, and one-of-a-kind illustrations, all pressed on machines that have been in service 50 to 100 years. The result is a print that is instantly recognizable.

The shop eventually outgrew its Broadway storefront and now operates inside the Country Music Hall of Fame and Museum. Visitors can tour the space, explore its history, and even create a keepsake print, with more than 100,000 guests visiting the shop every year.

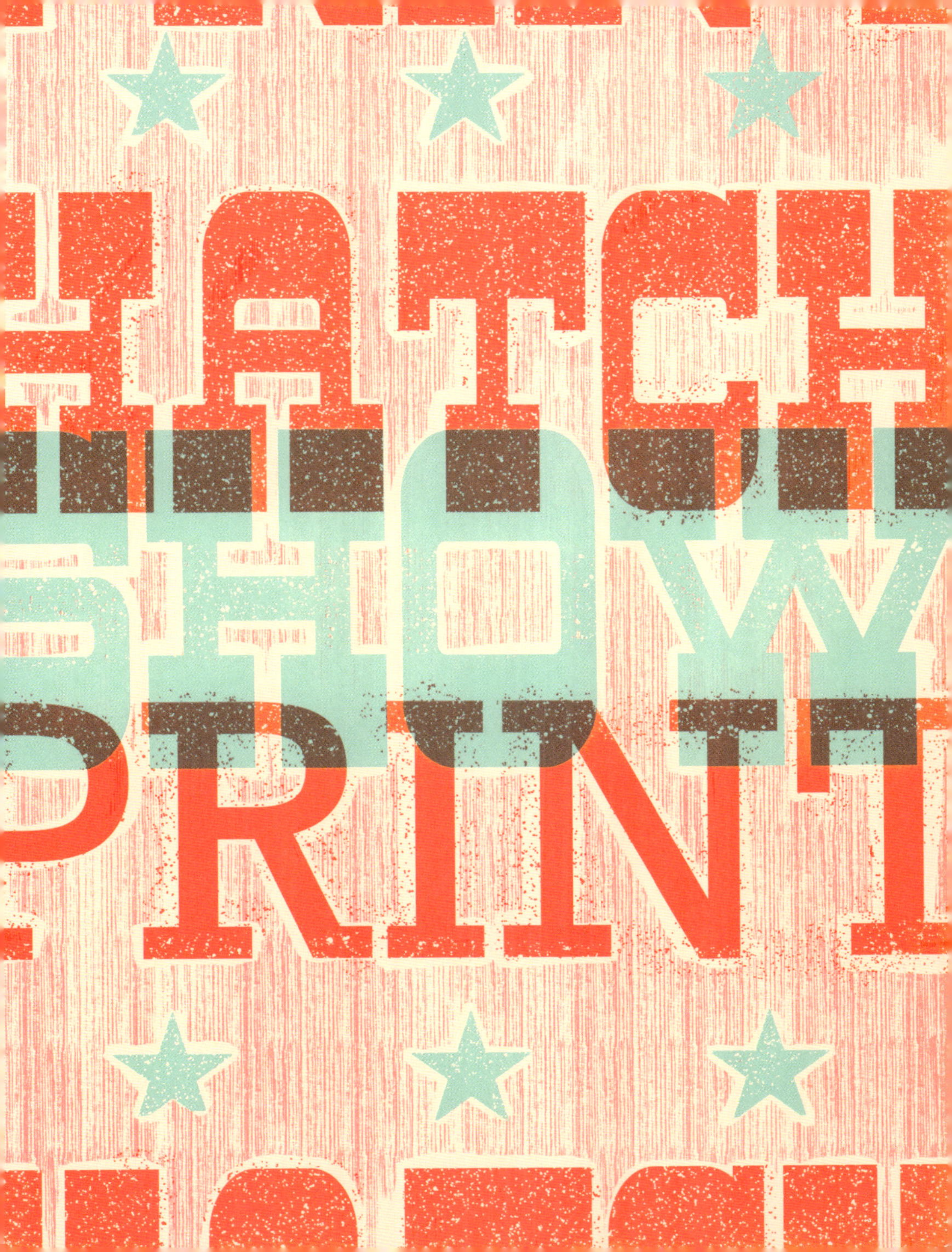

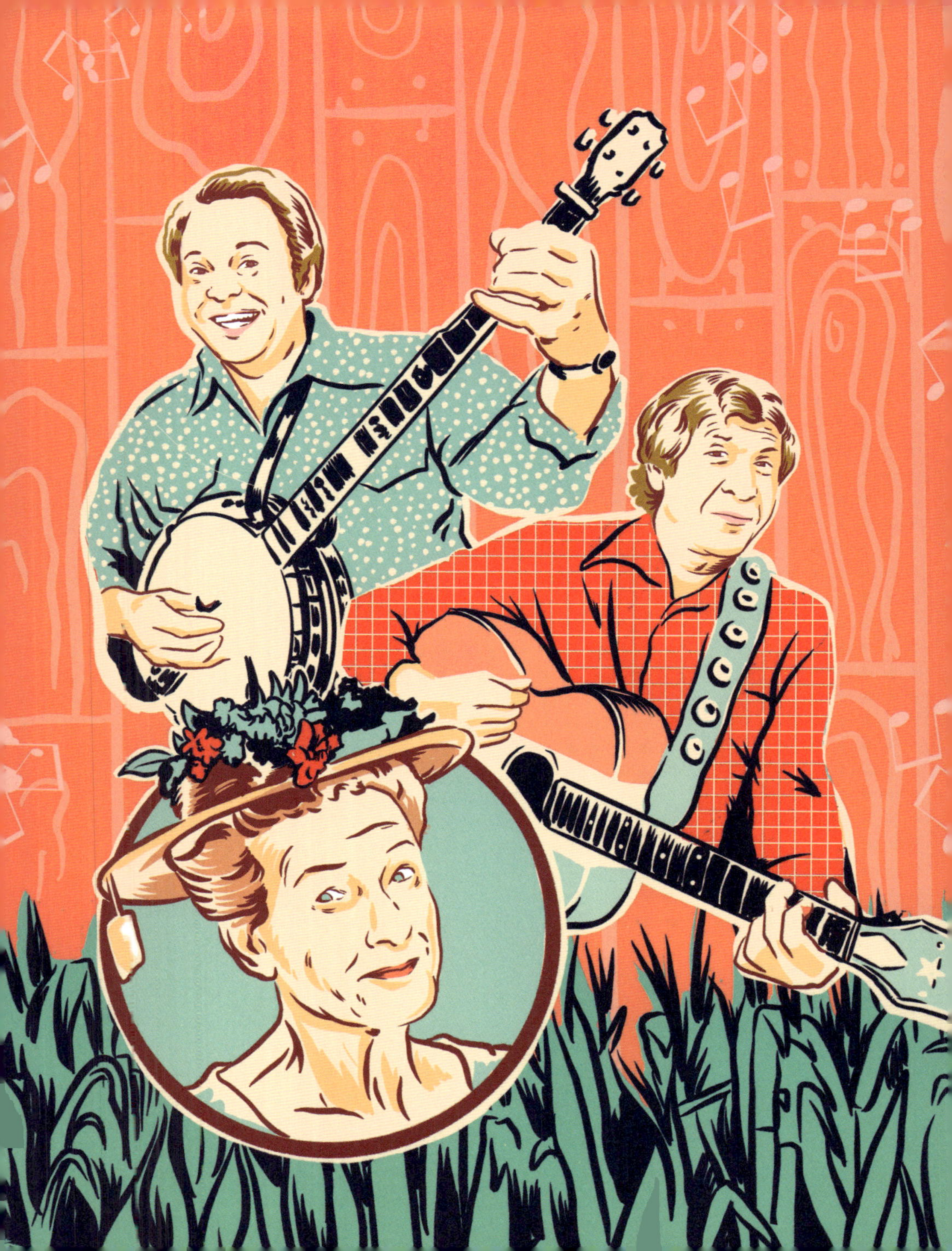

HEE HAW

In 1969, the country music variety show *Hee Haw* aired for the first time on CBS. Created by Frank Peppiatt and John Aylesworth, the one-hour program was initially broadcast as a test, but it proved so successful that the network quickly ordered it to series.

Hosted by country stars Buck Owens and Roy Clark, the weekly sketch show combined comedy, country music, and skits centered on rural life. *Hee Haw* was filmed backstage at the Grand Ole Opry House in Nashville for many years and set in the fictional "Kornfield Kounty," complete with cornstalks and hay bales. Cast members including Roy Acuff, Archie Campbell, Minnie Pearl, and Grandpa Jones wore stereotypical country attire, including overalls, plaid shirts, and gingham dresses.

The show gained a loyal fan base with its recurring comedic skits such as "The Cornfield," "Pickin' and Grinnin," "Pfft You Was Gone," and "Gloom, Despair, and Agony On Me," as well as a rotating lineup of guest stars and performers. There was no plot and no continuity, and according to cast members, none of the scenes were rehearsed.

During its broadcasting run of over 20 years, *Hee Haw* welcomed a slew of guest performers including Garth Brooks, Randy Travis, Alan Jackson, Loretta Lynn, and Tammy Wynette. Artists often jumped at the opportunity to appear on the show as it offered national television exposure and access to *Hee Haw*'s cultlike fanbase.

From 1969 to 1997, *Hee Haw* brought country music and rural humor to the masses every week. The show had a lasting impression on American pop culture and offered many country stars the chance to perform on a national stage. Vince Gill, a longtime fan and guest performer, once said *Hee Haw* was "The most massive exposure country music ever got," and it's hard to argue with that.

"The show had a lasting impression on American pop culture and offered many country stars the chance to perform on a national stage."

SEE ALSO:

ACUFF, ROY

GRAND OLE OPRY

H

HILL, FAITH

"Hill's mainstream success inspired artists like Taylor Swift to chase their own pop-country dreams."

SEE ALSO:

MCGRAW, TIM

NINETIES COUNTRY

SWIFT, TAYLOR

Faith Hill is a quintessential pop-country queen who rose to fame in the 1990s with her powerhouse vocals and girl-next-door charisma. She's a five-time Grammy winner and has sold more than 40 million albums worldwide.

Born in 1967, Audrey Faith Perry lived a simple life in Star, Mississippi, with her adoptive parents and two brothers. As a preschooler, she began singing in church and her parents encouraged her to keep performing. Her first public performance took place at a luncheon hosted by youth development organization 4-H when she was just seven.

At 19, Hill dropped out of college and moved to Nashville, where the first few years proved tough. She worked several dead-end jobs, including a stint at McDonald's, before landing a role as a receptionist at a publishing company. In 1988, she married music executive Daniel Hill, taking on what would become her stage name. Their marriage ended in divorce in 1994.

Faith Hill's big break came while she was singing backup vocals for Gary Burr at Nashville's Bluebird Cafe. A Warner Bros. executive spotted her and later signed her to the label. Her debut album, *Take Me as I Am*, arrived in 1993 and launched her to the top of the charts with hits like "Wild One" and "Piece of My Heart."

Around this time, Hill met a fellow rising star Tim McGraw at Country Radio Seminar. Two years later they went on tour together and, by the end of that tour, the couple had said "I do."

Hill continued to find success but her major breakout moment came in 1998 with her crossover hit "This Kiss." The song became a global success and her signature ballad, "Breathe," further cemented her international star status. "Breathe" went on to become the number one single of any genre on Billboard's year-end Hot 100 chart in 2000.

In addition to her solo career, Hill has found success through chart-topping duets with her husband and

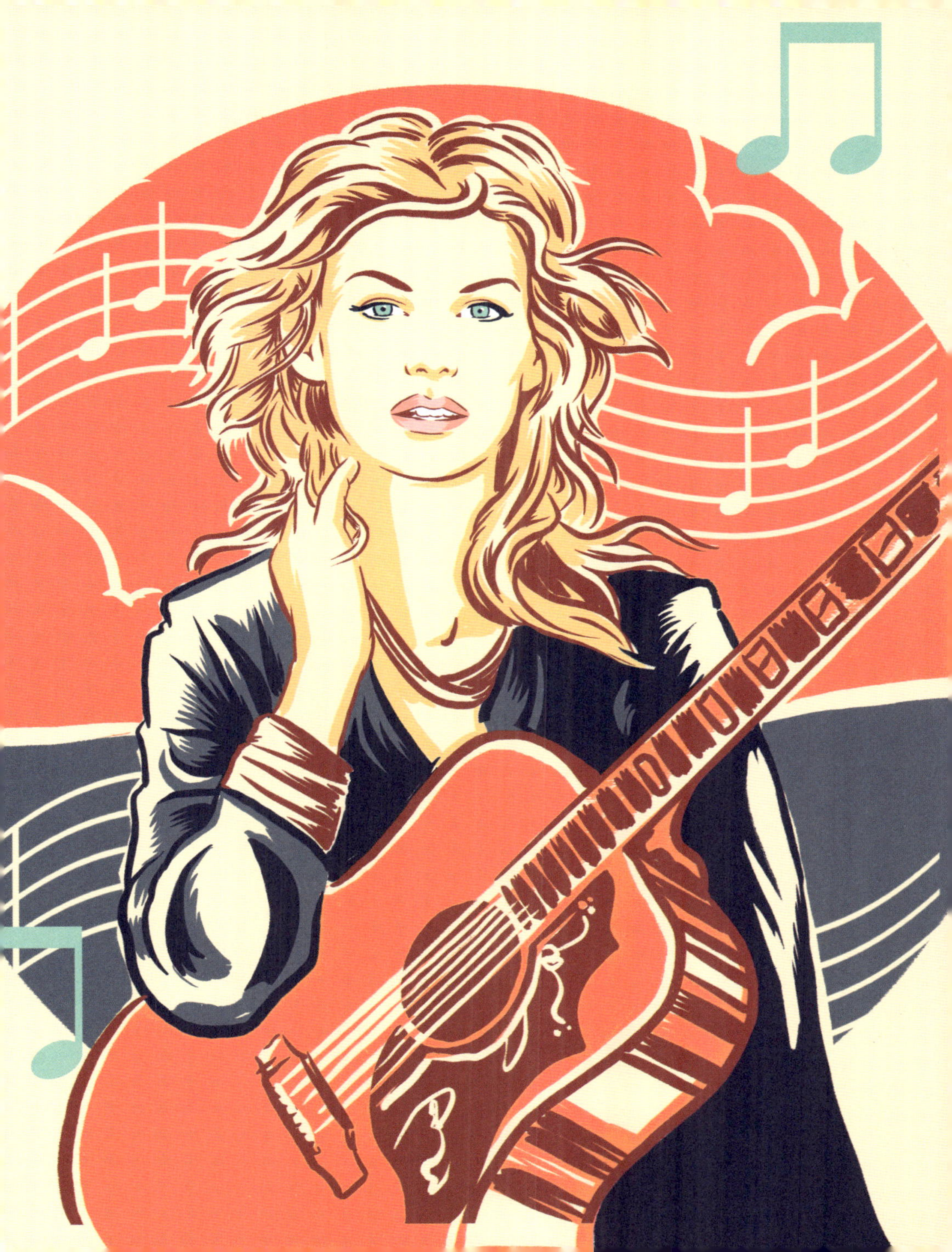

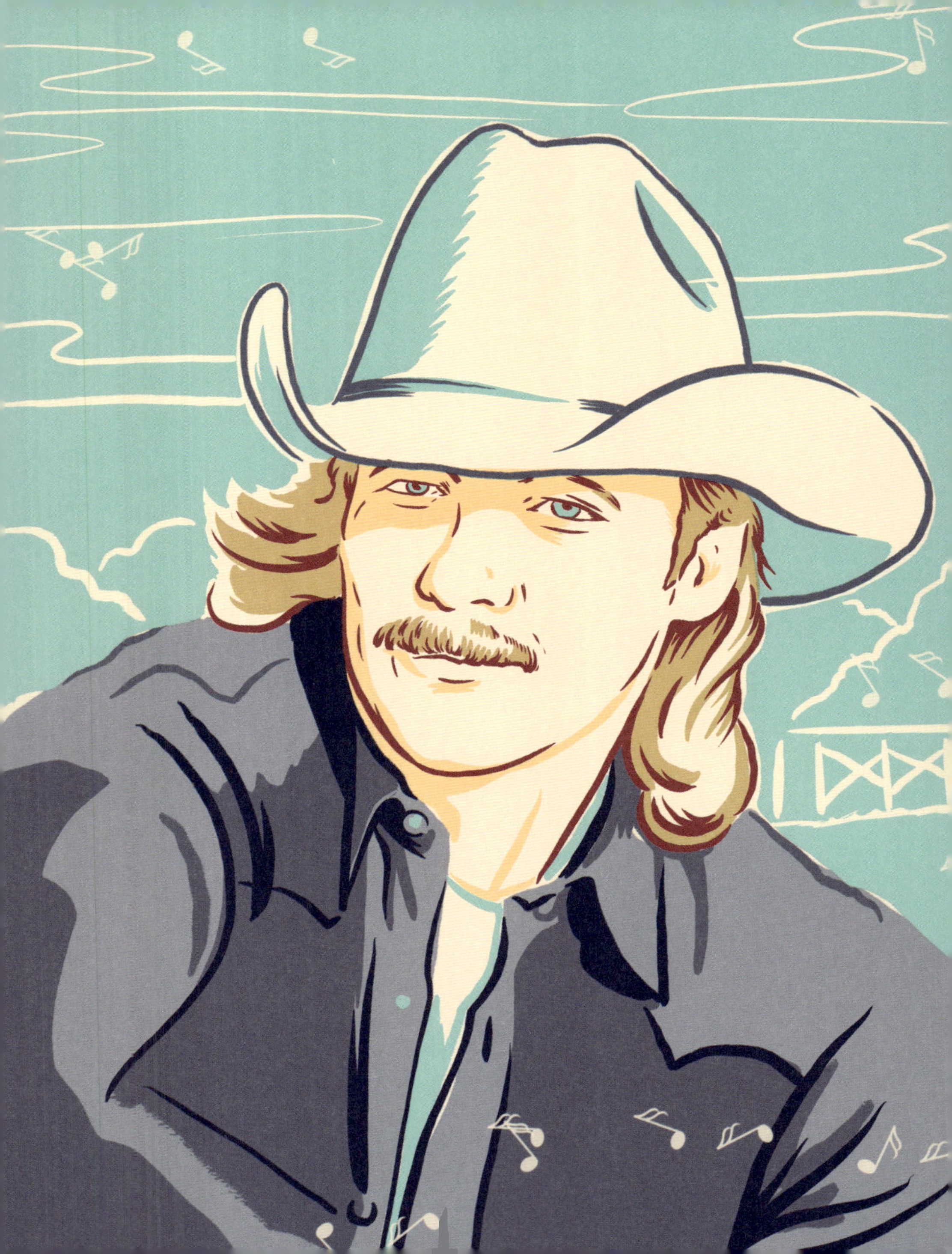

ventured into acting. She starred in *The Stepford Wives* and later co-starred with McGraw in the *Yellowstone* prequel, *1883*. From 2007 to 2012, Hill opened *Sunday Night Football* with her signature performance and even launched her own fragrance line in 2009.

She raised three daughters with McGraw, often stepping back from her recording career to focus on motherhood. Hill's mainstream success later inspired artists like Taylor Swift to chase their own pop-country dreams.

J

JACKSON, ALAN

Alan Jackson has been "Chasin' That Neon Rainbow" since he left his small town of Newnan, Georgia, in 1985. Little did he know that moving to Nashville would be one of the best decisions he'd ever make, launching a legendary country music career.

Country icon Glen Campbell played a pivotal role in Jackson's journey, thanks to a chance encounter with Jackson's wife, Denise. She told him all about her husband's musical talents and Campbell suggested that they move to Nashville, handing her his business card. Once in Music City, the budding singer-songwriter took a job in a mailroom and sang demos, performing at any gig he could find. With help from Campbell, he soon landed a publishing deal.

Jackson made his official debut in 1989, and the following year "Here in the Real World" marked the start of his reign on the charts. Hits like "Chattahoochee," "Mercury Blues," and "Livin' on Love" followed, firmly cementing his place in country music. A defining moment in his career came in 2001 with the release of "Where Were You (When the World Stopped Turning)," written just 47 days after the September 11 attacks. Jackson awoke at 4a.m. with the melody and lyrics in his head and later sat down to finish the song. He debuted it a few days later at the CMA Awards, leaving the audience speechless. The song captured what the entire nation felt on that dark day in history in words only Alan Jackson could write.

"Alan Jackson is as authentically country as it gets."

SEE ALSO:

CAMPBELL, GLEN

COUNTRY MUSIC HALL OF FAME AND MUSEUM

J

Jackson continued to deliver his neo-traditional country hits, including nostalgic "Drive (For Daddy Gene)" and emotional "Remember When" well into the early 2000s. In 2021, Jackson revealed that he was living with Charcot-Marie-Tooth disease, a neurological condition that impacts his muscle strength and mobility. He continued to perform and played his final tour show in May 2025, then marked the milestone with a star-studded finale concert in Nashville in June 2026.

Jackson's career highlights include 50 top 10 hits and 35 number one singles. He's taken home more than 150 industry awards, including several Entertainer of the Year trophies and the first-ever ACM Alan Jackson Lifetime Achievement Award, named in his honor. A member of both the Nashville Songwriters Hall of Fame and the Country Music Hall of Fame, Alan Jackson is as authentically country as it gets.

JELLY ROLL

"A voice and an advocate for the underdogs, he continues to bring country music to new audiences in a way no one else can."

Jelly Roll, born Jason DeFord, isn't your typical country music singer. He doesn't look like anyone else, he doesn't sound like anyone else, and his story isn't like anyone else's—but that's exactly what makes him special.

Born in 1984 and raised in Nashville, Tennessee, Jelly Roll had a troubled childhood and spent a decade in and out of detention centers and jail from the age of just 14. It was behind bars that he learned to write songs. Without access to instruments, he got creative, using a table to make beats. While incarcerated, he learned he had a daughter, a moment that changed everything.

After his release from jail at 24, he vowed never to go back. Using the childhood nickname his mom gave him, he began pursuing music. At first, Jelly Roll was a rapper, releasing several hip-hop albums and building a grassroots following. Over time, his sound evolved, blending hip-hop and rock with the storytelling elements

SEE ALSO:

JOHNSON, CODY

NASHVILLE

WILSON, LAINEY

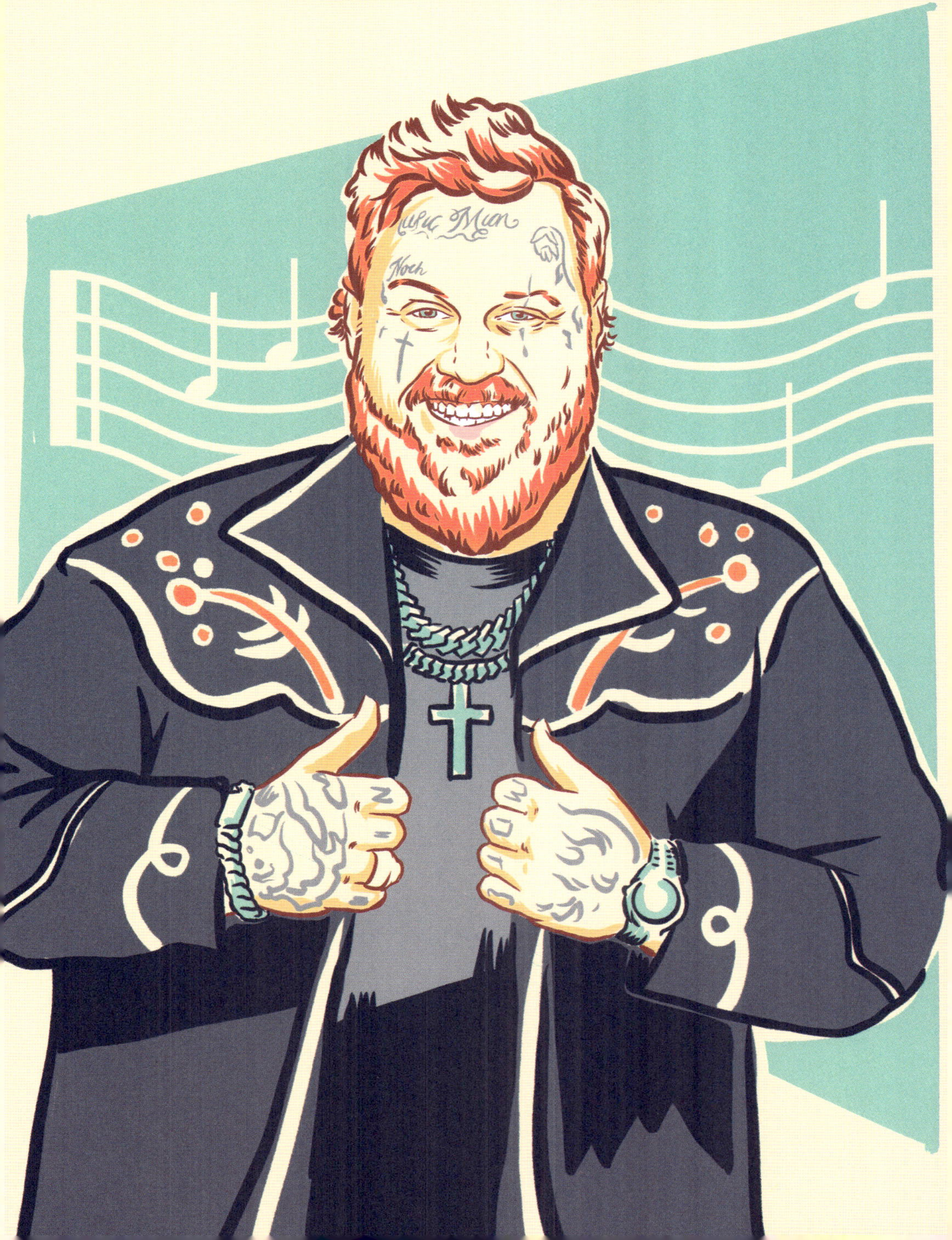

J

of country. His major label debut, *Ballads of the Broken* (2021), featured his first country number one, "Son of a Sinner," though much of the album still leaned into other genres.

His first full-length country album came in 2023 with *Whitsitt Chapel*, validating him as a true country music artist. Jelly Roll described it as "real music for real people with real problems," and fans instantly connected to it. With songs like "Need a Favor," "Save Me" (with Lainey Wilson), and "Halfway to Hell," the project spoke to those battling addiction, depression, and personal demons.

Along the way, Jelly Roll has sold out tours and collaborated with artists across many styles, from Eminem to Post Malone and Brandon Lake to Cody Johnson. He has used his platform for good, raising money for at-risk youth, people facing homelessness and food insecurity, and visiting juvenile facilities and prisons to inspire others to find a better path. He's also worked with the Nashville community to create vocational programs for at-risk teens and has previously helped to fund a new juvenile justice center in the area.

His music may not be for everyone, but it's hard not to admire Jelly Roll. He's turned his life around, even receiving a pardon from the Tennessee governor for his past criminal record, and has dedicated himself to making a difference. A voice and an advocate for the underdogs, he continues to bring country music to new audiences in a way no one else can, culminating in an invitation to become a member of the Grand Ole Opry.

JOHNNY & JUNE

Like a true country music fairytale, June Carter and Johnny Cash first met backstage at the Grand Ole Opry at Nashville's Ryman Auditorium on July 7, 1956, the night of Cash's Opry debut. That fateful evening sparked an undeniable connection that would later become the most epic love story in country music history.

June Carter had grown up in the spotlight, first performing with "The First Family of Country Music," the Carter Family, as a child and later with her mother and siblings as Mother Maybelle and the Carter Sisters. By the late 1950s, Johnny Cash had become one of country music's most promising stars with early hits like "Cry! Cry! Cry!" and "I Walk the Line."

When Carter began touring with Cash in the early 1960s, their chemistry inspired her to write "Ring of Fire," which her sister initially recorded. Cash released his own version in 1963, turning it into a multi-week number one hit.

During this time, both were married to other partners, and the details of their early relationship remain private. Carter Cash later admitted it was "not a convenient time" to fall in love. By 1966, both were divorced and in February 1968 Cash famously proposed on stage in London, Ontario, in front of 7,000 fans. They married shortly after in March 1968 in Franklin, Kentucky.

Their partnership extended into every part of their lives and both are members of the Country Music Hall of Fame. Johnny and June recorded beloved duets like the Grammy-winning "Jackson" and co-hosted *The Johnny Cash Show*, which featured guest appearances from country icons like Tammy Wynette and Glen Campbell.

"Many fans believe Cash died of a broken heart after losing his one true love."

SEE ALSO:

COUNTRY MUSIC HALL OF FAME AND MUSEUM

FILM & TV

GRAND OLE OPRY

RYMAN AUDITORIUM

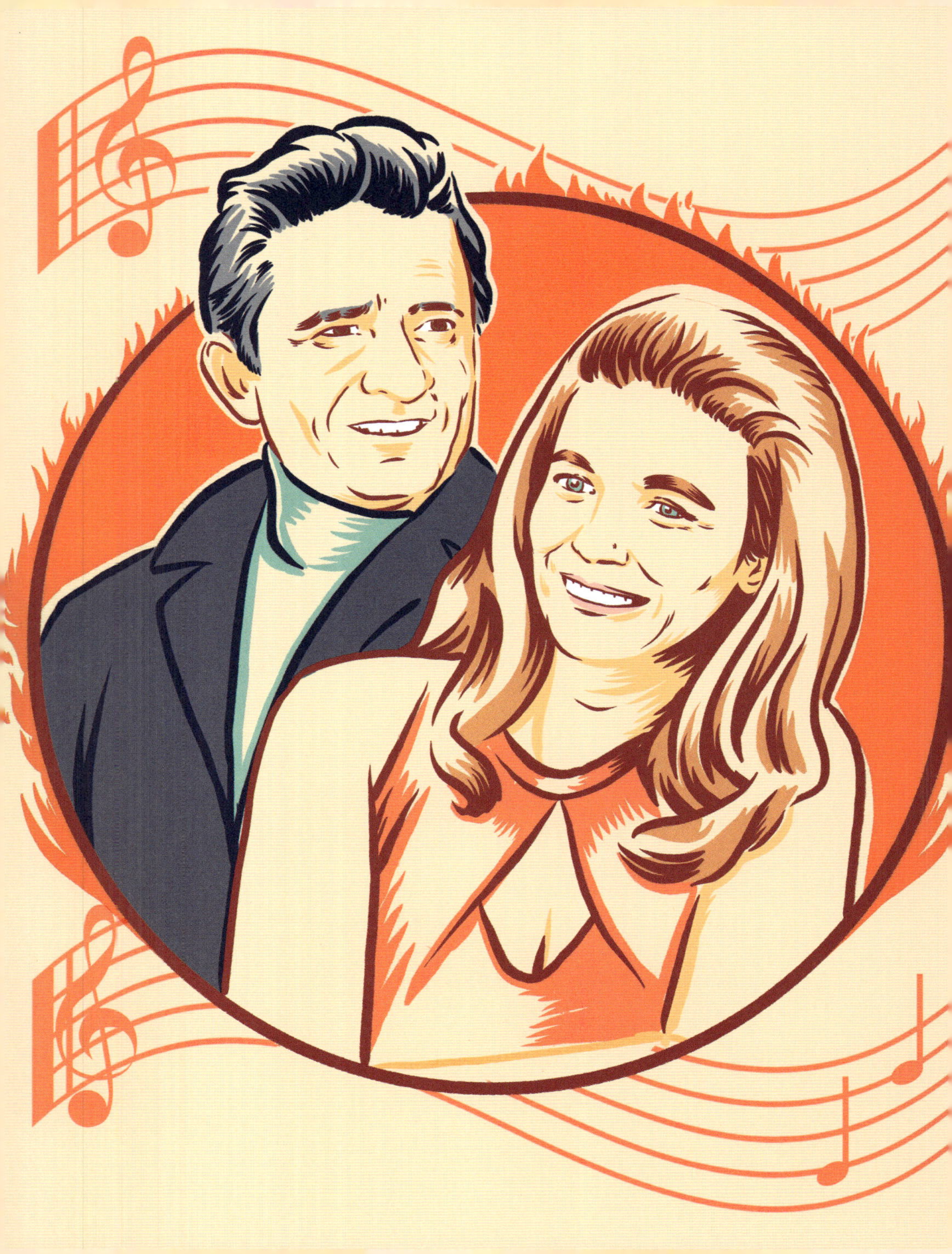

Together they raised their only child, John Carter Cash, who followed in their footsteps as a singer-songwriter and producer.

They remained married for the rest of their lives, passing away just four months apart—June on May 15, 2003 and Johnny on September 12, 2003—and their legendary love story was later immortalized in the 2005 movie *Walk the Line*. Although Johnny's death certificate lists other causes, many fans believe he died of a broken heart after losing his one true love.

J

JOHNSON, CODY

"Johnson built his career from the ground up, releasing music independently and building a loyal fan base."

SEE ALSO:

MCENTIRE, REBA

They say if you're going to talk the talk, you have to walk the walk, and Cody Johnson (CoJo) does just that. As a real cowboy living on a Texas ranch, his boots, jeans, and hat aren't for show; he's as authentic as they come.

Born in 1987 and raised in a tiny East Texas town of fewer than 500 people, Johnson's first love was rodeo. He took up bull riding as a teenager, and while he sang in church and at home, he dreamed of making it to the National Finals Rodeo. He even sold CDs at bull riding events just to fund his next ride. After several injuries and broken bones, he realized rodeo wouldn't pay the bills. He made the heartbreaking decision to quit and took a job at the local prison, while performing at clubs on the weekends.

At 21, Johnson met his wife Brandi, and they clicked instantly. Engaged within a year and married the next, she encouraged him to pursue music full time. Brandi dropped out of college and worked two jobs so he could focus on his music.

Johnson built his career from the ground up, releasing music independently and building a loyal fan base. In 2010, he met songwriter and producer Trent Willmon, who has produced him, and put out several albums on his own before finally signing with Warner Music Nashville in 2018. The deal was made on his terms and the label promised not to change him. His major debut, *Ain't Nothin' To It*, arrived in January 2019.

The album featured the deeply personal "Dear Rodeo," which inspired Johnson to share his story through the documentary *Dear Rodeo: The Cody Johnson Story*. Reba McEntire, who related to the song's message, co-starred in the film and joined Johnson for a duet version.

CoJo made his mark on country radio with hits like "'Til You Can't," "The Painter," and "Dirt Cheap," as his shows grew bigger and bigger. Johnson's live performances are electrifying, his stage presence reminiscent of a young Garth Brooks, as he's often seen running, jumping, and

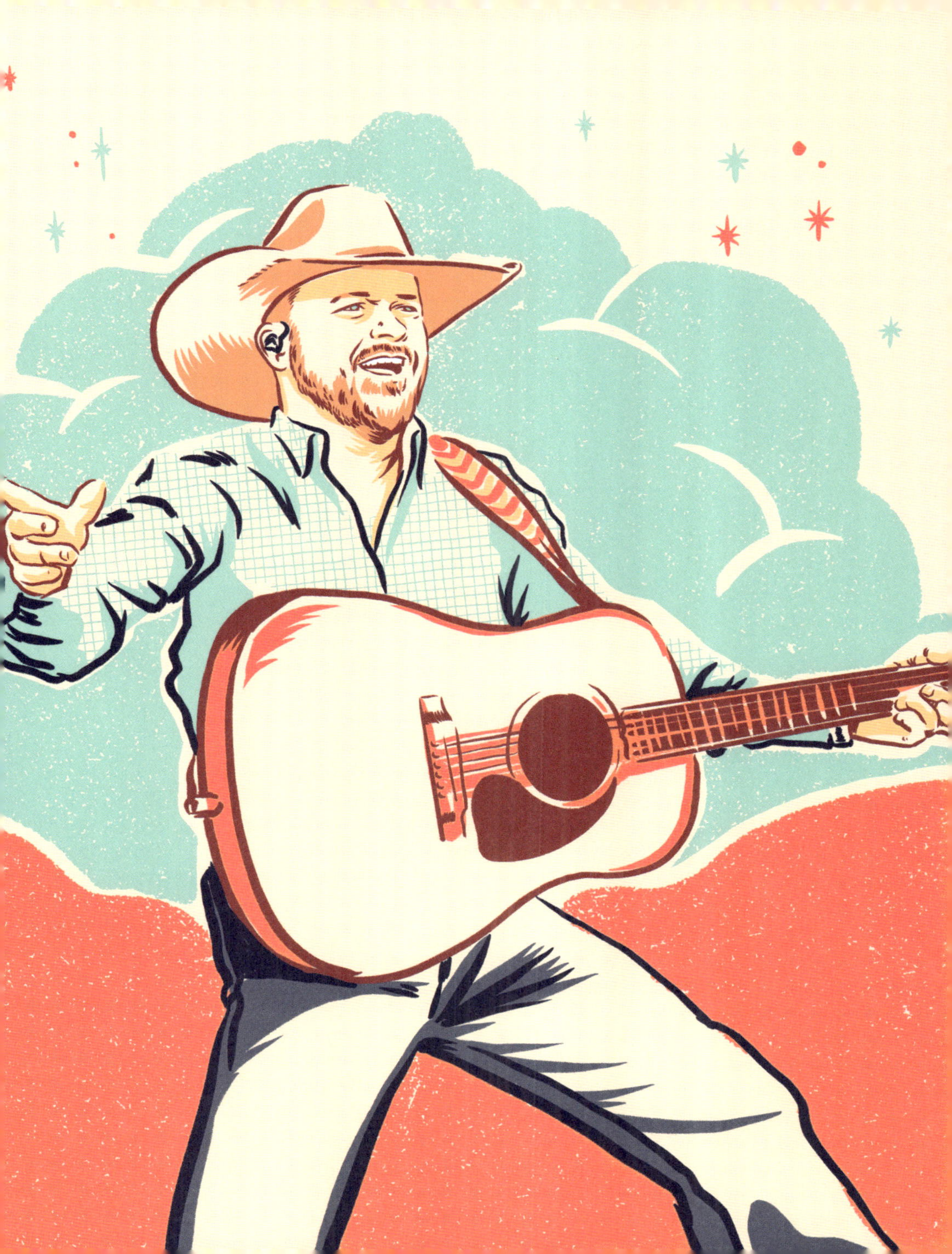

climbing across the stage. It's exactly what you'd expect from a self-described adrenaline junkie. Johnson's duet with Brooks & Dunn, "Long Live Country Music," feels quite fitting, because with artists like him, the genre is in good hands.

JONES, GEORGE

"Jones helped shape the sound of country music with his unmistakable voice and hard-hitting songs."

SEE ALSO:

COUNTRY MUSIC HALL OF FAME AND MUSEUM

DUETS

GRAND OLE OPRY

WYNETTE, TAMMY

When it comes to the greatest country singers of all time, George Jones is always in the mix. Lovingly known as "The Possum," a nickname inspired by his unique facial features, Jones helped shape the sound of country music with his unmistakable voice and hard-hitting songs. During his career, he charted 143 top 40 hits and inspired generations of artists.

Born in September 1931 in Saratoga, Texas, Jones's early life as the youngest of eight children was marked by poverty. He first discovered country music when he was seven by tuning in to the *Grand Ole Opry* on Saturday nights on his parents' radio. He had no idea he'd one day be welcomed into the Opry family.

When he was nine, his father gave him a guitar and Jones began singing for tips around Beaumont, Texas, where the family had settled. By his teens, he was performing on local radio. During that time, he briefly met his hero, Hank Williams, and later called him "the nicest guy" he'd ever met.

After two years in the Marine Corps, Jones returned to Texas and dove back into music. In 1955, "Why, Baby, Why" became his first top five hit. He scored his first number one with "White Lightning" in 1959, the same year he moved to Nashville. The 1960s brought more radio hits, including "She Thinks I Still Care," "Love Bug," and "The Race Is On," as Jones honed in on his signature sound.

He battled addiction and was divorced twice by the time he famously married Tammy Wynette. Dubbed "Mr. and Mrs. Country Music," the pair recorded several successful

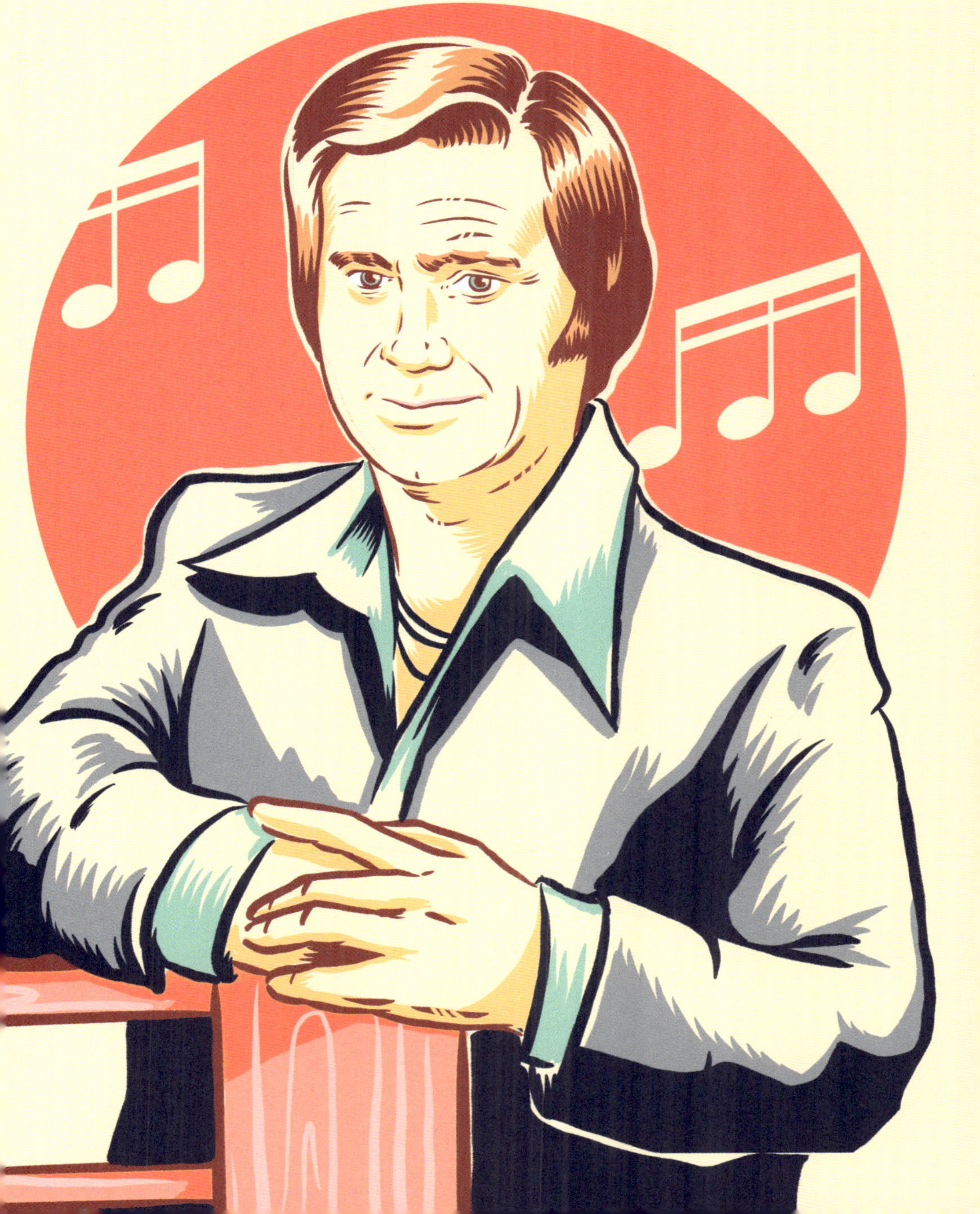

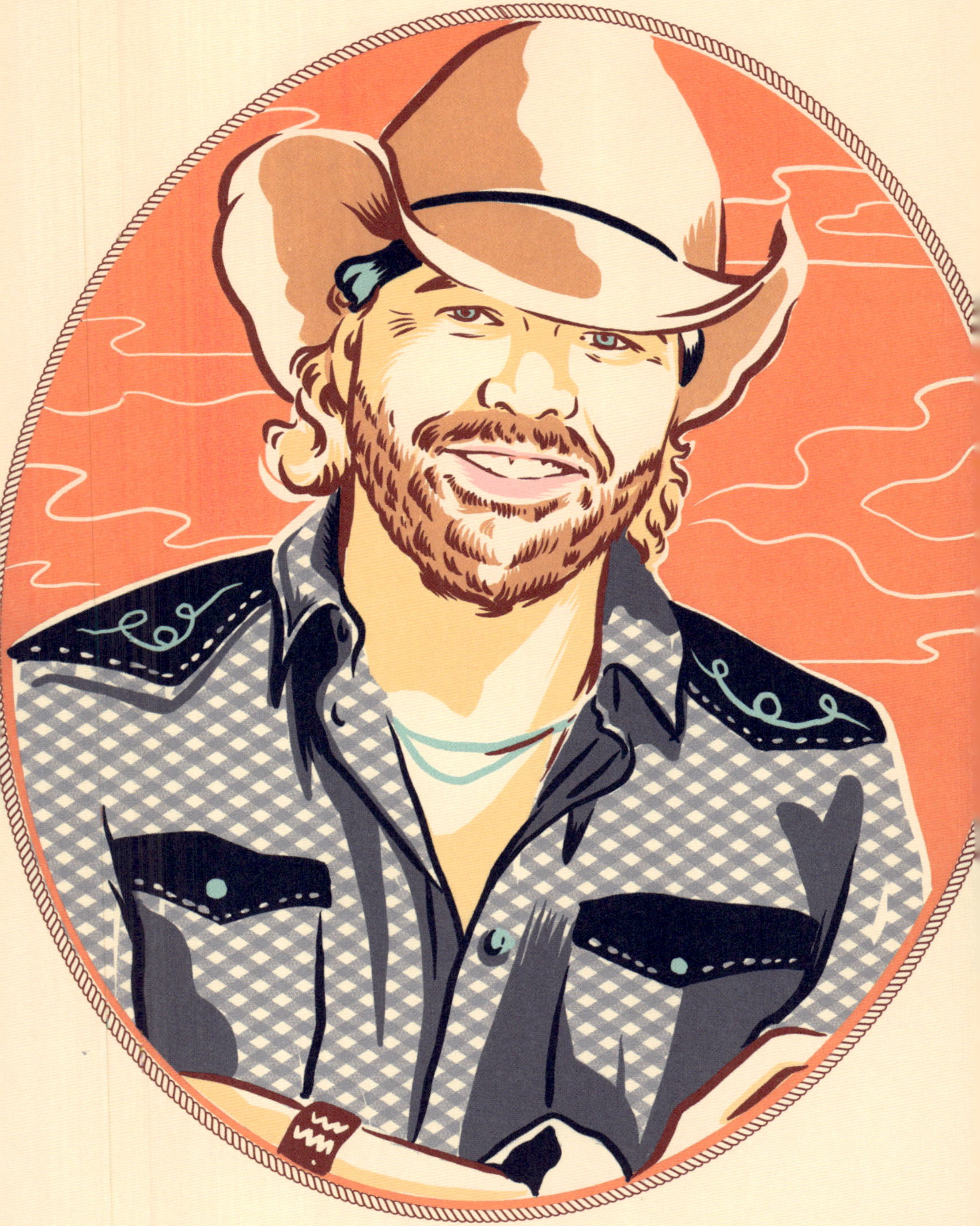

duets before divorcing in 1975. In the following years Jones's substance abuse spiraled, earning him the nickname "No Show Jones" due to him missing so many performances.

In 1980, he released the heartbreaking "He Stopped Loving Her Today," a career-defining hit that earned a Grammy and sparked a major resurgence in his career. His fourth wife, Nancy Sepulvado, helped him on his way to sobriety and he continued recording and touring into his senior years. His induction into the Country Music Hall of Fame came in 1992, and he received the National Medal of Arts in 2002.

He planned to retire after his farewell Grand Tour, which was announced in late 2012 and set to conclude with a star-studded Nashville show in November 2013. Sadly, he died on April 26, 2013, at age 81, in the midst of the tour, doing what he loved most: performing for his fans.

KEITH, TOBY

Few losses have rocked the country music community quite like the passing of Toby Keith. On February 5, 2024 Keith sadly died at the age of 62 following a brave battle with stomach cancer. Him impact on the genre was felt around the world as fans and fellow artists shared an outpouring of love and support for the singer. This was a testament to Keith's legacy as he built the kind of career many artists could only dream of with 33 number one singles and over 44 million albums sold.

Born in Clinton, Oklahoma, in July 1961, Keith was given his first guitar at just eight years old. After high school, he followed in his father's footsteps and went to work in the oil fields, although music and football were his true passions. He played semiprofessional football and took a gig as the frontman of a band called Easy Money. While working in the oil industry, Keith and the band played local gigs across Oklahoma and Texas throughout the mid-1980s.

"Toby Keith was a prolific songwriter whose unapologetic style of writing defined his career."

SEE ALSO:

COUNTRY MUSIC HALL OF FAME AND MUSEUM

MUSIC CITY

NINETIES COUNTRY

PHILANTHROPY

By the 1990s, Keith had his heart set on Nashville and began to make regular trips to Music City. One of his demo tapes eventually landed with a record executive who signed him to Mercury Records. Nashville may be a ten-year town for some, meaning it takes ten years to catch a big break, but that wasn't the case for Toby Keith. His self-written debut single, "Should've Been a Cowboy," was an instant hit, not only climbing to number one but also becoming the most-played country song of the decade.

Keith was a prolific songwriter whose unapologetic style of writing defined his career. His music blended humor, patriotism, and stories of love and loss throughout his diverse catalog. Known for his bold personality and distinct voice, Keith was also a savvy businessman, launching a successful record label, Show Dog Nashville, and venturing into several other endeavors.

Beyond music, the Oklahoma native had a passion for giving back. He formed the Toby Keith Foundation to support pediatric cancer patients and dedicated much of his spare time to his philanthropic efforts. He also embarked on 11 USO (United Service Organizations) tours, performing for close to 256,000 troops across 18 countries. Months after his passing, Keith was officially inducted into the Country Music Hall of Fame, a well-deserved honor that capped off his extraordinary career. Toby Keith may be gone, but he is certainly not forgotten.

LADY A

Dave Haywood, Charles Kelley, and Hillary Scott make up Lady A, one of the most successful groups in modern country music. With 11 number one singles and over nine billion streams, the trio is known for their stunning harmonies, irresistible melodies, and blend of country, rock, and pop.

Unlike some duos or groups, Lady A wasn't manufactured by a label or manager. The trio came together naturally after Scott discovered Kelley's music on the social media

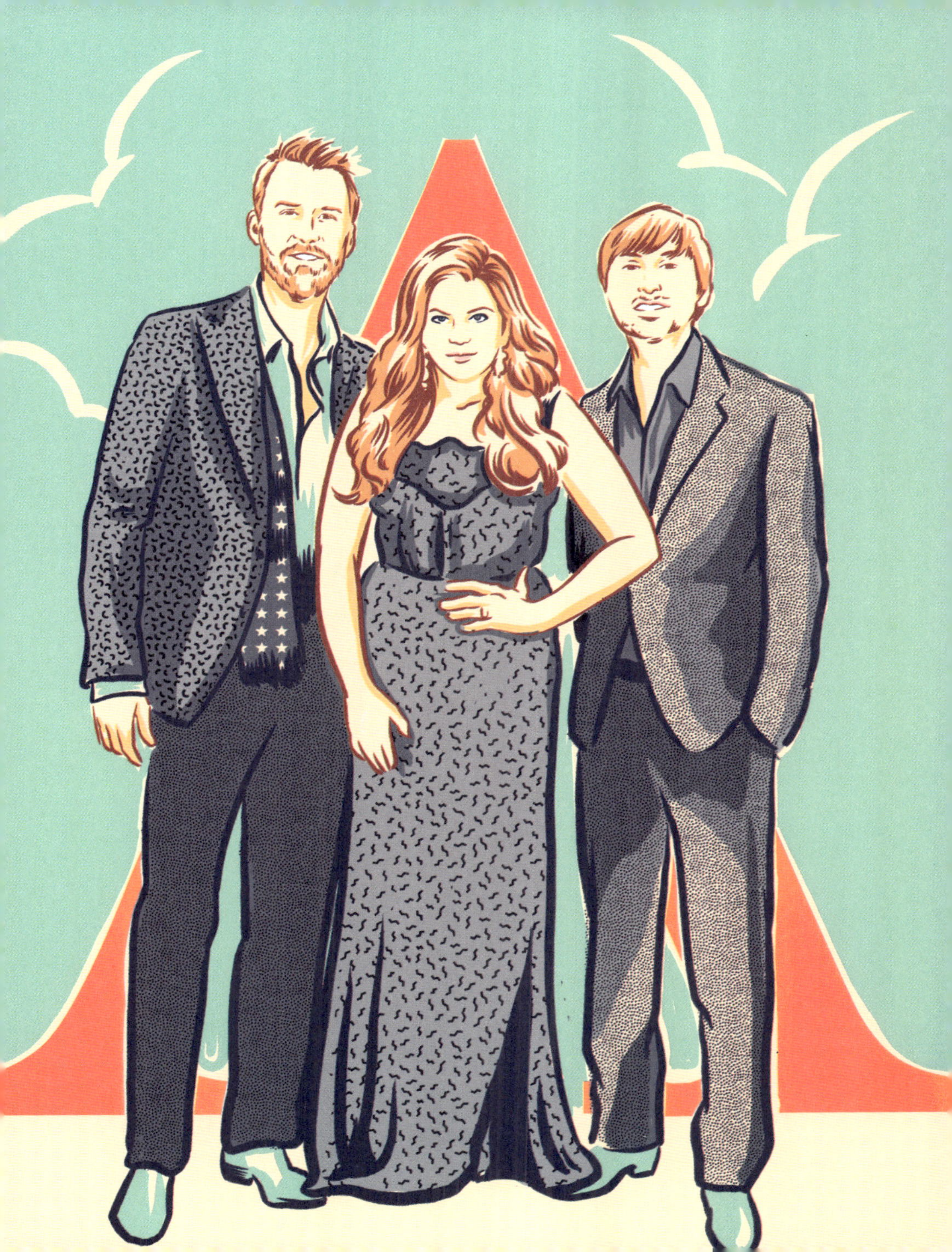

L

platform MySpace. As fate would have it, she ran into Kelley at a bar in Nashville soon after, and he invited her to join him and his college friend Haywood for a writing session.

That meeting was serendipitous. One of the first songs they wrote together, "Love Don't Live Here," became their debut single. Over the next six months, they wrote enough material to play a full live set. Word spread quickly, and by their final showcase, nearly every label in Nashville showed up. In early 2007, Lady A signed a record deal and released their first single that fall. Their self-titled debut album went on to produce three hits.

Then came "Need You Now," which would become their signature song. The lead single from their second album, the song became a multi-week number one, crossing over to the pop and contemporary charts and made waves around the world. It swept the 53rd Grammy Awards in 2011, taking home five wins, including all-genre nods Record of the Year and Song of the Year. It was the biggest country song since Faith Hill's "Breathe," and launched Lady A's career to a level of success that they could never have imagined.

Next, there were headlining tours, more chart-topping singles, and ACM and CMA Vocal Group of the Year trophies for three consecutive years. To date, the trio has collected seven Grammys. They were invited to become members of the Grand Ole Opry in 2021.

What's special about Lady A, much like Fleetwood Mac or the Eagles, is that they have multiple lead vocalists. There's just something magical when Kelley and Scott sing together. Add in Haywood's backing vocals and multi-instrumental skills, and you've got a recipe for country-pop gold.

"The trio is known for their stunning harmonies, irresistible melodies, and blend of country, rock, and pop."

SEE ALSO:
GRAND OLE OPRY

LAMBERT, MIRANDA

With Miranda Lambert, what you see is what you get. She sings what she knows and has never been anything but authentically herself: she's the real deal.

Her story began in Lindale, Texas, where she was born in 1983 and went on to perform at local talent shows and eventually on the Texas bar circuit. At 16, her father drove her to Nashville to record a demo, but she decided that the bubblegum pop-country songs pitched to her weren't her style. So she picked up a guitar and started writing her own material instead.

In 2003, she placed third on the TV competition *Nashville Star*, and by 2005 had released her major label debut, *Kerosene*. Her performance of the title track at the 2005 CMA Awards was a make-or-break moment in her career. Naturally, she nailed it, lighting the stage on fire in more ways than one.

The year 2010 brought what Lambert calls a "career maker" song, "The House That Built Me." Although she didn't write it, she felt every word, delivering a performance so personal it became the fastest-rising single of her career and earned her a Grammy.

Like her hero Loretta Lynn, Lambert never shies away from tough topics, from domestic violence in "Gunpowder & Lead" to a small-town cheating story in "White Liar." Nothing is off-limits. She's become an award show favorite, collecting over 80 honors and becoming the most-awarded artist in the Academy of Country Music history.

"A champion for women in country music, Lambert uses her platform to stand up for what she believes in."

SEE ALSO:

LOWER BROADWAY

LYNN, LORETTA

PHILANTHROPY

TATTOOS

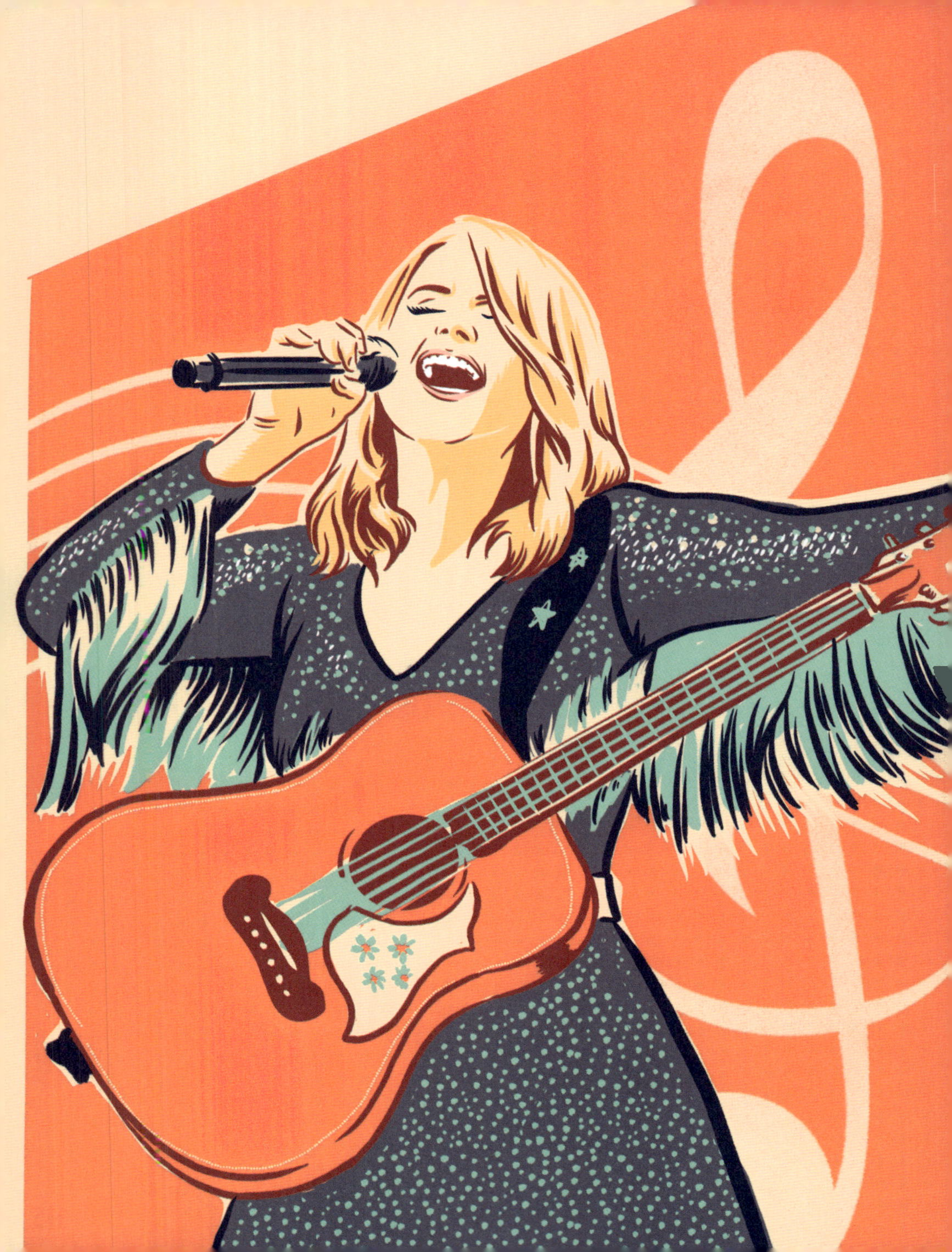

A champion for women in country music, Lambert uses her platform to stand up for what she believes in. Her legacy includes co-founding the nonprofit MuttNation Foundation with her mom, Bev, supporting animal rescue.

Lambert has diversified her career with her "Velvet Rodeo" residency in Las Vegas, co-founding a record label and becoming the first female artist to open a venue on Nashville's Lower Broadway. She's also a best-selling author and has even launched her own clothing line.

I respect Miranda Lambert not just for her talent, but also for the way she's carved her own path and remained a true artist in every sense of the word.

LOVELESS, PATTY

"Her chart success was not instant, but once she found her footing, Loveless became unstoppable."

SEE ALSO:

COUNTRY MUSIC HALL OF FAME AND MUSEUM

GRAND OLE OPRY

LYNN, LORETTA

Patty Loveless has left a lasting mark on country music with her powerful, emotive vocals, and her unique blend of country, rockabilly, and bluegrass. She emerged onto the scene in the late 1980s, just as artists like Randy Travis were leading the neo-traditionalist movement, and her timing couldn't have been better. She went on to become a member of the Country Music Hall of Fame, the Kentucky Music Hall of Fame, and the Georgia Music Hall of Fame. Impressively, she's also a five-time CMA winner, a three-time ACM winner, and a two-time Grammy winner.

Born in Pikeville, Kentucky, in 1957, Loveless was one of seven children. Like her distant cousin Loretta Lynn, she was also the daughter of a coal miner. Her earliest musical memories include listening to the *Grand Ole Opry* on Saturday nights and singing alongside her brother, Roger. The siblings later formed a duo, performing at local events.

As a teenager, Loveless traveled to Nashville with Roger, hoping to sing for the Wilburn Brothers. Though the duo was on the road, a chance meeting with Porter Wagoner led to an introduction to Dolly Parton, and even an invitation to attend the Opry as their guest. Loveless later described the experience as "hillbilly heaven."

Still in high school, she began performing with the Wilburn Brothers, who also signed her to a publishing deal. After graduation, she toured extensively with the duo. Following a stint fronting a pop-rock cover band, Loveless returned to Nashville ready to find her place in country music. It wasn't long before legends like George Jones and Willie Nelson took notice, inviting her on their tours.

Her chart success was not instant, but once she found her footing, Loveless became unstoppable. Between 1988 and 2003 she charted 34 top 40 singles. Some of her best-known hits include "Blame It on Your Heart," "Timber, I'm Falling in Love," and "I Try to Think About Elvis."

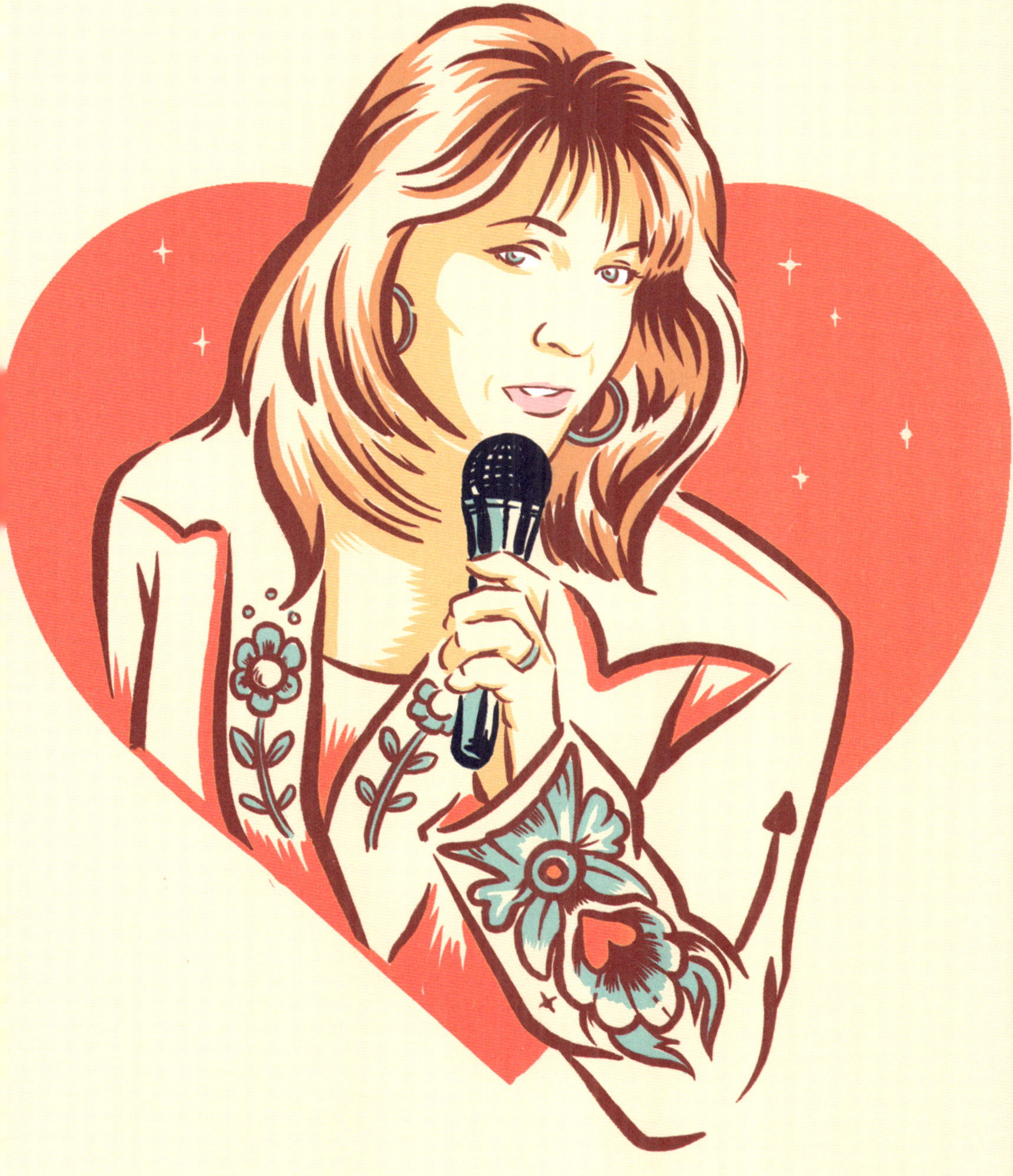

L

In a full-circle moment, Wagoner invited her to become a member of the Grand Ole Opry in 1988. Later in her career, Loveless leaned into her Appalachian roots, releasing several bluegrass records. Though semiretired, she has recently collaborated with artists such as Carly Pearce, Chris Stapleton, and Miranda Lambert.

Patty Loveless never chased trends or tried to fit into what was popular. She's always made music true to herself, and that authenticity is what has kept her songs timeless.

LOWER BROADWAY

"It's loud, and at times it's wild and a bit crazy, but it's the heartbeat of Music City."

SEE ALSO:

FRIED BOLOGNA SANDWICH

NASHVILLE

Nashville's Lower Broadway has seen a complete transformation over the years. What began as a bustling commercial district has become a lively hub for tourists filled with restaurants, stores, and, most famously, honky-tonks.

Nicknamed "Honky-Tonk Highway," Lower Broadway is known for its nonstop party atmosphere and live music that plays from 10a.m. to 3a.m. daily. Tootsie's Orchid Lounge was Lower Broadway's very first honky-tonk and remains a staple on the famed stretch. Drawing its name from its purple exterior, Tootsie's became a hub for country music with artists like Patsy Cline, Kris Kristofferson, and Mel Tillis performing there on a regular basis. Willie Nelson even landed his first songwriting job after a show at Tootsie's. Honky-tonks continued to fill the famous strip with iconic establishments like Robert's Western World, The Stage, and more lining the block.

In recent years, Lower Broadway has been taken over by celebrity owned and affiliated bars and restaurants. Alan Jackson led the charge with AJ's Good Time Bar, followed by Dierks Bentley's Whiskey Row, Blake Shelton's Ole Red, and Jason Aldean's Kitchen and Rooftop Bar, to name but a few. Miranda Lambert made history as the first female artist with a bar on Broadway when she opened Casa Rosa, and Lainey Wilson followed with Bell Bottoms Up.

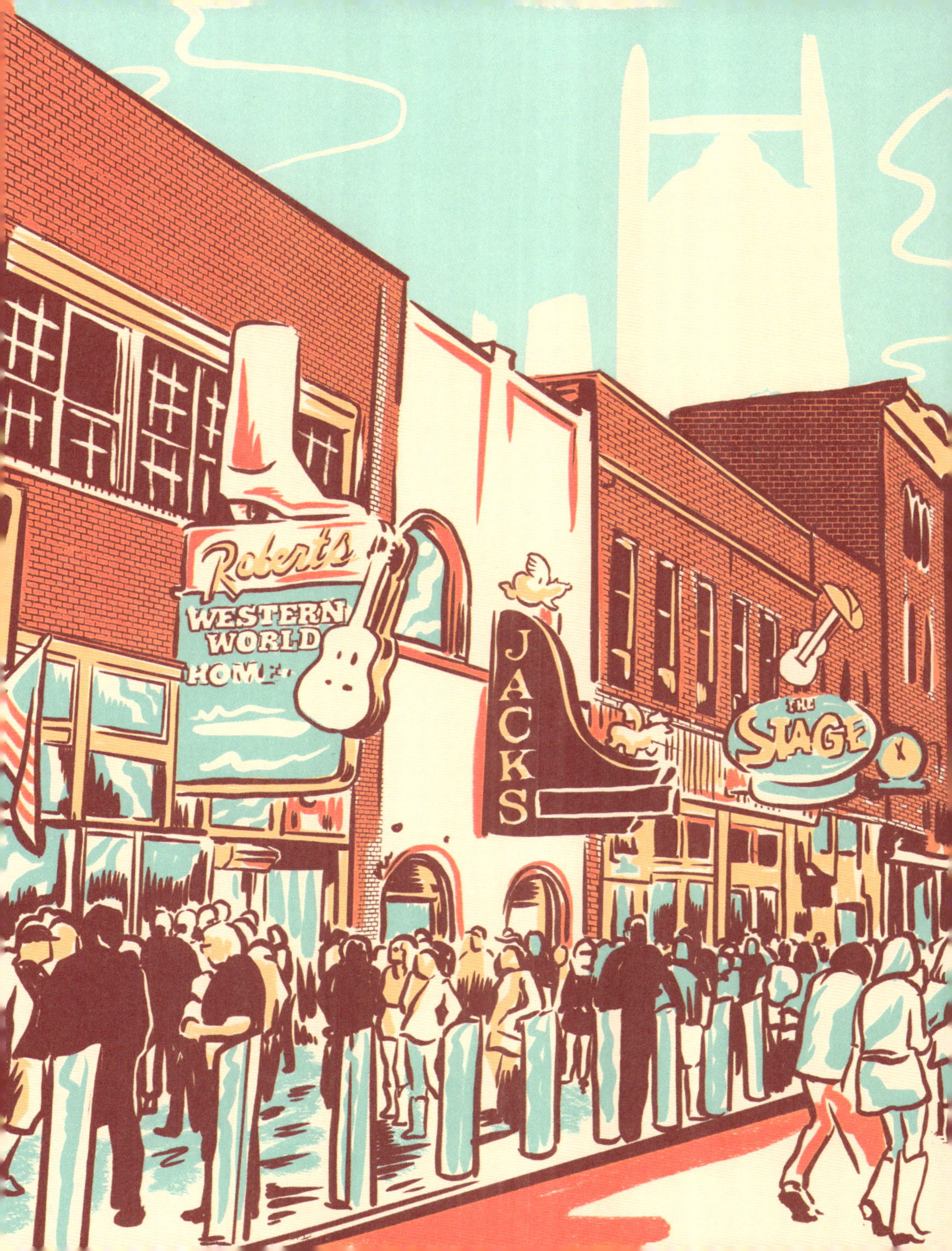

Robert's
WESTERN
WORLD
HOME
JACKS
THE
STAGE

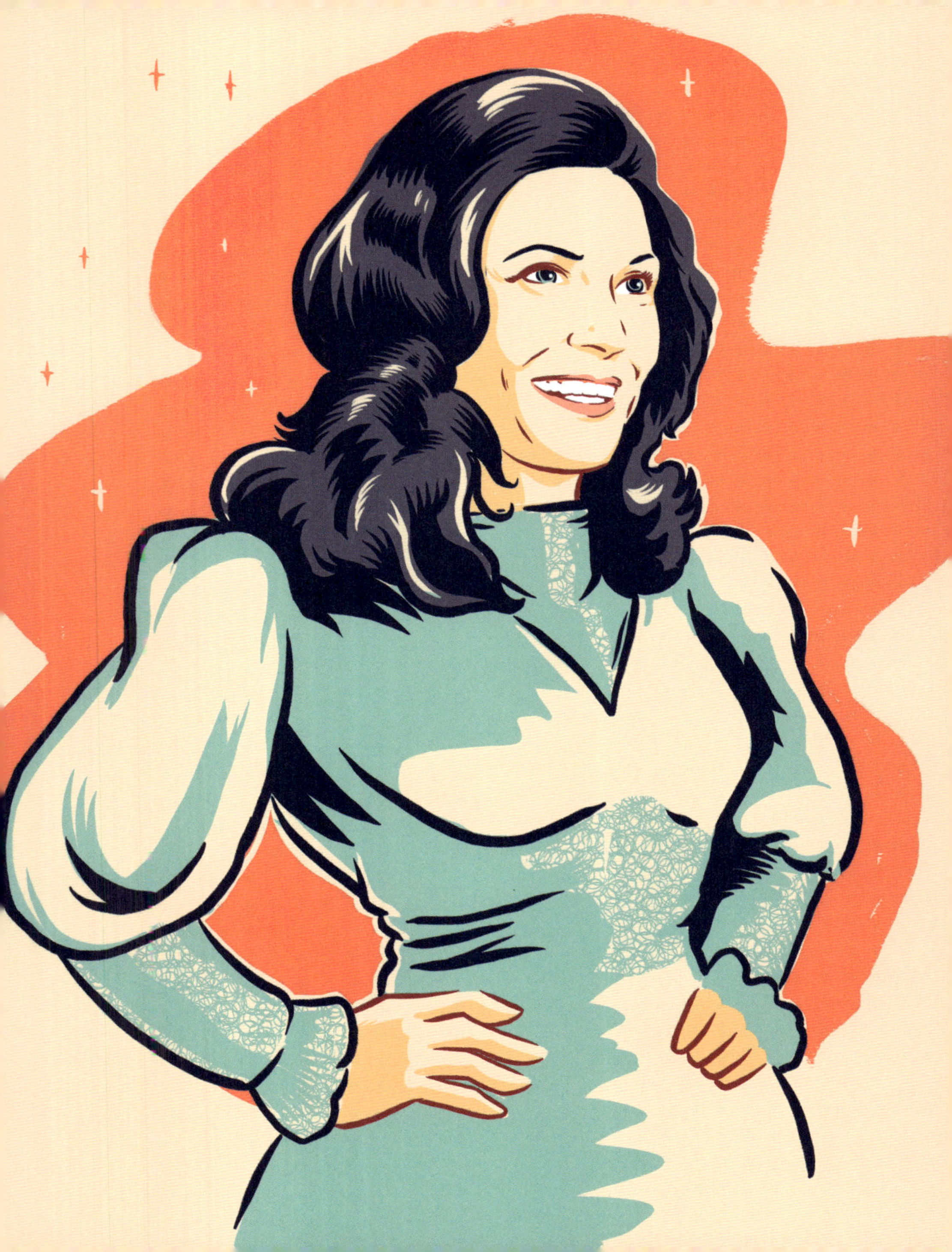

Artists outside of country music are also getting in on the action—Jon Bon Jovi and Post Malone are among those who have added their names to venues along the strip. No matter the season or the day of the week, Broadway is filled with people hopping from one honky-tonk to the next. Neon lights line the street and live music echoes through every open door. It's loud, and at times it's wild and a bit crazy, but it's the heartbeat of Music City.

Fun fact: There's no cover charge for any of the establishments on Broadway. Patrons are simply encouraged to tip the band.

LYNN, LORETTA

One of the most iconic and influential women in country music, Loretta Lynn broke down barriers for female artists with her daring and honest lyrics, some so controversial they were banned from radio play.

Born in 1932 in Butcher Hollow, Kentucky, Lynn married Olive "Doolittle" Lynn when she was just 15. Although she was raised in a musical family, it was Doolittle who encouraged her to pursue music, buying her a guitar and helping her book shows. They drove across the country together visiting radio stations to promote her first single, "I'm a Honky Tonk Girl." This grassroots effort landed them in Nashville.

With Doolittle serving as her manager, Lynn dove into the country music scene and began to perform regularly at the Grand Ole Opry. She signed a record deal, became a member of the Opry, and began her rise to superstardom. During her early days in Nashville, Lynn formed a tight-knit friendship with Patsy Cline, a bond she said changed her life forever.

Over her 60-year career she amassed a whopping 51 top ten singles. A fearless songwriter, Lynn wrote about her life and sometimes forbidden topics: "Don't Come Home a Drinkin' (With Lovin' on Your Mind)" is about a woman

"Lynn is the most awarded woman in country music, garnering every available accolade."

SEE ALSO:

CLINE, PATSY

COUNTRY MUSIC HALL OF FAME

GRAND OLE OPRY

TWITTY, CONWAY

standing up to her drunk husband; "Fist City" was a direct response to her husband's infidelity; and she wrote "The Pill" about birth control. These songs may have been banned, but they still found widespread success.

Her signature song, "Coal Miner's Daughter," was written about her experiences growing up poor in rural Kentucky. The story later came to life on the big screen through the award-winning movie *Coal Miner's Daughter*, introducing her music to a new generation of fans.

Lynn also found success in collaborations, charting a dozen top tens with Conway Twitty and teaming up with Dolly Parton and Tammy Wynette on the collaborative album, *Honky Tonk Angels*.

Lynn is the most awarded woman in country music, garnering every accolade available in music. She was the first woman to win the ACM and CMA Awards for Entertainer of the Year and is a member of the Country Music Hall of Fame.

She built a wildly successful career, all while raising six children and enduring the ups and downs of a tumultuous marriage. Lynn passed away at the age of 90 in October 2022, leaving behind a legacy that will impact country music forever.

MCBRIDE, MARTINA

Martina McBride remembers the exact moment she knew she wanted a career in country music. After performing with her family's band, The Schiffters, in a battle of the bands contest, she listened back to their performance on tape and realized this was what she was meant to do. A few months later, she moved to Nashville and never looked back.

McBride, born Martina Mariea Schiff in 1966, started out performing with The Schiffters around her home state of Kansas. Her father, Daryl Schiff, was instrumental in

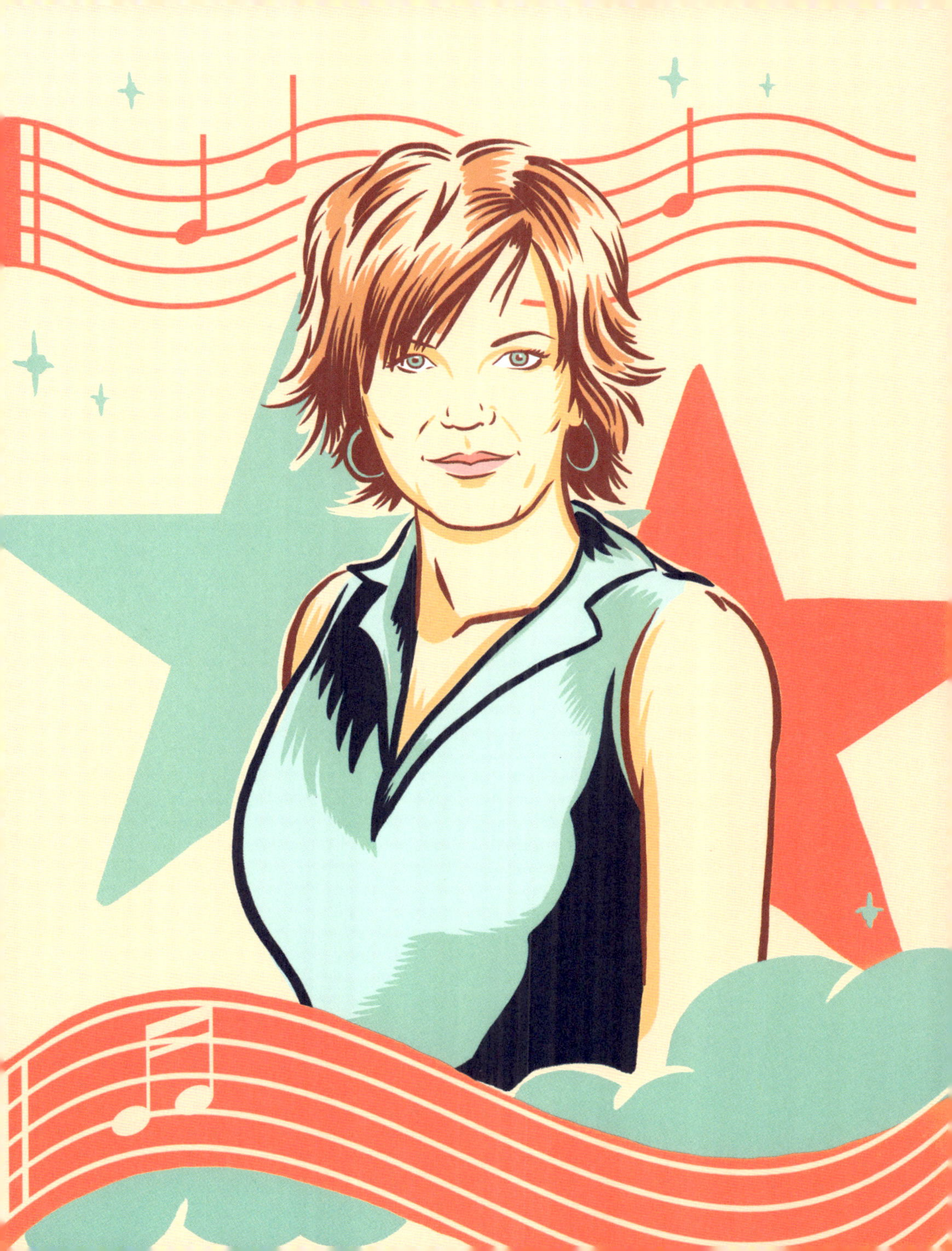

M

"Her legacy lies with 'Independence Day,' a powerful anthem about domestic violence."

SEE ALSO:

DEMOS

GRAND OLE OPRY

NINETIES COUNTRY

her journey, forming the band, teaching her to play and sing, and giving her invaluable stage experience. In 1990, McBride and her husband, John, moved to Nashville. A year later John, a music engineer, became Garth Brooks's production manager and Martina tagged along on tour, selling T-shirts.

Determined to land her big break, Martina borrowed money to record a demo tape. After facing countless rejections, she heard that RCA Records was searching for a female artist. Taking a chance, she placed her demo into a purple envelope labeled "requested material" and delivered it to RCA. Her clever move paid off; she landed a record deal and her debut album was out within a year.

Among her six number one hits and 20 top ten singles are the joyful "My Baby Loves Me," the empowering "This One's for the Girls," and the heart-wrenching "I'm Gonna Love You Through It." Her legacy, however, lies with "Independence Day," a powerful anthem about domestic violence. Though it never landed in the top ten due to its subject matter, the song earned the CMA Song of the Year award in 1995.

Beyond music, McBride has released two cookbooks, *Martina's Kitchen Mix: My Recipe Playlist for Real Life* (2018) and *Around the Table: Recipes and Inspiration for Gatherings Throughout the Year* (2014), and hosted a cooking show, *Martina's Table*, on Food Network.

With her show-stopping vocals, Martina McBride has sold more than 23 million albums and earned four CMA Awards and three ACM Awards as Female Vocalist of the Year. She's a member of the Grand Ole Opry and continues to advocate for female country artists receiving more airplay on country radio.

MCENTIRE, REBA

One of the most successful female recording artists of all time, Reba McEntire has built a career that touches nearly every corner of entertainment. She's a Kennedy Center Honors recipient, a member of the Grand Ole Opry and the Country Music Hall of Fame, and has won over 50 major awards. With 35 number one singles and more than 58 million albums sold worldwide, she rightfully holds the title "Queen of Country Music."

An Oklahoma native, Reba was born into a rodeo family in 1955 and raised on a ranch. In high school she performed in a family band, the Singing McEntires, performing at rodeos and local honky-tonks. She was discovered in 1974 by fellow singer Red Steagall after singing the national anthem at the National Finals Rodeo. Impressed by her voice, he helped finance her first recordings and helped her land a record deal the following year.

Her early singles struggled, but by the late 1970s and early 1980s her songs were steadily climbing higher on the charts. Her first number one arrived with 1982's "Can't Even Get the Blues." With label executives pushing her toward a pop-leaning sound, Reba decided to take control of her career. Wanting to return to her country roots, she changed labels and gained more creative freedom. Her 1984 album *My Kind of Country* marked a major turning point. That same year, she was crowned CMA Female Vocalist of the Year, a title she would go on to win four years in a row.

Reba continued her chart dominance in the 1990s with hits like "Fancy," "Is There Life Out There," and her duet "Does He Love You" with Linda Davis. During this time, she also launched her acting career, landing roles in major films and lending her voice to animated TV shows and

"Reba McEntire has built a career that touches nearly every corner of entertainment."

SEE ALSO:

COUNTRY MUSIC HALL OF FAME AND MUSEUM

GRAND OLE OPRY

FILM & TV

M

movies. In 2001, she took on the role of Annie Oakley in the Broadway revival of *Annie Get Your Gun*. That same year, she debuted her sitcom *Reba*, which ran for six seasons and remains a fan favorite through reruns and streaming.

She's conquered Las Vegas, authored books, hosted awards shows, opened a restaurant in her hometown, and reinvented herself with each chapter of her career. Reba remains a powerhouse to this day. There's seemingly nothing she can't do, and we're so proud to call her one of our own.

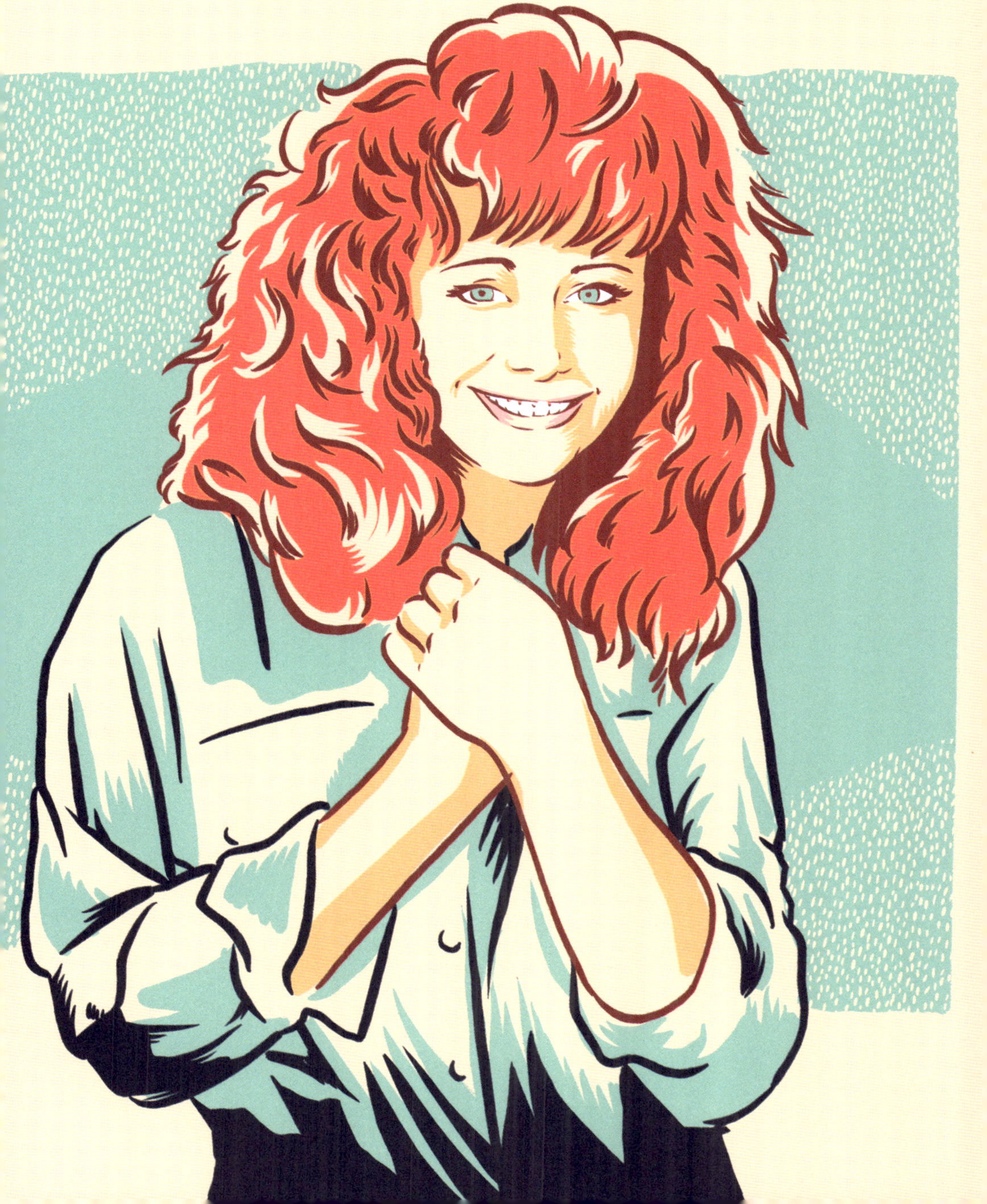

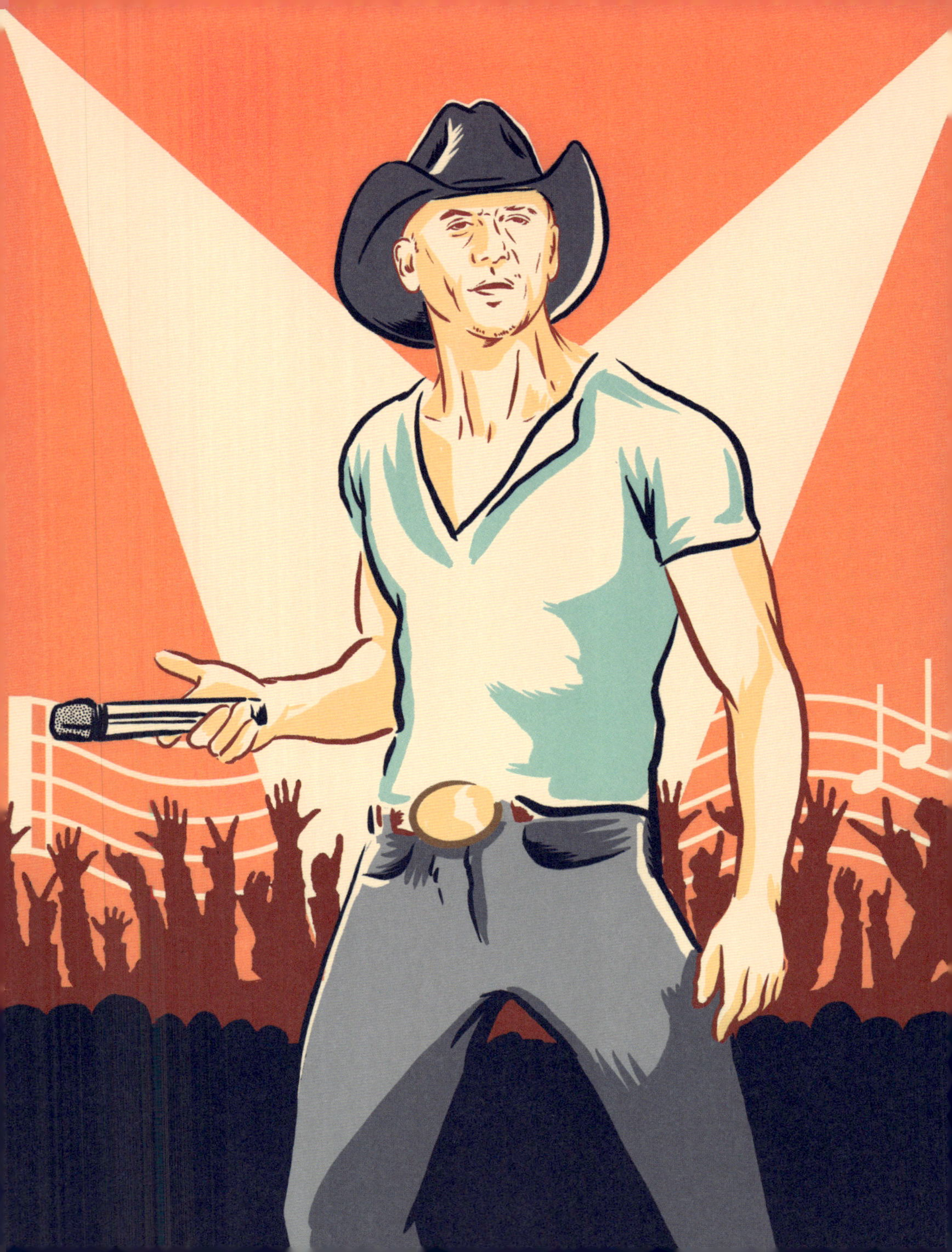

M

MCGRAW, TIM

Tim McGraw has built a reputation as one of modern country music's most consistent hitmakers. With a career spanning decades and defined by meaningful songs like "Live Like You Were Dying" and "Humble and Kind," he has sold over 103 million albums, scored 47 number one singles, and earned more accolades than you can count.

Born Samuel Timothy McGraw in 1967 in Delhi, Louisiana, he was raised by his mother and stepfather, whom he believed was his biological father. At 11, McGraw learned that his real father was professional baseball player Tug McGraw, who initially refused to acknowledge him; the two eventually formed a relationship.

As a rising country singer, McGraw idolized Keith Whitley. After meeting Whitley at a concert in Jacksonville, Florida, the legend told McGraw that he hoped to see him in Nashville someday. Eventually, McGraw dropped out of college and arrived in Nashville on a Greyhound bus on May 9, 1989, the same day Whitley tragically died of alcohol poisoning at just 34. In a twist of fate, a contact of Tug McGraw who worked as an executive at Curb Records heard Tim's demo and offered him a record deal.

The early years weren't easy. His first singles flopped, and his 1993 self-titled debut album failed to make much of an impact. Everything changed in 1994 with "Indian Outlaw" and the follow-up single "Don't Take the Girl," which became his first number one hit. This success propelled his sophomore release to become the year's best-selling country album. From there, the hits kept coming and McGraw built a powerhouse touring career alongside his radio success.

In 1996, McGraw invited Faith Hill to join him on tour. They fell in love, he proposed backstage, and the couple married on October 6 that same year. Today, they remain one of country music's most beloved couples, even spending several years touring together.

"Despite his success in Hollywood, Nashville (and country music) will always be home."

SEE ALSO:

HILL, FAITH
SWIFT, TAYLOR
WHITLEY, KEITH

M

Once McGraw established himself as a bona fide star, he branched into acting, landing roles in films *The Blind Side* and *Friday Night Lights*, as well as the hit series *1883*, where he starred alongside Hill. Despite his success in Hollywood, Nashville (and country music) will always be home.

MUSIC CITY WALK OF FAME

"Music City Walk of Fame is free, open to the public, and available to view 24/7."

SEE ALSO:
NASHVILLE

No trip to Nashville is complete without a visit to the Music City Walk of Fame. Similar to the Hollywood Walk of Fame, this landmark was created in 2006 and features star-shaped medallions that honor generations of individuals who have made a lasting impact on music and have a connection to Nashville.

Along the legendary 1 mile (1.6km) stretch, you will see stars honoring the likes of country greats such as Reba McEntire, Vince Gill, Alan Jackson, Patsy Cline, and Johnny Cash, as well as modern country stars like Eric Church, Miranda Lambert, Dierks Bentley, and Luke Combs.

The Walk of Fame also honors artists from other genres, including guitar legend Jimi Hendrix (who spent his early years performing in Nashville), rock band Kings of Leon (who started out in Nashville and continue to call Music City their home), and Christian singer Michael W. Smith (a longtime Nashville resident).

And it's not just celebrities who are recognized here: Lula C. Naff, the manager of the Ryman Auditorium who was instrumental in the venue becoming a world-renowned concert hall, Jo Walker-Meadow, who reigned as the director of the Country Music Association (CMA) for nearly 30 years, and E.W. "Bud" Wendell, former general manager of the Grand Ole Opry, are among the industry pioneers who are honored along the Walk of Fame.

Located on Demonbreun Street between 4th and 5th Avenues South, the Music City Walk of Fame is free, open to the public, and available to view 24/7.

MUSIC ROW

In Nashville, the parties happen on Lower Broadway, but the work gets done on Music Row. Centered around 16th and 17th Avenues South, this stretch is home to record labels, publishing companies, management offices, booking agencies, recording studios, and countless other music-related businesses. It's the heartbeat of Nashville's music industry.

The hub's story began in 1954 when brothers Owen Bradley (a legendary producer) and Harold Bradley (a sought-after session musician) opened the first recording studio on Music Row. Soon after other businesses followed, including the historic RCA Studio B in 1957. By 1979, more than 600 music-related companies lined the streets. It became the place where deals were signed, songs were written, and legendary careers were launched. The Country Music Hall of Fame and Museum even had its first home here.

Music Row's creative community has been behind thousands of hits, including timeless classics like Patsy Cline's "Crazy" and George Jones's "He Stopped Loving Her Today." The National Trust for Historic Preservation has named Music Row a "National Treasure."

Years ago, Music Row felt like a neighborhood, with craftsman-style homes serving as offices and only a few large buildings in between. Today, it looks much different. Along with Nashville's growth came developers building apartments and condos, knocking down pieces of country music history along the way. As a result, Music Row was added to the list of America's 11 Most Endangered Historic Places in 2019.

While many major labels—including Universal Music Group's MCA and Sony Music Nashville—have moved downtown,

"Banners line the streets celebrating the latest number one songs and albums, reminding everyone that Music Row is still the heart of Nashville's music industry."

SEE ALSO:

LOWER BROADWAY

NASHVILLE

RECORDING STUDIO

Music Row remains a vital hub for the business of country music. On any given day, banners line the streets celebrating the latest number one songs and albums, reminding everyone that Music Row is still the heart of Nashville's music industry.

N

NASHVILLE

"Every day in Nashville, someone's dream comes true."

SEE ALSO:

CMA FEST

GRAND OLE OPRY

LOWER BROADWAY

MUSIC ROW

RYMAN AUDITORIUM

Affectionately known as Music City, Tennessee state capital Nashville is "The Home of Country Music." It's a city filled with people from all over who share the same dream: to make it big. Some hope they'll be discovered while playing for tips on Broadway, others aim to land a job behind the scenes in the music industry, and many come to write the next number one hit.

Nashville's evolving music scene has deep roots. In the late 1700s, the first settlers along the Cumberland River played fiddle music and buck danced. Then in 1873 Fisk University's Fisk Jubilee Singers famously performed for Queen Victoria, putting Nashville's music on an international stage. By the early 1900s, the city's clubs came to life with R&B, jazz, and orchestras, helped by the opening of the Ryman Auditorium in 1892, which drew musicians from every genre, including Louis Armstrong and Nat King Cole. The Grand Ole Opry found its home at the former church, welcoming future country icons and earning a national audience through WSM's broadcasts. Nashville soon became the birthplace of bluegrass and the epicenter of country music.

Recording studios, publishing houses, record labels, and management offices set up shop along 16th and 17th Avenues South, an area now known as Music Row. And Nashville soon became the songwriting capital of the world, a place where poets share stories of life, love, loss, and everything in between.

Today, there's live music on nearly every corner. Nashville is home to more than 250 venues, and the music plays almost around the clock 365 days a year. Fans travel

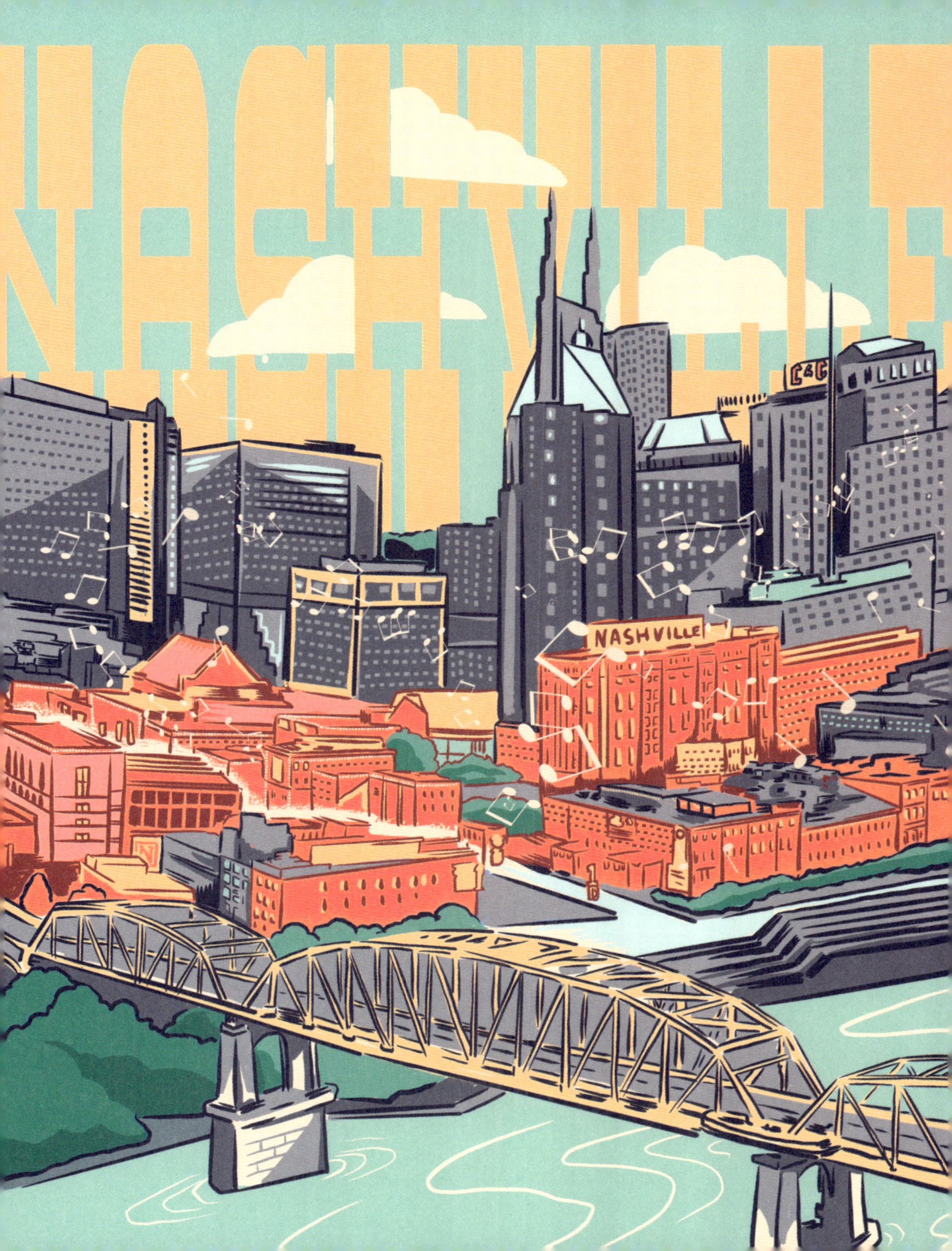
NASHVILLE
NASHVILLE

N

from across the globe to experience CMA Fest and enjoy hearing artists play in the round at The Bluebird Cafe, as well as to take in the sights and sounds of Lower Broadway: the "woo" girls on bachelorette parties riding by on pedal taverns, the shouts of people on party buses, live music spilling out of honky-tonks from every angle, crowds strolling by in cowboy boots, and the bright neon lights flashing from every bar and venue.

Every day in Nashville, someone's dream comes true: a songwriter gets their first cut, an artist hears themselves on the radio for the first time, a musician nails a solo. There's truly no place like it.

NELSON, WILLIE

"Nelson remains one of the oldest active recording and touring musicians of all time."

SEE ALSO:

CLINE, PATSY

COUNTRY MUSIC HALL OF FAME AND MUSEUM

GUITAR

OUTLAW COUNTRY

TOUR BUS

Willie Nelson is one of music's most beloved singers, songwriters, guitarists, authors, activists, and pop culture icons. His career spans seven decades, with a whopping 78 solo albums to his name. A member of the Country Music Hall of Fame and Rock & Roll Hall of Fame, Nelson has left his mark with hits such as "Blue Eyes Crying in the Rain," "Always on My Mind," and, of course, "On the Road Again."

Nelson was born in April 1933 in Central Texas and was surrounded by music from a young age. He sang in church, wrote his first song at seven and played in local bands before he was ten. Raised by his grandparents, he helped support the family by performing in honky-tonks and even promoted shows and booked acts around his hometown.

After arriving in Nashville in 1960 he landed a publishing and record deal within two years. He penned hits for artists including Patsy Cline ("Crazy") and Billy Walker ("Funny How Time Slips Away") while beginning to climb the charts himself. Although he had modest chart success in the 1960s, his style and phrasing didn't quite fit the Nashville mold. On Christmas Eve in 1969 his Nashville home burned down. He managed to save his guitar, Trigger, but took the fire as a sign to return to Texas. The next decade would redefine his career.

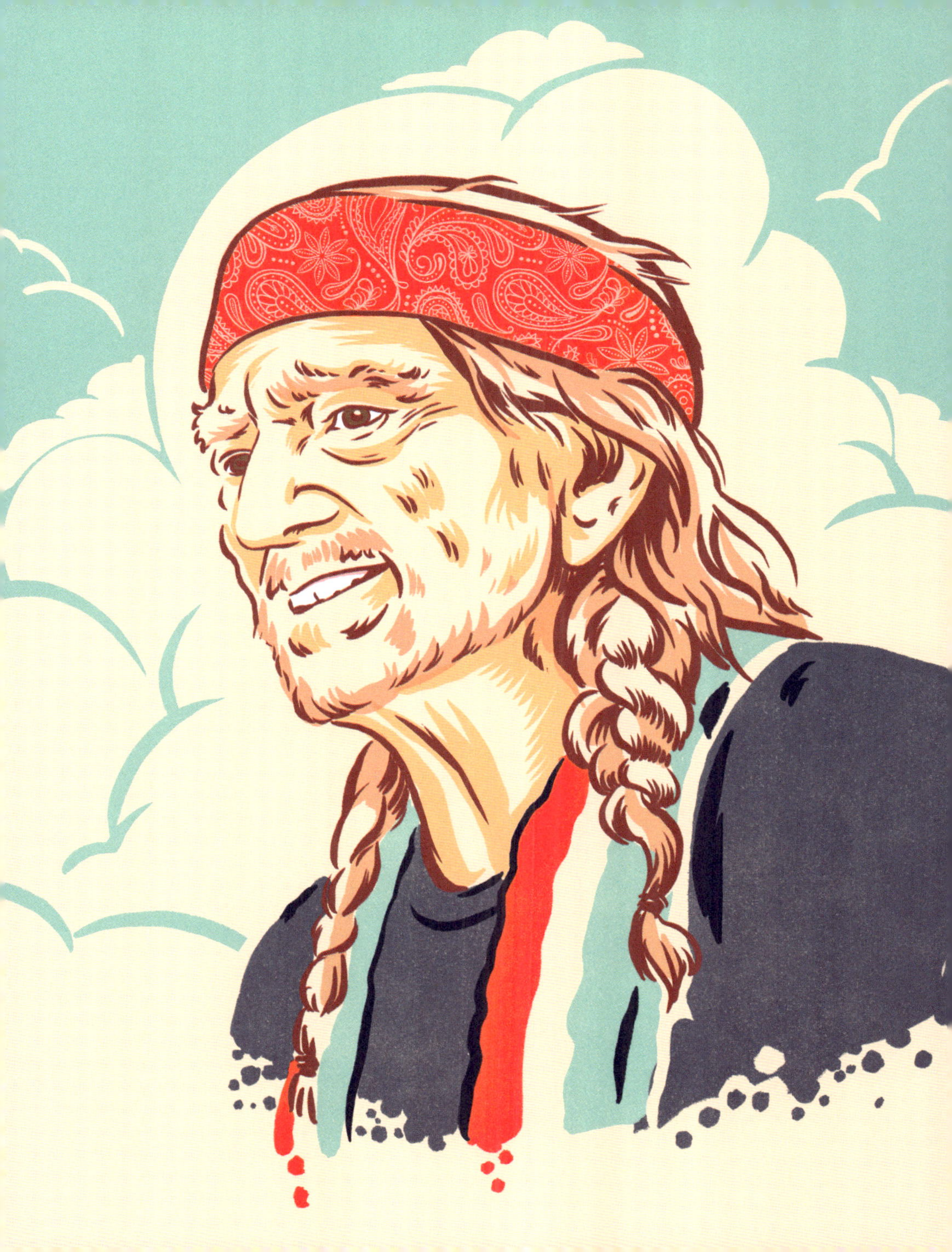

In the early 1970s, Nelson and Waylon Jennings became the faces of country music's outlaw movement, making music on their own terms with full creative control. Nelson's 1975 album, *Red Headed Stranger*, recorded in Texas, would prove to be the turning point in his career. He also transformed his look, growing out his hair and beard, and by the late 1970s, Nelson had become a true powerhouse artist.

While Nelson is celebrated for his contribution to country music, his legacy extends much further. In 1978, he surprised fans with *Stardust*, an album of classic pop songs, and soon ventured into film. His annual Fourth of July Picnic, launched in 1973, has hosted thousands of fans over the years, becoming a Woodstock-like event for country and Americana fans alike. He is also a co-founder of Farm Aid with Neil Young and John Mellencamp, a concert series started in 1985 to support farming families. And at the time of writing, Nelson remains one of the oldest active recording and touring musicians of all time.

NINETIES COUNTRY

Garth Brooks. Shania Twain. Alan Jackson. Faith Hill. George Strait. Brooks & Dunn. These are just a few of the country music icons who rose to fame during what is widely considered to be the best decade in country music history: the 1990s. As someone whose earliest musical memory is hearing Trisha Yearwood's "She's In Love With The Boy" on FM radio, I can attest that the 1990s was country music's golden era.

The cowboy hats were tall, the jeans were tight, fierce women ruled the airwaves, and the music had a perfect blend of traditional and modern sounds. Country music reached a new level of popularity in this decade, climbing so high that the 1994 Super Bowl halftime show featured the first-ever full country music lineup with Clint Black, Tanya Tucker, Travis Tritt, Wynonna Judd, and The Judds all taking the stage.

Garth Brooks was the poster child for nineties country, rising to the top with mega hits like "Ain't Goin' Down ('Til the Sun Comes Up)," and "Friends In Low Places," but it wasn't just Brooks who shaped this period of music. Songs like Alan Jackson's "Chattahoochie," George Strait's "Check Yes or No," Brooks & Dunn's "Boot Scootin' Boogie," and Billy Ray Cyrus's "Achy Breaky Heart" took the country craze to new heights.

Powerhouse females also took charge and even crossed genres, bringing country to the masses. Twain became a global sensation, and Hill reigned as the queen of pop-country with "This Kiss" and "Breathe." Martina McBride tackled the taboo subject of domestic abuse with "Independence Day," and Deana Carter delivered a major dose of nostalgia with "Strawberry Wine." Heartthrobs like Tim McGraw and Kenny Chesney began to find success, laying the groundwork for wildly successful careers that continue to this day.

The latter half of the decade introduced fans to The Chicks, who burst onto the scene with stunning harmonies and tunes that blended country, pop, and bluegrass, creating a sound all their own. Nineties country has seen a resurgence in recent years as country music fans find themselves craving the nostalgia and traditional sounds that are sometimes absent from modern country music. This is the decade that continues to have influence, with artists like Jon Pardi, Carly Pearce, Zach Top, Jake Worthington, and others paying homage to the beloved era through their latest releases.

N

"The cowboy hats were tall, the jeans were tight, and fierce women ruled the airwaves."

SEE ALSO:

BROOKS & DUNN
BROOKS, GARTH
CHESNEY, KENNY
HILL, FAITH
JACKSON, ALAN
MCGRAW, TIM
THE CHICKS
TWAIN, SHANIA

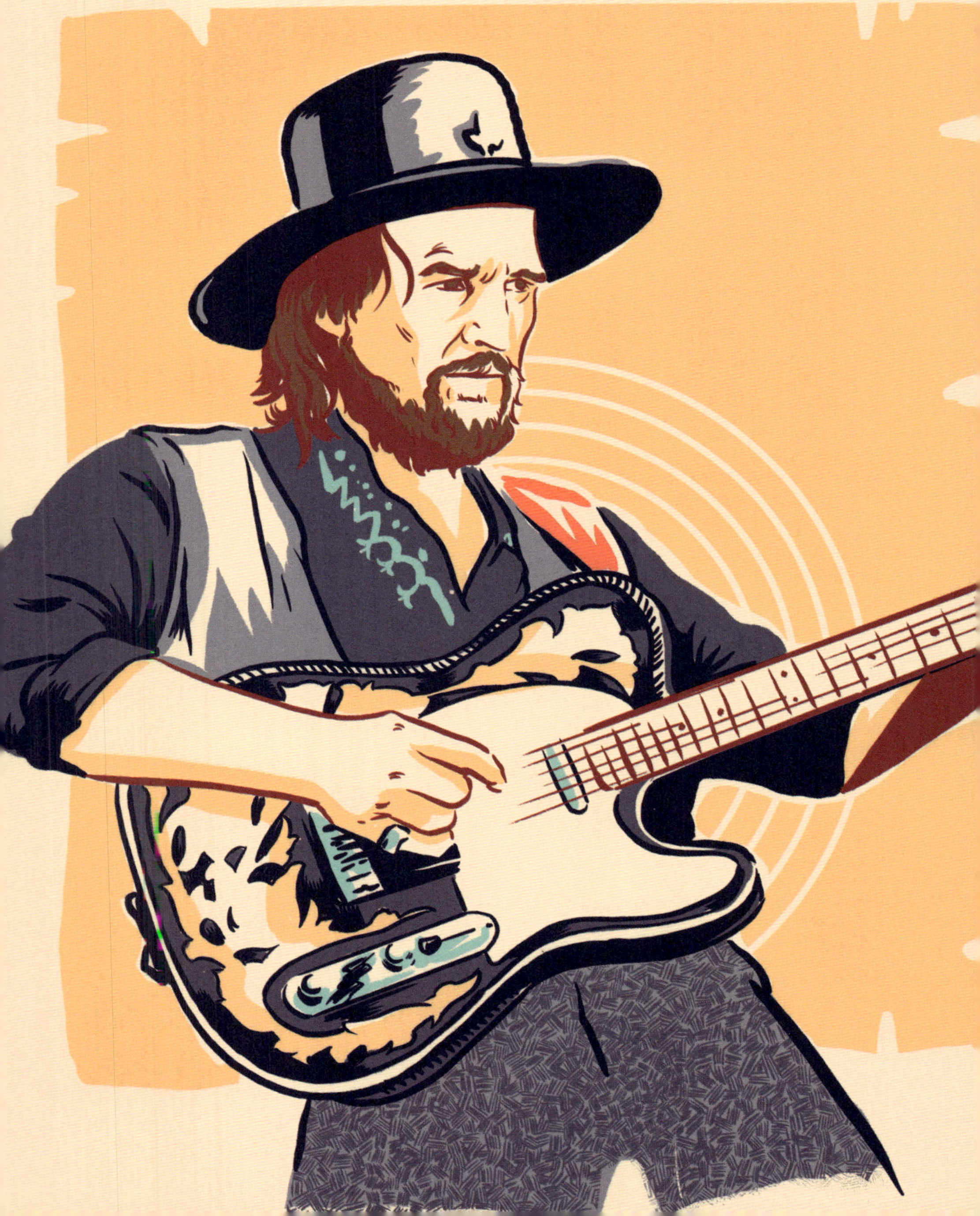

OUTLAW COUNTRY

O

Singer-songwriter Bobby Bare kick-started what would become country music's outlaw movement when he self-produced his 1973 album, *Ride Me Down Easy*. At a time when the polished, pop-leaning Nashville Sound dominated and producers and label executives controlled every detail, from the music to the artists' looks, Bare's move opened the door for musicians to take creative control of their work.

This shift in control also gave artists the freedom to record in the studios of their choosing, drawing many to Austin, Texas, where they faced fewer rules and fewer executives watching over their every move. Their image began to change too, trading clean-cut styles for long hair, beards, and a rougher, more rebellious look. They worked hard and partied even harder.

With Bare leading the charge, Waylon Jennings co-produced his *Honky Tonk Heroes* album that same year. In 1974, Jennings and Willie Nelson teamed up to self-produce *This Time*. Jennings later joked that he had "beat the system" when he renegotiated his record deal, securing the freedom to make music his way on his own terms. In 1975, Jennings released the self-penned and co-produced "Are You Sure Hank Done It This Way," tipping his hat to the great Hank Williams and detailing his frustrations with the Nashville machine. The song became an anthem for the outlaw era.

The pinnacle of the movement came in 1976 with the release of *Wanted! The Outlaws*, a compilation album featuring Jennings, Nelson, Jennings' wife Jessi Colter, and Tompall Glaser. It was a massive success and the first country album in history to be certified platinum, selling over one million copies. Jennings, Nelson, and Johnny Cash would go on to form supergroup The Highwaymen with Kris Kristofferson.

The outlaw movement began to die down by the end of the decade, but it left a lasting mark on the genre, emphasizing the importance of authenticity in country music.

"The outlaw movement opened the door for musicians to take creative control of their work."

SEE ALSO:

HAIR

NELSON, WILLIE

PAISLEY, BRAD

"Brad Paisley is one of country music's most recognizable artists and gifted storytellers."

SEE ALSO:

BELMONT UNIVERSITY

GRAND OLE OPRY

GUITAR

UNDERWOOD, CARRIE

Known for his heartfelt ballads, cheeky sense of humor, and unparalleled guitar skills, Brad Paisley is one of country music's most recognizable artists and gifted storytellers. His musical journey began while growing up in West Virginia, where he inherited his love for country music and the guitar from his Pawpaw, who gave him a guitar for Christmas when he was eight. At the age of 12, he made his live radio performance debut on WWVA's *Jamboree USA*, and by the time he was in high school, Paisley was already opening shows for artists like Charley Pride and George Jones.

In his junior year of college, he moved to Nashville to attend Belmont University, where he often skipped class and logged many late nights in the studio. He graduated in 1995 and his career quickly took off after landing a publishing deal. Three years later he signed a record deal with Arista and Paisley's debut album, *Who Needs Pictures*, arrived in 1999. He earned his first number one single with the heartfelt "He Didn't Have to Be" later that year.

George Jones wrote a letter to welcome Paisley to the Grand Ole Opry family, which was read aloud during his induction on February 17, 2001. In part, the letter read, "I am counting on you to carry on the tradition." Paisley took those words to heart and has continued to embody country music's traditional sounds while pushing the envelope in a lane that's all his own.

Paisley is well known for his versatility. He can deliver humorous tracks like "I'm Gonna Miss Her (The Fishin' Song)" and "Me Neither," while also tapping into more emotional lyrics with "Letter to Me" and "She's Everything." Additionally, "Whiskey Lullaby" with Alison Krauss is regarded as one of the greatest country songs of all time, and "Mud on the Tires" set the bar high for every truck song that followed.

When it comes to the guitar, Paisley is among the best of the best. His skills are on full display on his 2008 release

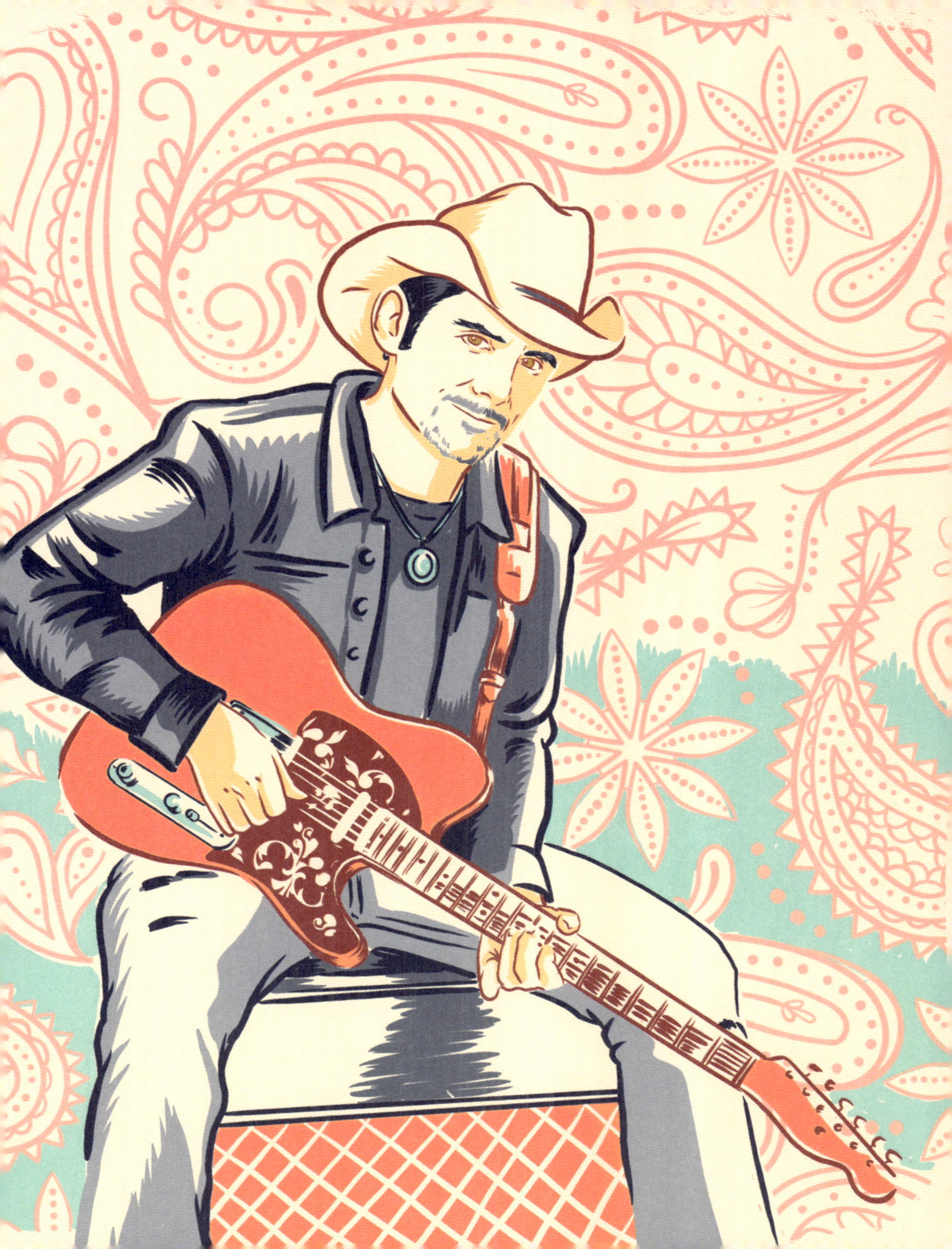

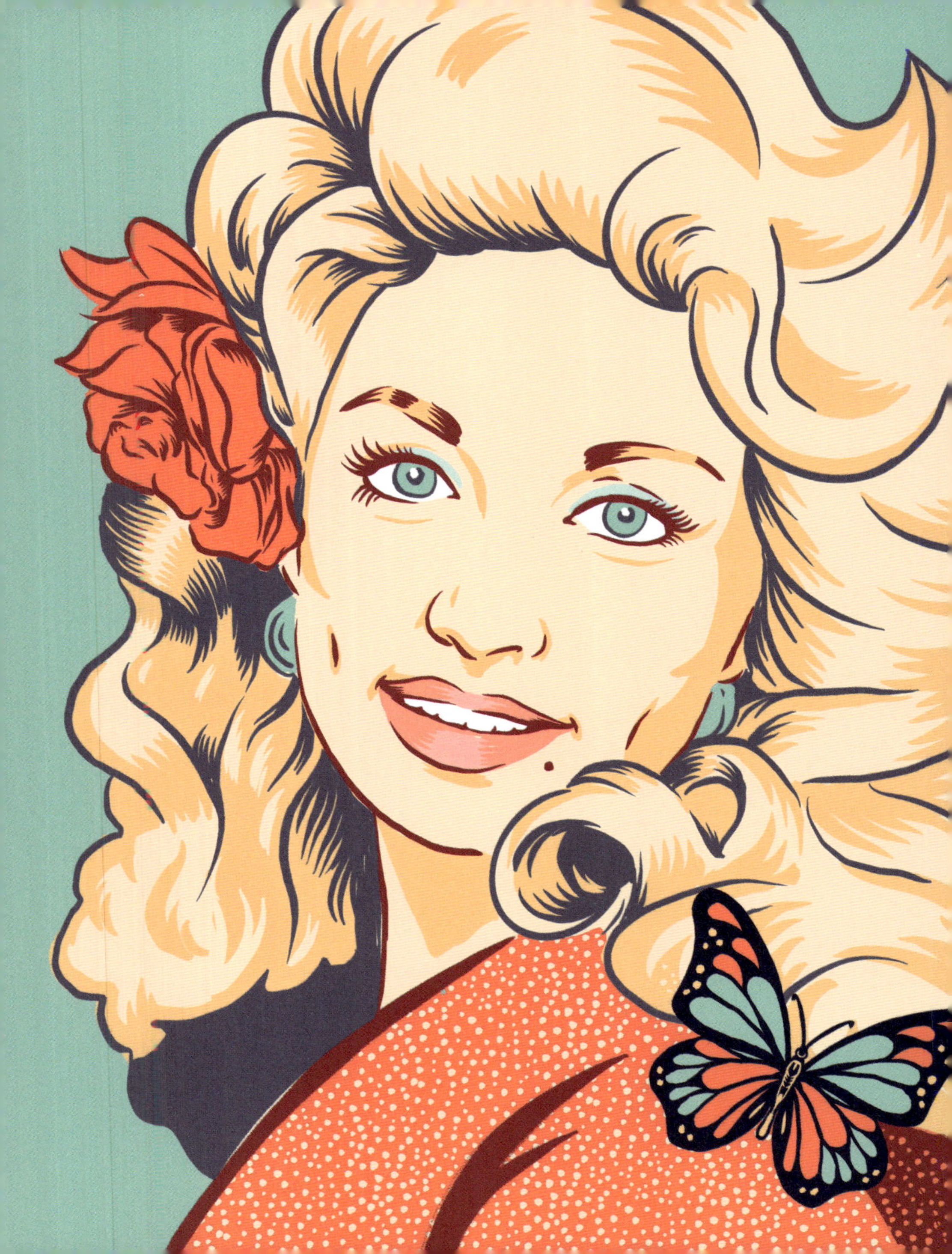

Play: The Guitar Album and during his live shows. He's won countless awards, including the coveted title of CMA Entertainer of the Year, written 21 of his 25 number one hits, and gone down in history for his 11-year run as a CMA Awards co-host with Carrie Underwood.

Something I'll always remember about Brad Paisley is that after I first had the chance to spend a few minutes with him, he took the time to go on Twitter (now X) and encourage his followers to check out my then-independent country music website. It was a small gesture but one I'll never forget, and it really shows the kind of person he is, willing to go out of his way to do something kind for someone else.

PARTON, DOLLY

Dolly Parton is nothing short of an entertainment icon. Her skills—as a singer, songwriter, entrepreneur, actress, author, philanthropist, and so much more—know no bounds, and she has touched fans around the world with her songs, humor, genuine spirit, and kindness.

A Tennessee native, Dolly was born the fourth of 12 children in Locust Ridge on January 19, 1946. Her family lived in a small, two-room cabin with no electricity or running water—she didn't grow up with much, except a dream to be a singer and songwriter. Dolly credits her uncle, Bill Owens, for the launch of her career. He encouraged her to write songs, play guitar, and sing, and eventually drove her back and forth to Nashville to make connections. She wrote "Puppy Love" with Owens, releasing it via Goldband Records in 1959 and marking the beginning of a legendary career.

In 1964, the day after graduating from high school, Dolly moved to Nashville to chase her dreams. That same day, she met her future husband, Carl Dean, outside a laundromat. Her big break came when Porter Wagoner invited her to join his syndicated television show; she

"She is a once-in-a-lifetime artist and human being, and we are truly lucky to live in a world where she exists."

SEE ALSO:

DOLLYWOOD

GRAND OLE OPRY

HAIR

PHILANTHROPY

ROGERS, KENNY

WAGONER, PORTER

P

agreed to stay for five years, then stayed for seven. In 1974, she ended the partnership and famously wrote "I Will Always Love You" as a goodbye. She later formed a musical partnership with Kenny Rogers and they recorded several duets together, among them "Islands in the Stream" and "Real Love."

While she's known for hits like "9 to 5," "Jolene," and "Coat of Many Colors," Dolly's timeless influence goes far beyond her music. She's starred in several movies—*9 to 5* and *Steel Magnolias*, to name just two—and she's bringing her songs and stories to Broadway with *Dolly: An Original Musical*.

Her giving spirit shines through Dolly Parton's Imagination Library, which has given over 300 million free books to children around the world. She's stepped up in times of natural disaster, offered aid to her community, and awarded scholarships to students from her hometown. She's also a fashion icon, known for her big hair, elaborate outfits, and high heels, and she holds the role of "Dreamer-in-Chief" at her beloved theme park, Dollywood.

An international treasure, Parton is one of the most honored entertainers of all time. She is a member of the Grand Ole Opry, the Country Music Hall of Fame, and the Rock & Roll Hall of Fame. When it comes to Dolly Parton, the sky's the limit. There's seemingly nothing she can't do. She is a once-in-a-lifetime artist and human being, and we are truly lucky to live in a world where she exists.

PHILANTHROPY

One of the things that makes me proud to be a country music fan is the genre's tradition of giving back. Honestly, there could be an entire book written on country music's giving heart because there are countless instances of artists stepping up in times of need, donating their time, money, and talent to help their neighbors.

No effort better represents country music's giving spirit than Alabama's Randy Owen stepping up in 1989 to help launch Country Cares for St. Jude Kids. What began as his idea quickly grew into one of the genre's longest-running charitable traditions, uniting artists across country music to encourage donations from fans and working with country radio partners to host fundraisers all so that families never receive a bill for their child's treatment at St. Jude Children's Research Hospital in Memphis, Tennessee. To date, the program has raised over $1 billion.

Dolly Parton is the queen of giving back. When her hometown faced devastating wildfires and floods, she donated millions to help rebuild. Since 1995, her Imagination Library has sent free books to children across the globe, instilling a love of reading in children everywhere.

Many artists have also launched their own foundations to support causes close to their hearts. The Morgan Wallen Foundation supports youth sports and music, the Toby Keith Foundation provides support for children with cancer, and Miranda Lambert channels her love for animals into MuttNation, which supports shelter pets nationwide. Chris Stapleton and his wife, Morgane, support various causes through their charitable fund, Outlaw State of Kind.

Others give back through music itself. When hurricanes devastated parts of North Carolina in 2024, Luke Combs and Eric Church rallied their friends for a massive benefit concert, raising nearly $25 million for affected communities. Meanwhile, Luke Bryan supports farming families through his annual Farm Tour, which funds scholarships for children of farmers. Giving back isn't just something country music stars do; it's truly part of who they are.

P

"Giving back isn't just something country music stars do; it's truly part of who they are."

SEE ALSO:

ALABAMA

BRYAN, LUKE

CHURCH, ERIC

COMBS, LUKE

KEITH, TOBY

LAMBERT, MIRANDA

PARTON, DOLLY

STAPLETON, CHRIS

WALLEN, MORGAN

P

PRIDE, CHARLEY

"Pride left a lasting mark on country music and paved the way for other Black artists."

SEE ALSO:

BARITONE

COUNTRY MUSIC HALL OF FAME AND MUSEUM

GRAND OLE OPRY

The late Charley Pride was a beloved artist and trailblazer who became country music's first Black superstar. Born in 1934, Pride grew up working on his family's 40-acre (16-hectare) farm in Sledge, Mississippi, playing baseball in his spare time. His love for country music was thanks to his father, who would often listen to the *Grand Ole Opry* on the radio. As a teenager, Pride began to sing and play guitar.

He began pitching for the Negro American League in 1953, moving between several teams until 1956, when he was drafted into the Army. When he was discharged after two years, Pride continued to chase his dreams of playing Major League Baseball while exploring a career in country music. In 1963, after letting go of his MLB dreams, Pride stopped in Nashville on his way home to Montana. During this visit, he met Jack Johnson, who became his manager. Johnson eventually introduced Pride to producer "Cowboy" Jack Clement, who recorded several demos for the soon-to-be-star.

Initially, they were met with some resistance when seeking out a record label. This was during the height of the Civil Rights Movement when opportunities for Black artists were still very limited. In 1965, those demos landed in the hands of RCA Records' Chet Atkins, who agreed to sign Pride to the label.

By the time he released his third single, "Just Between You and Me," in late 1966, it was clear that Pride was on a fast track to success. For the next two decades, he amassed 52 top ten hits and became RCA's top-selling country artist, with tens of millions of albums sold worldwide. He earned three Grammys and several CMA Awards, including the top honor of CMA Entertainer of the Year.

His love for the Grand Ole Opry came full circle when he became the first Black solo singer to perform there, becoming an official member in 1993. He was inducted into the Country Music Hall of Fame in 2000 and honored with the Willie Nelson Lifetime Achievement Award during

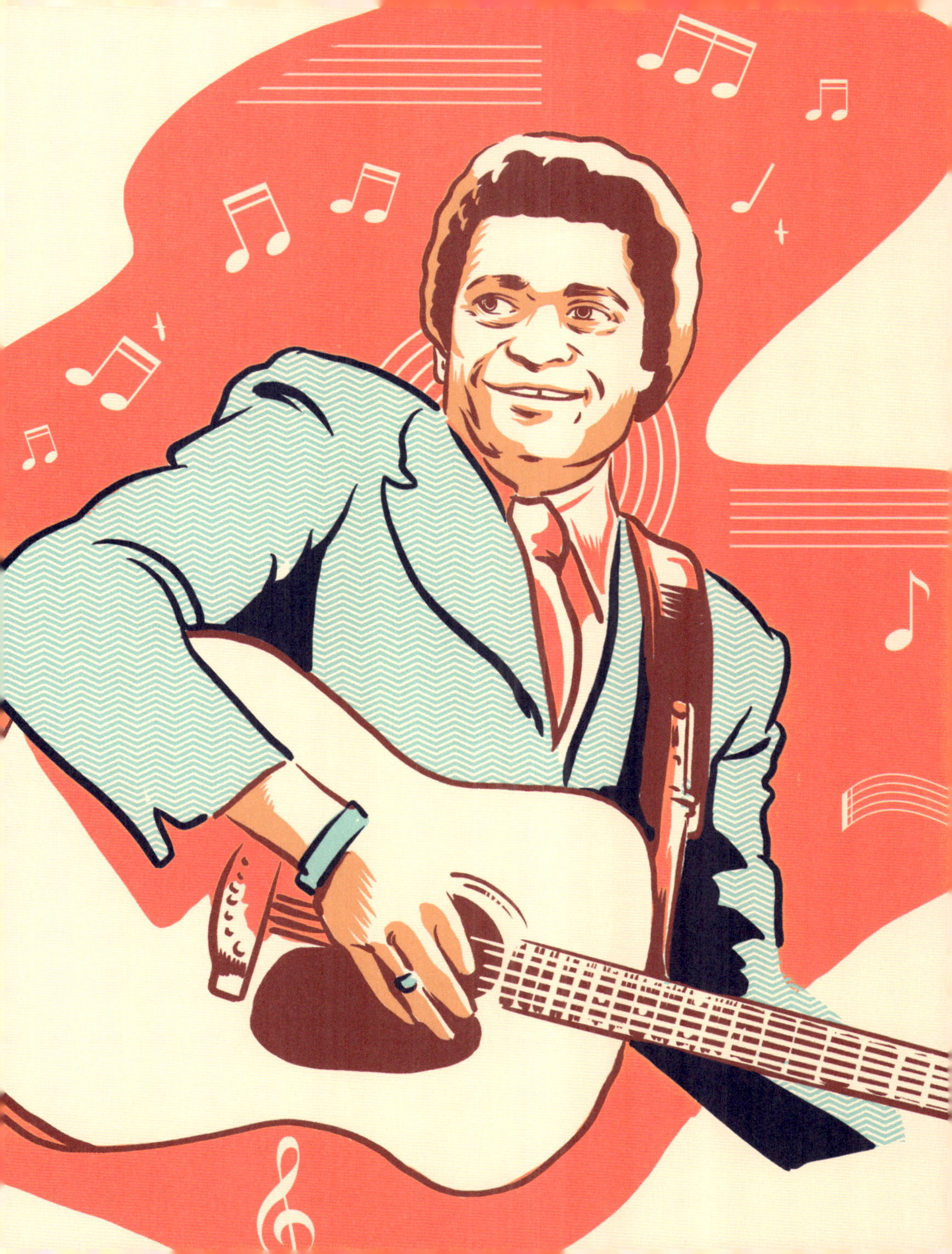

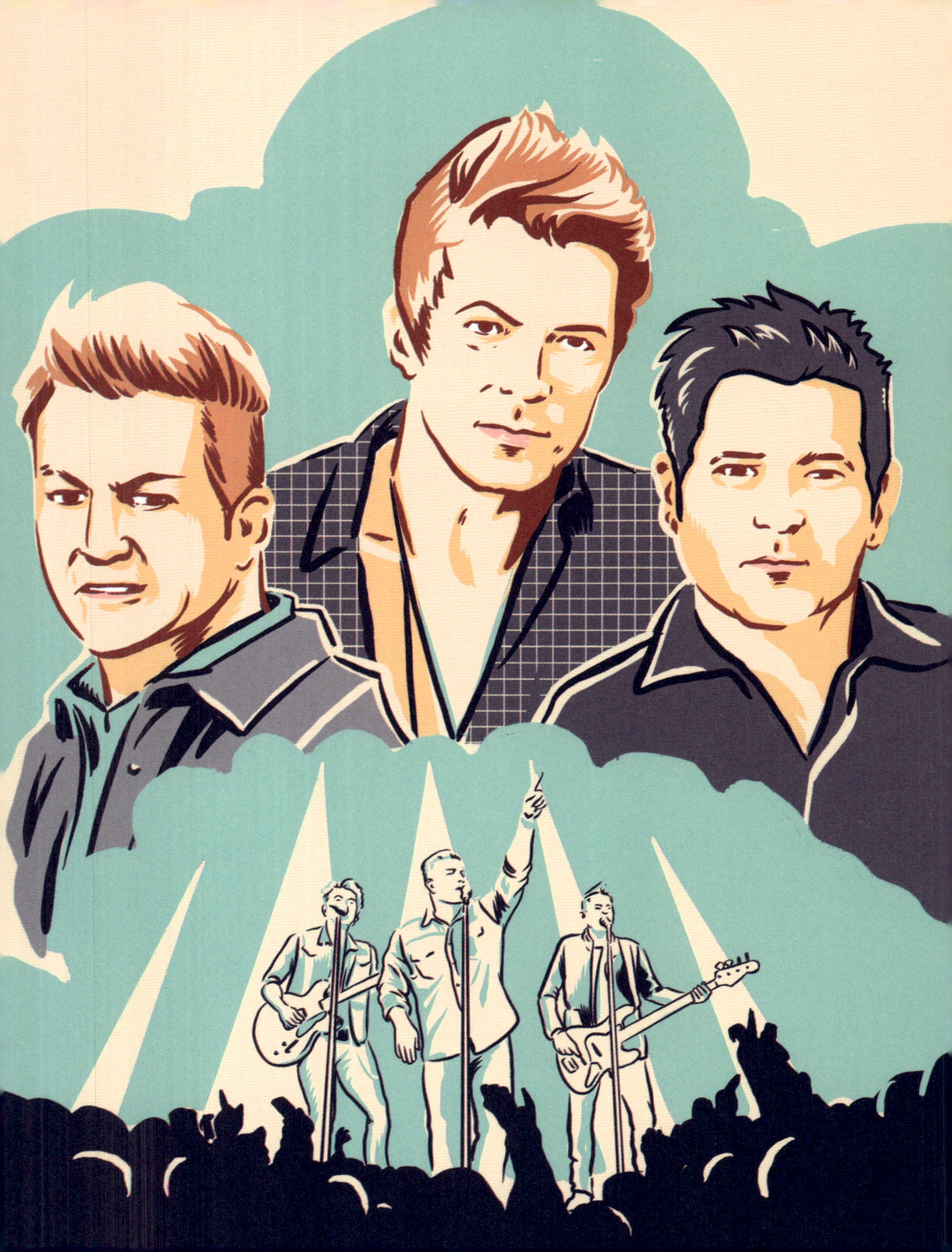

the 54th Annual CMA Awards in 2020. He passed away just a month later, at the age of 86. With songs like "Kiss an Angel Good Mornin'," "Is Anybody Goin' to San Antone," and "All I Have to Offer You (Is Me)," Pride left a lasting mark on country music and paved the way for other Black artists.

I never had the opportunity to meet Charley Pride or see him perform, but when he was posthumously honored with the RIAA (Recording Industry Association of America) Lifetime Achievement Award in 2021, his son Dion accepted the honor on his behalf. I was inspired by the way Dion spoke about his dad and struck by how much they resembled each other. We truly lost a legend when we said goodbye to Charley Pride.

RASCAL FLATTS

If you turned on country radio in the early 2000s, it was almost guaranteed you'd hear a Rascal Flatts song. Composed of Gary LeVox, Jay DeMarcus, and Joe Don Rooney, the group dominated the airwaves, ultimately pushing the boundaries of the genre with their distinct harmonies and pop-country hits.

The trio made their country radio debut with "Prayin' for Daylight" in 2000. While their self-titled debut album saw early success, it was their second record, *Melt*, that proved their staying power. The album included their first number one single, "These Days," as well as the beloved "I Melt" and "Mayberry," marking a true turning point for the band.

Their crossover triumph began with "Bless the Broken Road" in 2004, continued with "What Hurts the Most," and peaked with the massive success of their cover of the Tom Cochrane hit "Life Is a Highway," featured on the *Cars* movie soundtrack. While carefree anthems like "Summer Nights" and "Me and My Gang" became staples in their

"As true masters of the pop-country sound, their songs became the soundtrack to so many moments in fans' lives."

SEE ALSO:

GRAND OLE OPRY

high-energy live shows, Rascal Flatts' bread and butter has always been emotional power-ballads that tug at the heartstrings.

As their popularity soared, the trio was met with criticism for their pop-leaning sound and often drew comparisons to boy bands. But the band never let the critics get to them and always remained true to who they were. After a successful 20-year run, Rascal Flatts announced plans to embark on a farewell tour, but this was canceled due to the Covid-19 pandemic, and the group officially disbanded in 2021. Following the multi-year hiatus, they reunited for a 25th anniversary tour in 2025, allowing fans to relive their iconic catalog of hits once again. I attended the opening night of the tour, and it felt like taking a trip down memory lane, reliving the songs that have been such a huge part of my life.

With 17 number one singles and over 40 industry awards to their name, the Grand Ole Opry members remain one of the most successful groups in country music history. As true masters of the pop-country sound, their songs became the soundtrack to so many moments in fans' lives, including my own, and that's the kind of legacy that never fades.

RECORDING STUDIOS

Nashville is home to some of the most iconic recording studios in the world. What's more, some of the legendary spaces where artists like Johnny Cash, Elvis Presley, and Patsy Cline once recorded are still in operation today, continuing to shape the sound of country music.

The Quonset Hut was the first professional studio built on Music Row, opened by brothers Owen and Harold Bradley in 1954. Along with neighboring Columbia Studio A, it became the place where Loretta Lynn, Brenda Lee, George Jones, and countless others laid down vocals. Both studios were later purchased and restored by Mike

Curb of Curb Records and now serve as a classrooms and labs for students from nearby Belmont University.

RCA Studio B followed in 1957 and soon became known as the "Birthplace of the Nashville Sound." For two decades it produced hit after hit, including Charley Pride's "Kiss an Angel Good Morning" and Dolly Parton's "Jolene," along with more than 240 songs by Elvis Presley. Today, the studio is open for tours and is a classroom for students visiting the Country Music Hall of Fame and Museum.

A few blocks away, Ocean Way Nashville Recording Studios opened in 1996 inside a 100-year-old church. Known for its acoustics, it has hosted country stars such as Morgan Wallen, Jelly Roll, and HARDY, as well as icons like Lionel Richie and Bon Jovi. Belmont acquired the studio in 2001, and it now operates as both a commercial studio and a laboratory for students.

Outside of Music Row, Castle Recording Studio in Franklin operates from an extraordinary building that, true to its name, looks just like a castle. Once a Chicago mobster's hideaway and later a restaurant, it is now a state-of-the-art studio that has welcomed music greats including Chris Stapleton, Brooks & Dunn, and Miley Cyrus.

Other notable Nashville-area recording studios include Bradley's Barn, a barn-turned-studio founded by Owen Bradley where dozens of icons have recorded, and Blackbird Studio, established by Martina McBride and her husband, John, is also home to a sound and studio engineering school.

From the historic halls of RCA Studio B to the modern acoustics of Ocean Way, Nashville's recording spaces are as diverse as the artists who walk through their doors, each one a living part of country music history.

"Nashville's recording spaces are as diverse as the artists who walk through their doors."

SEE ALSO:

BELMONT UNIVERSITY

COUNTRY MUSIC HALL OF FAME AND MUSEUM

MUSIC ROW

R

RILEY GREEN'S THE GOLDEN SAW

"Named after the family's nearby sawmill, The Golden Saw welcomed local musicians for intimate Saturday night performances."

SEE ALSO:

HAGGARD, MERLE

JONES, GEORGE

Many country artists started out singing in church, but country superstar Riley Green cut his teeth in a very different place: The Golden Saw Music Hall in his hometown of Jacksonville, Alabama. As a teenager, Green watched his great grandparents' former home transform into a small live music venue. Named after the family's nearby sawmill, The Golden Saw welcomed local musicians for intimate Saturday night performances.

Operated by Riley's grandfather, Buford Green, the space was very low-key with rough-cut pine walls, a small stage, and a homemade banner that read "The Golden Saw" hanging behind it. A mismatched collection of chairs filled the room; it wasn't fancy, but it meant everything to Riley.

Surrounded by country, bluegrass, and Southern gospel, Green learned to sing and play guitar at The Golden Saw. Inspired by legends like George Jones and Merle Haggard, he soon began writing and recording his own music, releasing songs independently by 2013. He framed houses for a day job, earning $500 a week, and played shows at the weekend. Five years later, his hard work paid off when he signed a record deal with Big Machine Label Group in Nashville.

In 2019, Green honored both of his grandfathers, Buford Green and Lendon Bonds, with the heartfelt single "I Wish Grandpas Never Died." The song became a career-defining hit and is now certified three-times platinum. Riley returned to The Golden Saw in 2020 for a live acoustic performance series, sharing stripped-down sets from the place where it all began and giving fans a glimpse into his humble hometown roots.

Now, Riley Green is one of country music's biggest stars, known for his traditional country influences and for his

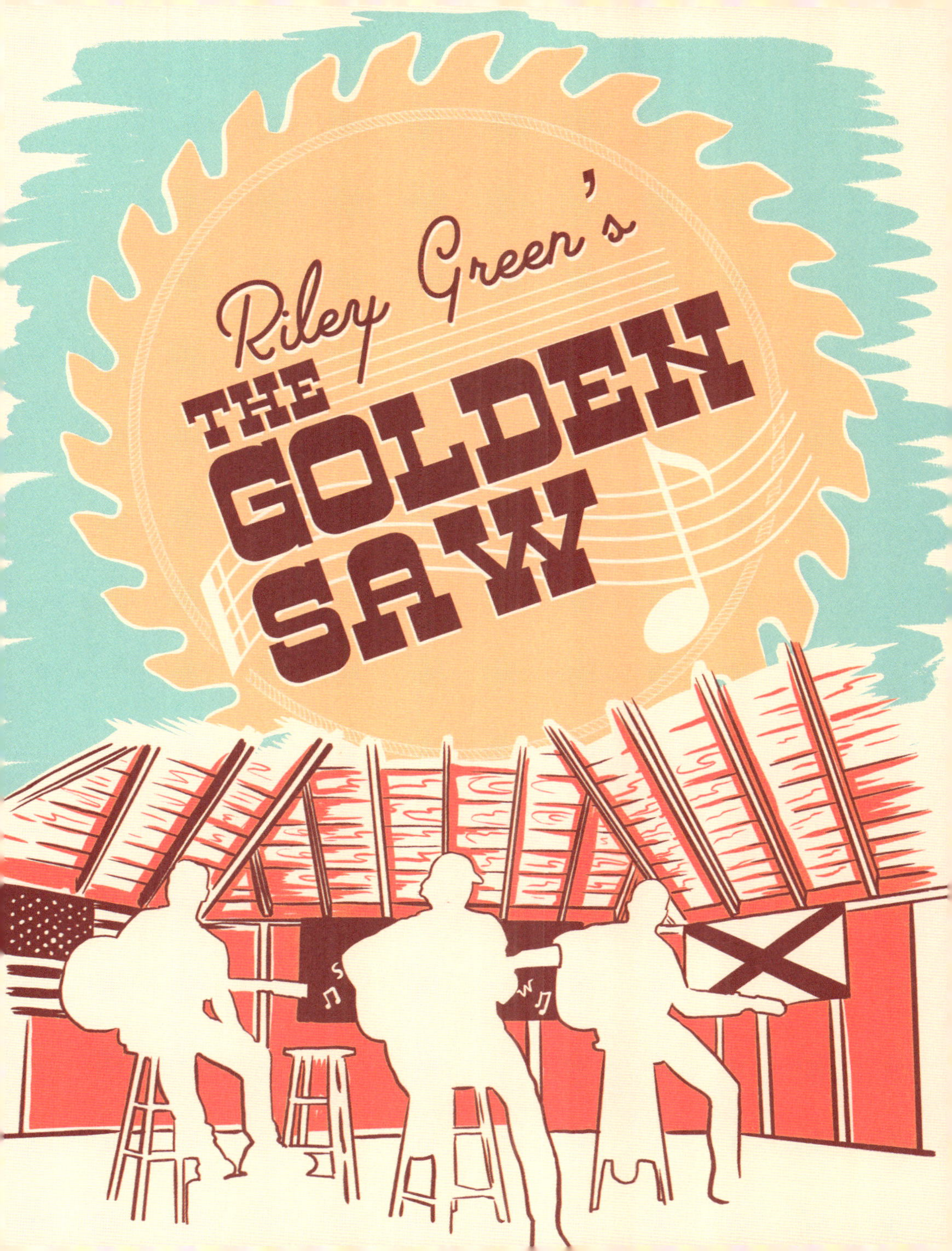
Riley Green's
THE GOLDEN SAW

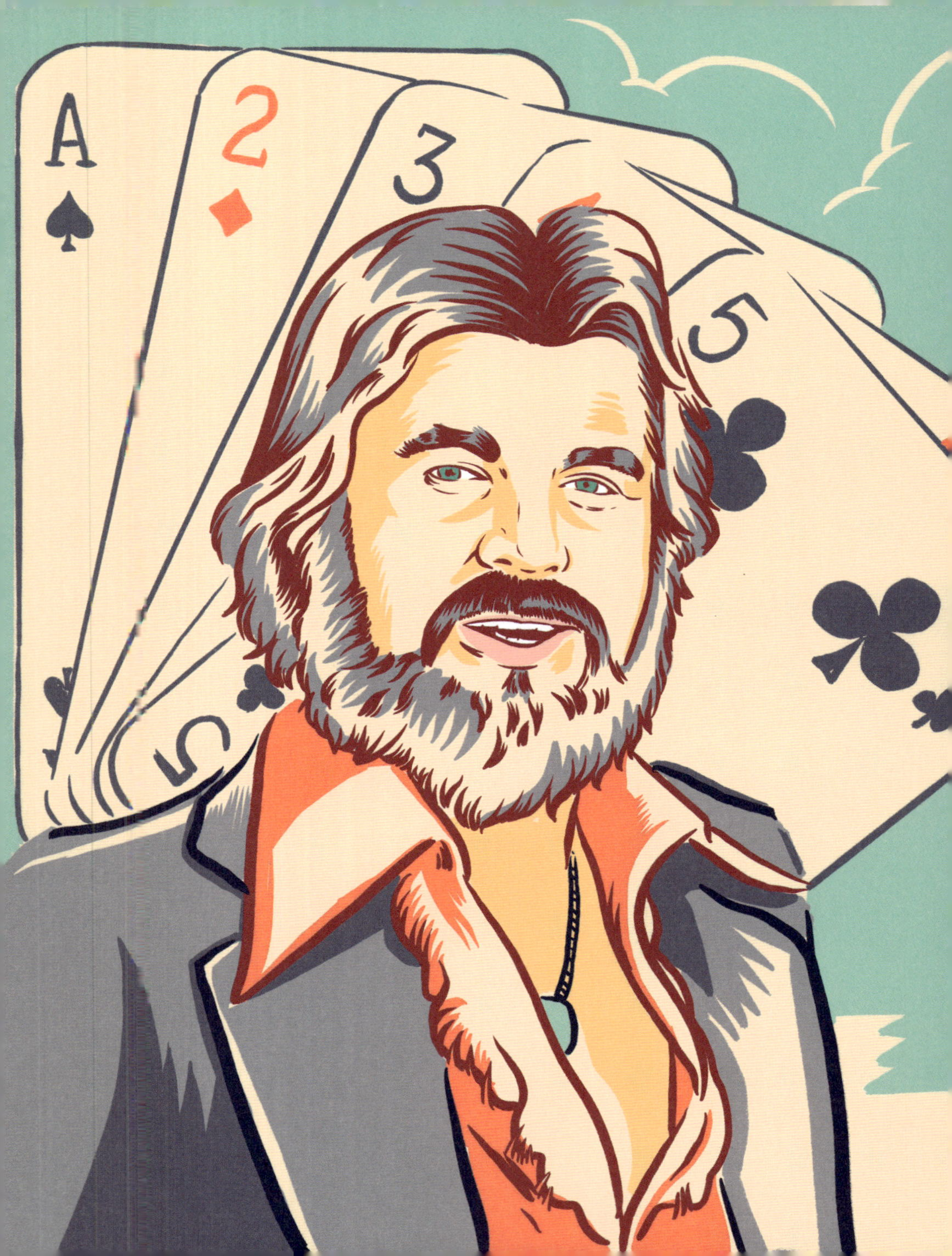

ability to tell powerful stories through his songs. And it all started at The Golden Saw. There's no doubt Grandpa Buford would be proud.

R

ROGERS, KENNY

During his extraordinary career Kenny Rogers sold over 120 million albums, notched up 24 number one hits, and won nearly every music award imaginable. A 2013 inductee into the Country Music Hall of Fame, Rogers left a lasting mark with his timeless, genre-crossing hits.

A native of Houston, Texas, where he was born in 1938, Rogers began his career playing in various bands, spanning jazz, pop, folk, rock, and country. His best-known group was First Edition who popularized songs including "Just Dropped In (To See What Condition My Condition Was In)" and hosted the syndicated TV series *Rollin'*. They disbanded in the mid-1970s, and Rogers launched his solo career soon after.

The release of "Lucille" in 1977 was a defining moment for the gravelly-voiced singer, securing his first number one on the country charts. The single was also a worldwide success, setting the stage for Rogers' international star status. The following year he released "The Gambler," the career-defining hit that charted globally and inspired a series of TV movies. It's still widely regarded as one of the best country songs of all time.

His hit-filled run continued with tracks "She Believes in Me," "Coward of the County," and the beloved "Lady." Written by Lionel Richie, "Lady" became a multi-week number one, dominating not just the country charts but also pop, adult contemporary, and R&B. Rogers remained a mainstay on the charts through the 1980s, including his unforgettable duet with Dolly Parton, "Islands in the Stream."

"'The Gambler' is widely regarded as one of the best country songs of all time."

SEE ALSO:

COUNTRY MUSIC HALL OF FAME AND MUSEUM

PARTON, DOLLY

R

As the first country star to routinely sell out arenas, Rogers toured the world and had a successful run in Branson, Missouri, at a 4,000-seat theater he co-owned. A renaissance man, Rogers was also an actor, a photographer, and a businessman who co-founded a chain of chicken restaurants dubbed Kenny Rogers Roasters.

In 2015, he announced his farewell tour, "The Gambler's Last Deal," citing declining mobility as his reason for stepping away from the road. Unfortunately, the tour was cut short due to health challenges and Rogers passed away in March 2020 at the age of 81.

With a sound that straddled country and pop, Rogers appealed to a wide audience. He rose to fame during the height of the pop-country era, when twangy country was fading and a more cosmopolitan sound was taking over. Rogers once described himself as a country singer with many other musical influences and his work truly reflected that.

RUCKER, DARIUS

"Rucker's live performances are a treat. His onstage energy is infectious."

SEE ALSO:

GRAND OLE OPRY
PHILANTHROPY

When Hootie & the Blowfish frontman Darius Rucker announced plans to make a country music album, fans weren't quite sure what to expect. Often when artists outside the field cross into country music, it's a flash in the pan; they're here one minute and gone the next. But that was not the case with Rucker. The South Carolina native was welcomed into the country music family with open arms and has since become one of the most prominent Black artists in country music history.

Born in 1966 in Charleston, Rucker became a fan of Dwight Yoakam and credits Radney Foster for changing the way he listened to music. In the late 1980s he made a promise to himself that he'd make a country album one day. That dream came true in 2008 with the release of *Learn to Live*. The success of the project was fueled by his number one debut single, "Don't Think I Don't Think About It," making

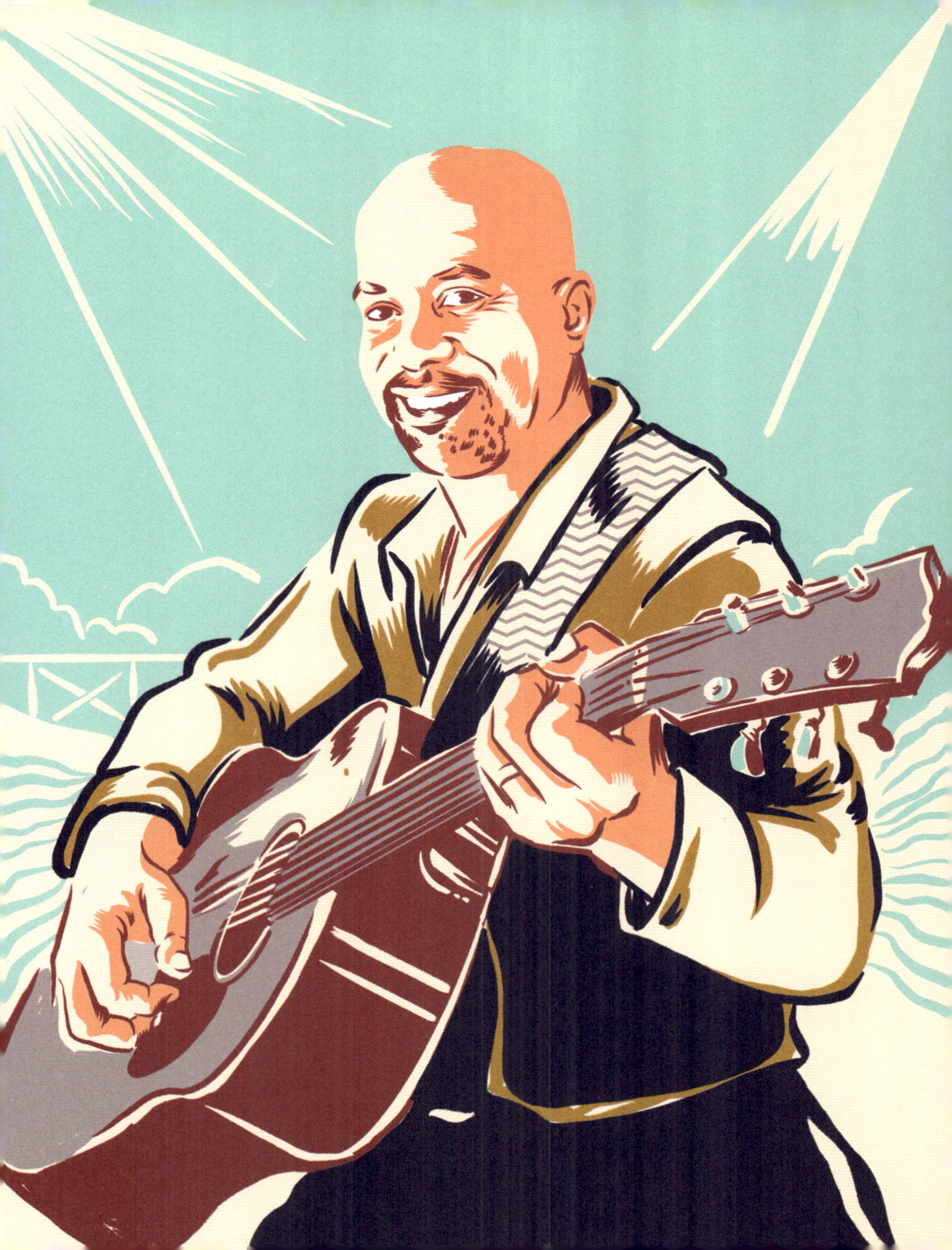

R

Rucker the first Black artist to have a chart-topping single at country radio since the great Charley Pride. Since then, Rucker has earned ten number one singles on country radio and even took home a Grammy for Best Solo Country Performance with his beloved version of "Wagon Wheel."

Rucker's live performances are a treat. His onstage energy is infectious, and you can't help but smile when he starts swaying his hips. In 2012, he received the great honor of becoming a member of the Grand Ole Opry, a moment that he says made him truly feel like he was part of the country music family.

Outside of music, Rucker has built a legacy through his philanthropic work, which began during his Hootie & the Blowfish days. Rucker has raised over $5.1 million (and counting) for St. Jude Children's Research Hospital through his annual benefit concert and golf tournament in Nashville. He may have started out as a rocker, but country music is lucky to have him, and we're certainly proud to call him one of our own.

RYMAN ALLEY

"This narrow stretch connects the iconic venue to the backdoors of several legendary honky-tonks."

SEE ALSO:

LOWER BROADWAY

RYMAN AUDITORIUM

Between Nashville's famous Ryman Auditorium, the former home of the Grand Ole Opry, and the buzzing lights of Lower Broadway sits an inconspicuous alleyway that has been traveled down by dozens of country music legends through the years.

Known as Ryman Alley, this narrow stretch connects the iconic venue to the backdoors of several legendary honky-tonks, giving performers a discreet path to slip out of the Ryman and into their favorite watering holes, most notably Tootsie's Orchid Lounge, before or after shows.

Stopping by Tootsie's became a rite of passage for singers and songwriters performing at the "Mother Church of Country Music." Patsy Cline, Johnny Cash, Little Jimmy Dickens, and Willie Nelson were said to be regulars. Nelson even joked, "It's 17 steps to Tootsie's and 34 back," a nod to the extra effort required after a night of drinks at the famous honky-tonk. Legend has it that Hank Williams, who was fired from the Opry after missing several performances, still haunts the alleyway to this day.

Even now, you never know who you might run into. Kenny Chesney and Steve Miller caused a stir when they wandered into Tootsie's for an impromptu jam session after taping a special episode of *CMT Crossroads* at the Ryman. That's Nashville for you, you never know who's going to pop up.

Today, visitors can retrace the steps of country icons in this historic passage between Fourth and Fifth Avenues in Downtown Nashville. Look down as you walk, and you'll see the footsteps of this journey immortalized on the alley's pavement.

RYMAN AUDITORIUM

In the heart of Music City lies one of the most famous venues in the world: the Ryman Auditorium. Known as the "Mother Church of Country Music," the brick building with colorful stained-glass windows has a storied history dating back to 1892.

The idea to construct the Ryman came after a riverboat captain Thomas Green Ryman attended a Nashville tent revival. Inspired by Reverend Sam Jones' sermon, Ryman vowed to use his fortune to build a place where religious gatherings could take place. The Union Gospel Tabernacle opened seven years later and became a community gathering place for worship and other events, just as Ryman had envisioned.

"Attending a concert at the Ryman is like a religious experience."

SEE ALSO:

GRAND OLE OPRY

NASHVILLE

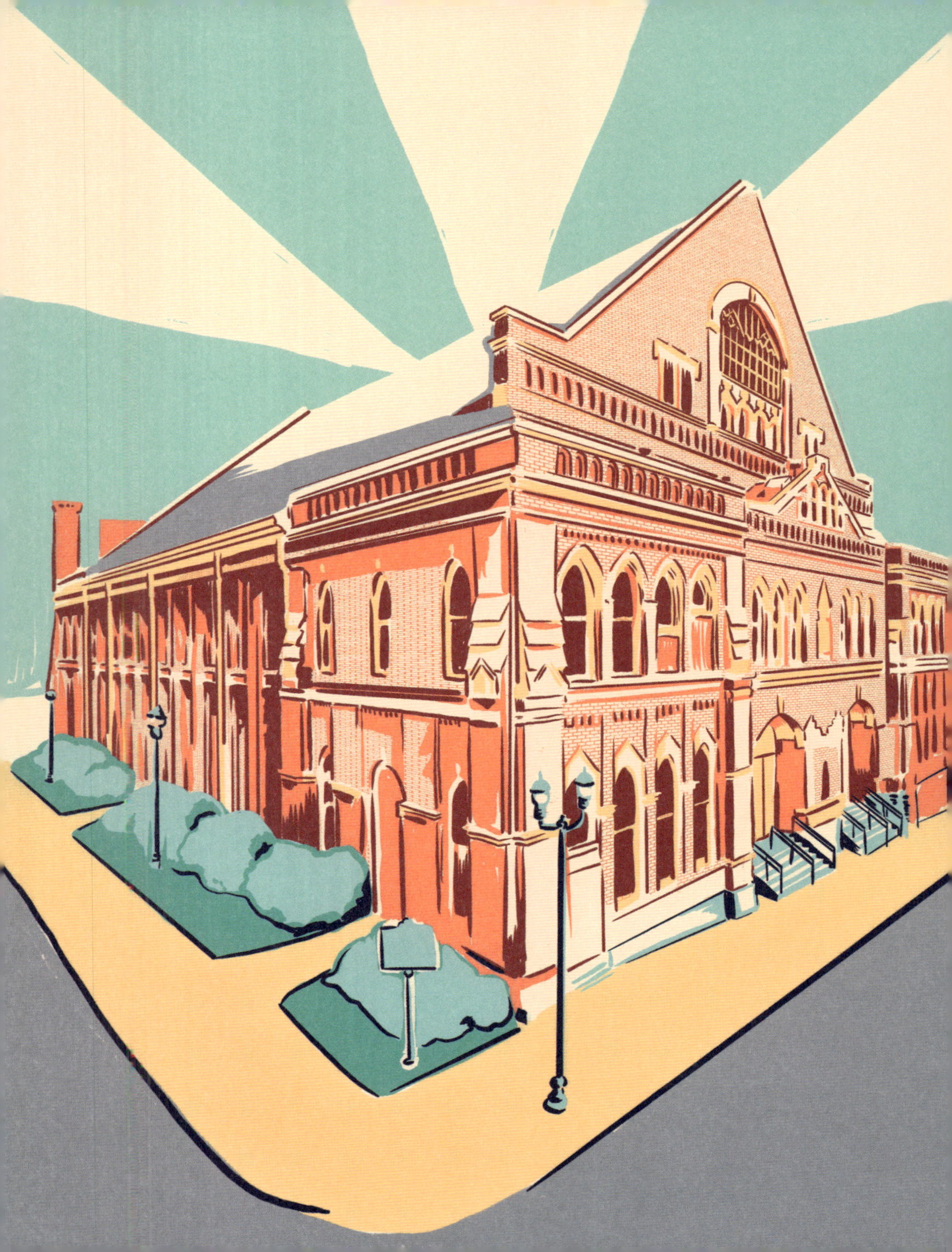

The first concert held at the venue was the May Music Festival with the Theodore Thomas Orchestra, followed by a debut from the Fisk Jubilee Singers, who have been performing at the Ryman ever since. Ryman passed away in 1904, and the building was renamed in his honor. The now-famous venue began to attract national attention under Lula Clay Naff, who took over as general manager in 1920. In 1943, Lula helped bring the Grand Ole Opry to the Ryman, where the famous show remained for close to 31 years.

Many significant moments in country music have happened at the Ryman: Johnny Cash joined the Opry and later met June Carter; Patsy Cline became an Opry member; and Elvis Presley famously made his Opry debut. After Earl Scruggs stepped onto the stage for his Opry debut in 1945 with Bill Monroe's Bluegrass Boys, the Ryman also became known as the birthplace of bluegrass music.

Following the Opry's departure, the Ryman sat empty for nearly two decades. There was a time that it was rumored to have faced demolition; however, local groups rallied to save the venue. After undergoing renovations, it reopened in 1992 and became a National Historic Landmark in 2001.

Attending a concert at the Ryman is like a religious experience. When you sit in the wooden pews and listen to the supreme acoustics, it's impossible not to think about all the legendary performers who once stood on the fabled stage. As they say, if these walls could talk...

S

SHELTON, BLAKE

"Throughout his career, Shelton has balanced boundary-pushing hits with nods to traditional country storytelling."

SEE ALSO:

FILM & TV
GRAND OLE OPRY
HAIR
TATTOOS

Blake Shelton has built his career on heartfelt ballads, light-hearted tunes, and barn burners, becoming a household name thanks to an incredible 23-season run on *The Voice*. Along the way, he's racked up ten CMA Awards, six ACM Awards, and has become a member of the Grand Ole Opry, but the road to success wasn't always easy. Early in his career, his chart performance was literally hit and miss, and at one point he thought his shot at stardom was over.

Shelton grew up in Ada, Oklahoma, where he was born in 1976. He began performing as a child and his mom entered him in pageants to give him a stage to showcase his talents, something he later joked was the "worst experience" of his life. For a while, it even made him want to quit singing. But by his early teens, he was back at it, performing at "Opry-type" shows around his hometown and realizing music was what he wanted to do forever.

After graduating high school in 1994, Shelton moved to Nashville at just 17. He spent years taking odd jobs, painting houses, moving furniture, and recording demos for $40 a song, all while chasing his dream. In 1998, he signed with Giant Records and in 2001 his debut single, "Austin," was released. Just as it hit the radio, the label folded. Thankfully, Warner Bros. stepped in, and "Austin" went on to top the charts.

The years that followed were a bit rocky as hits came and went, but Shelton eventually found his stride. By 2008, he had dropped his cowboy hat, cut his mullet, and started working with a new producer, Scott Hendricks, who proved to be instrumental in Shelton's success. The stars aligned and the chart-topping singles kept coming. Then in 2011 *The Voice* took his career to an entirely new level, introducing fans to his charming personality and unfiltered humor.

Throughout his career, Shelton has balanced boundary-pushing hits like "Boys 'Round Here" and "God's Country,"

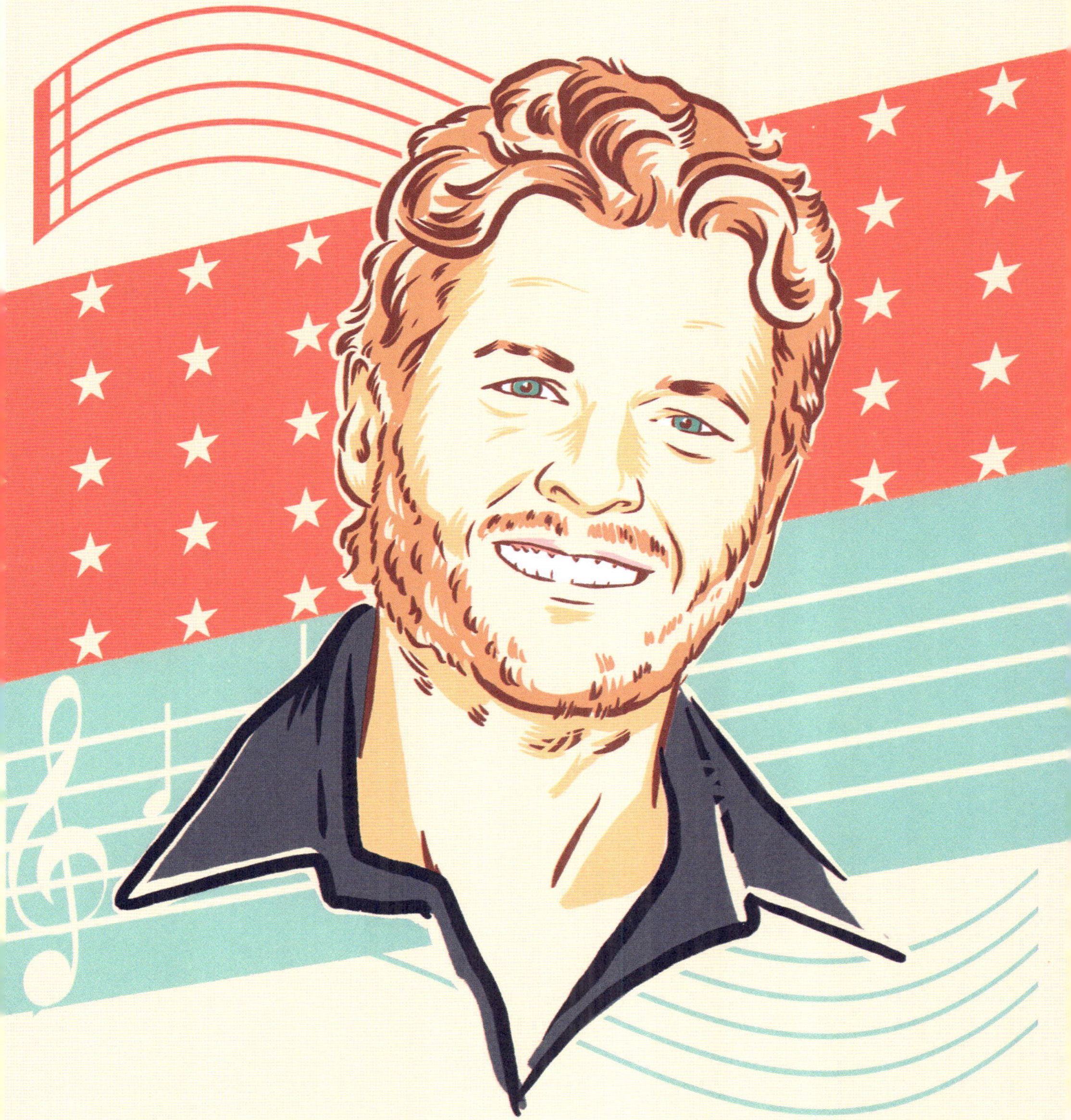

with nods to traditional country storytelling with "The Baby" and his signature "Ol' Red." To date, he's earned 30 number one singles and sold over 13 million albums.

Despite his superstar status and his marriage to pop icon Gwen Stefani, Shelton remains down to earth. He spends most of his time at his Oklahoma ranch, planting crops, tending the land, and enjoying family time with Stefani and her three sons.

SIGNATURE STYLE

"These artists have turned their style into part of their story, creating unique looks that are just as unforgettable as their songs."

SEE ALSO:

CHURCH, ERIC
CLINE, PATSY
COMBS, LUKE
STYLE
WAGONER, PORTER
WILSON, LAINEY

Many country artists have taken their style to the next level, creating a signature look that's instantly recognizable. In a genre flooded with talent, it's a smart way to stand out.

Patsy Cline adopted hers early in her career, wearing custom cowgirl dresses designed and sewn by her mother, Hilda. These intricate outfits, complete with appliqués, fringe, and sequins, left a lasting impression on fans.

Some male stars like Porter Wagoner and Little Jimmy Dickens were known for their flashy rhinestone suits, while Johnny Cash went the opposite direction. Known as "The Man in Black," he performed head-to-toe in his dark, rebellious look that set him apart from his peers.

Not all signature styles were deliberate; Eric Church's started by accident. Early in his career, stage lights dried out his contacts, so he started wearing Ray-Ban aviators. The shades stuck, and now he never performs without them. These days, he's traded aviators for Wayfarers, but the look is just as iconic. His American flag scarf also became a staple after his stylist, Katy Robbins, made it a last-minute addition to his "Springsteen" music video. Fans loved it so much that many now copy the look at his shows.

Luke Combs is rarely seen without his black Columbia PFG (Performance Fishing Gear) Bahama II shirt. In 2025, he doubled down on his love for the shirt, rocking a custom PFG suit to the 18th Annual ACM Honors. When you see that black PFG, you instantly know it's Luke Combs.

For Lainey Wilson, picking her style was completely strategic. Opting to wear wide-brimmed hats and bell bottoms was her way of setting herself apart from other female artists in the format. Her unique, throwback style became part of her brand, so much so she called her 2022 album *Bell Bottom Country* and named her Nashville bar Bell Bottoms Up.

These artists have turned their style into part of their story, creating unique looks that are just as unforgettable as their songs.

SONGWRITERS

Songwriters are the heartbeat of Nashville. Every day, countless writers head to Music Row, pouring their hearts into lyrics they hope might one day become country music's next big hit. While their names may not always be recognized by fans, their work is everywhere, shaping the sound of country music with stories of love, heartbreak, and joy.

Some artists are legendary songwriters in their own right: Hank Williams, Dolly Parton, Merle Haggard, and Alan Jackson among them. But many performers rely on or collaborate with Nashville's songwriting community, recognizing the incredible talent working tirelessly behind the scenes to get their songs heard.

Harlan Howard was one of the first true professional songwriters in Nashville, laying the foundation for today's songwriters. Over his career, he wrote more than 4,000 songs, proving that songwriting could, in fact, be a profession.

"If you ever find yourself in Nashville, stop by The Bluebird Cafe to experience a songwriter's round. There's nothing else like it."

SEE ALSO:

BLUEBIRD CAFE

MUSIC ROW

THREE CHORDS AND THE TRUTH

S

Following in his footsteps came a new generation of greats. Dean Dillon, best known for his long partnership with George Strait, has written more than 75 of Strait's hits. Ashley Gorley has become a modern powerhouse, with over 80 number one songs (and counting) recorded by artists such as Luke Bryan, Thomas Rhett, and Morgan Wallen.

Songwriting circles have also left their mark. The Peach Pickers (Dallas Davidson, Rhett Akins, and Ben Hayslip) dominated the 2000s and 2010s with a run of chart-toppers. The Love Junkies (Hillary Lindsey, Lori McKenna, and Liz Rose) have crafted memorable songs, including Little Big Town's "Girl Crush" and Carrie Underwood's "Cry Pretty."

A new wave of songwriters continues to shape country music today, with songs penned by Michael Hardy, Jessie Jo Dillon, Ernest Keith Smith, Jessi Alexander, Josh Phillips, Trannie Anderson, Jonathan Singleton, Randy Montana, and others dominating the charts.

As a song lover, I always found myself flipping through CD inserts, scanning the credits to learn who the writers were. In today's digital world, it isn't as easy, but I still make a point to look. I encourage you to do the same. And if you ever find yourself in Nashville, stop by The Bluebird Cafe to experience a songwriter's round. There's nothing else like it.

STAPLETON, CHRIS

Chris Stapleton is the male vocalist of his generation. No modern country artist can match his soulful delivery, blending influences from country and blues to soul and R&B. He's one of the most decorated artists of all time, with multiple ACM, CMA, and Grammy Awards, and is among music's most respected singers, songwriters, and entertainers.

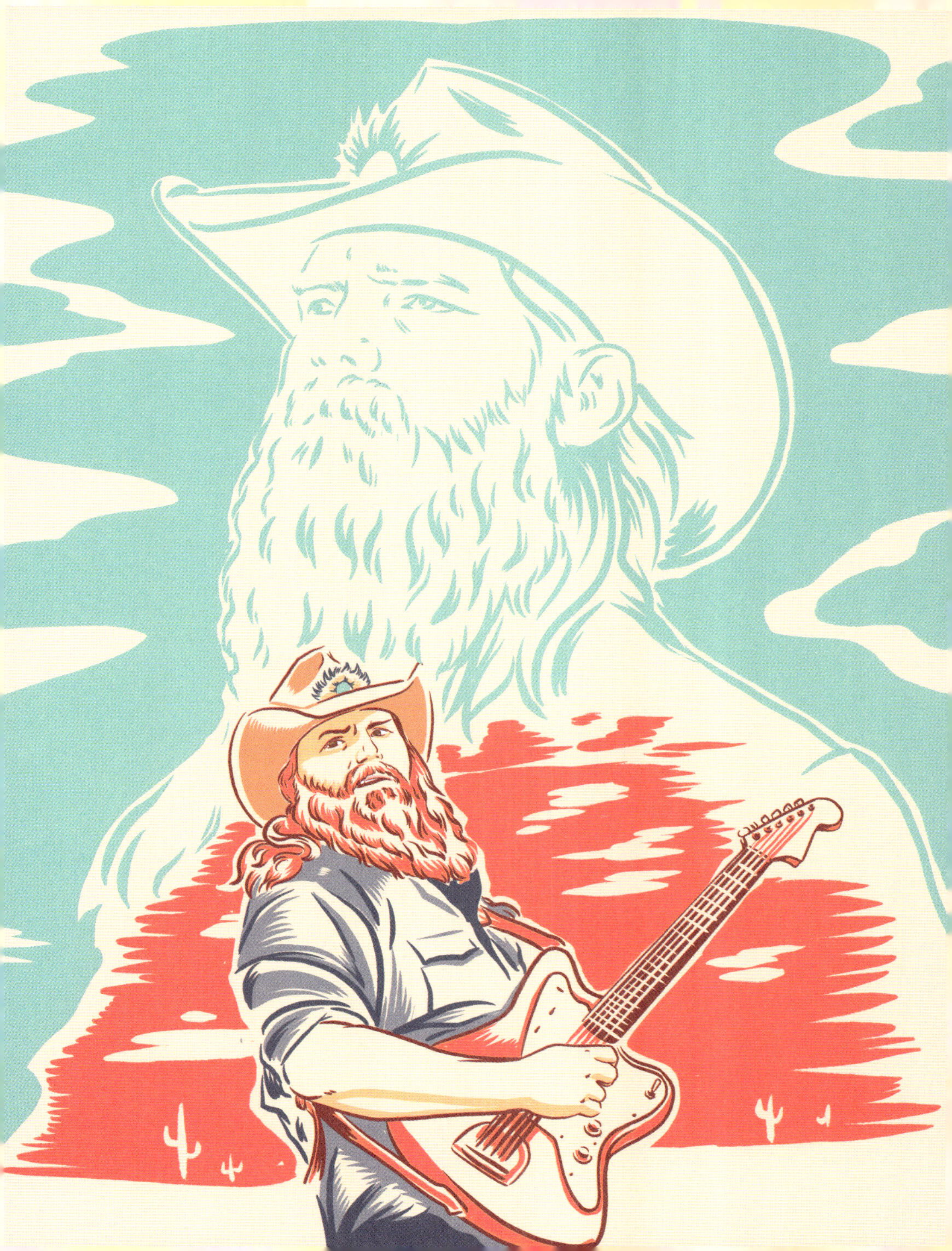

S

"No modern country artist can match his soulful delivery, blending influences from country and blues to soul and R&B."

SEE ALSO:

GILL, VINCE

PHILANTHROPY

Born in Eastern Kentucky in 1978, Stapleton grew up surrounded by all kinds of music. As a teenager, he taught himself guitar and began writing songs. After graduating high school as valedictorian, he moved to Nashville in 1996 to study engineering at Vanderbilt University. A year in, he realized it wasn't for him, returned home, and worked various jobs while pursuing music.

His second shot at Music City came in 2001 when he signed a publishing deal and began writing full-time. His early cuts include Josh Turner's "Your Man" and Kenny Chesney's "Never Wanted Nothing More." Stapleton fronted the bluegrass band The SteelDrivers and later the blues-rock group The Jompson Brothers while continuing to rack up songwriting credits.

In 2013, he made his solo debut with "What Are You Listening To?," but the single didn't make much of an impact. After losing his father, Stapleton took a cross-country road trip, reflecting on the music his dad would have wanted him to make. The song "Traveller" was born from that journey, inspiring the rest of his debut album. The project also included his now-iconic cover of George Jones's "Tennessee Whiskey," famously performed with Justin Timberlake at the 2015 CMA Awards, where Stapleton became the first artist to win Album of the Year, Male Vocalist of the Year, and New Artist of the Year in the same night. That performance turned him into an instant superstar and *Traveller* went on to become the best-selling country album of the 2010s.

Some of his best-known songs include "You Should Probably Leave," "Starting Over," "Broken Halos," and "White Horse." Known for his electrifying live shows, Stapleton plays sold-out venues across the globe. His wife, Morgane, an accomplished singer-songwriter, joins him on stage with stunning harmonies. He's collaborated with everyone from Taylor Swift and P!nk to Dua Lipa and Post Malone, and set the bar for national anthem performances with his jaw-dropping rendition at Super Bowl LVII in 2023.

When he first started singing, Stapleton tried to mimic Vince Gill. Eventually, he found his own voice, and we're lucky he did.

STATION INN

Nashville is widely known as the home of country music, but bluegrass, a subgenre of country, has a rich history in Music City, too. The "Father of Bluegrass" Bill Monroe cemented the genre's place in history with his 1945 performance at the Grand Ole Opry, then held at the Ryman Auditorium.

The Station Inn has drawn visitors from across the globe to experience the magic of bluegrass music. Its intimate, listening-room atmosphere highlights the sounds of banjo, fiddle, mandolin, guitar, dobro, and upright bass, showcasing some of the most talented musicians in the world.

The Station Inn was founded in 1974 by bluegrass musicians Bob and Ingrid Fowler, Marty and Charmaine Lanham, Jim Bornstein, and Red and Bird Lee Smith. It was created as a place where musicians could gather, play, and share their love of music. The owners often played in the house band and pop-up performances were welcome at any time. Originally located near Centennial Park, the venue moved in 1978 to its longtime home in The Gulch. Surrounded by luxury hotels, boutiques, and trendy restaurants, the 175-seat club stands out with its stone-covered exterior, neon signs, and walls lined with Hatch Show Print posters. Stepping into the Station Inn almost feels like you're stepping back in time.

The venue began regularly booking bluegrass bands and quickly earned a reputation as one of the best bluegrass stages in the world. Legends like Bobby Osborne and Jimmy Martin became regulars, often stopping by after weekend performances at the Grand Ole Opry.

A fan-favorite tradition at the Station Inn is its Sunday night bluegrass jam, where all pickers and players are invited to join. There's no cover charge as the venue wants everyone to be able to experience the fun.

Over more than 50 years, the Station Inn has welcomed countless icons including Vince Gill, Dierks Bentley, Alison

S

"The Station Inn has drawn visitors from across the globe to experience the magic of bluegrass music."

SEE ALSO:

GRAND OLE OPRY

HATCH SHOW PRINT

NASHVILLE

RYMAN AUDITORIUM

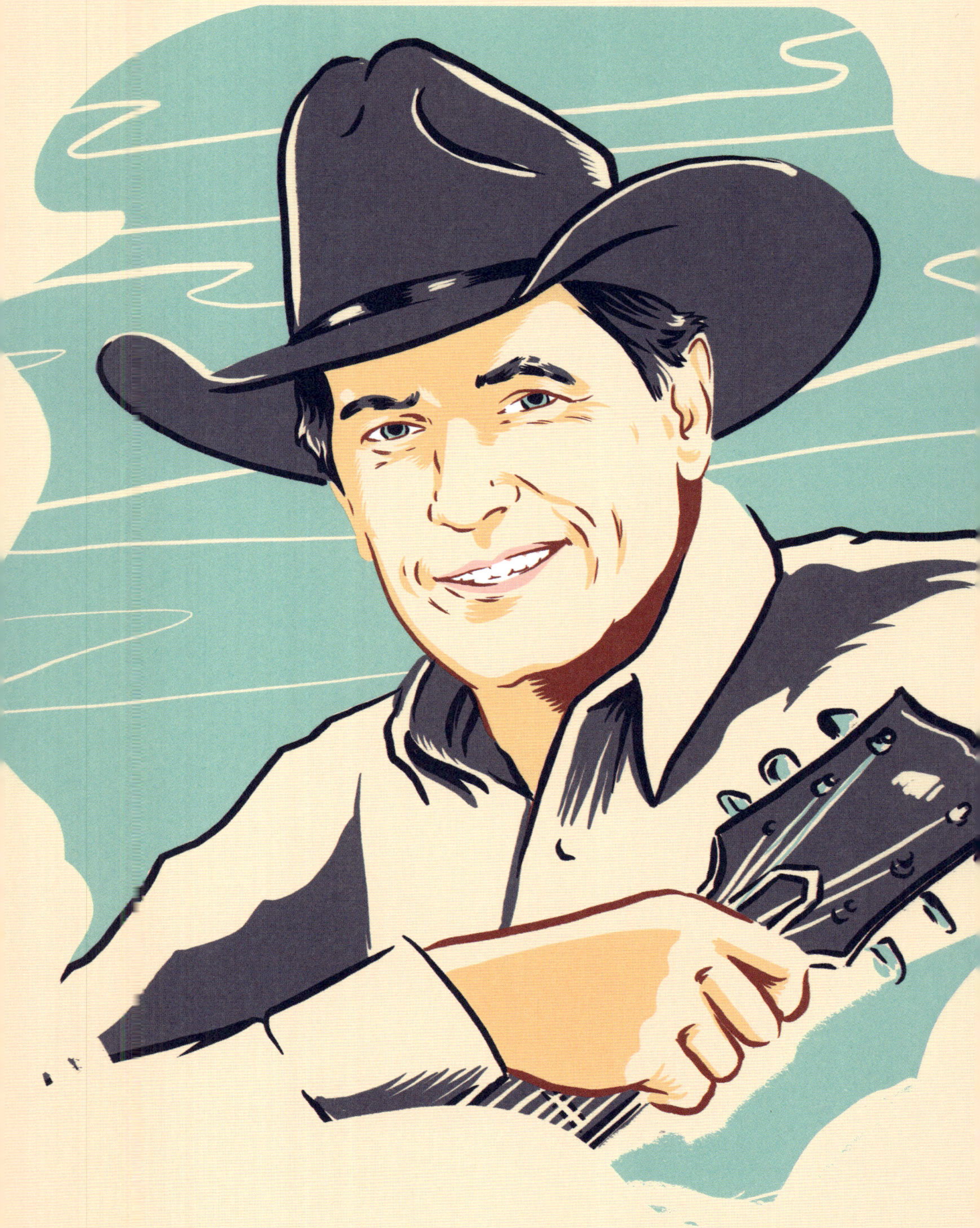

Krauss, Dolly Parton, and Randy Travis. What makes the venue truly special is that it welcomes both legends and newcomers. Any night of the week, you might be in the crowd as a future star steps onto the stage for the first time. And after a fantastic performance, you might even hear the ring of a cowbell, thanks to a Swedish fan who gifted the Station Inn a massive cowbell, now hanging above the bar for patrons and staff to ring in celebration.

STRAIT, GEORGE

"The King of Country Music" George Strait is one of the most successful and influential country artists of all time. Born and raised in Texas, Strait is a cowboy through and through. He learned to ranch from his father on his family's 2,000-acre (800-hectare) cattle farm but, despite his rural upbringing, Strait didn't catch the country music bug until he joined the service and performed with the U.S. Army-sponsored band, Rambling Country.

After being honorably discharged from the Army, Strait pursued a degree in agriculture at Southwest Texas State University (now Texas State University). Upon graduation in 1979, Strait still had music on the mind and began building an impressive regional following in Texas. As fate would have it, a music industry executive named Erv Woolsey crossed paths with Strait in 1981. Believing strongly in Strait's talent, Woolsey convinced MCA Records label head Jim Foglesong to sign him. Strait eventually signed with MCA, the label he continues to call home to this day.

Strait is best known for his cowboy hat, smile, and traditional brand of country music. Throughout his storied career, he has stayed completely true to who he is, never once compromising his music and artistry. A beloved entertainer, Strait's live performances are famously no frills, allowing the music to speak for itself.

He's sold over 105 million albums (and counting!) and has earned more than 60 industry awards. He was inducted

S

"Strait is best known for his cowboy hat, smile, and traditional brand of country music."

SEE ALSO:

COUNTRY MUSIC HALL OF FAME AND MUSEUM

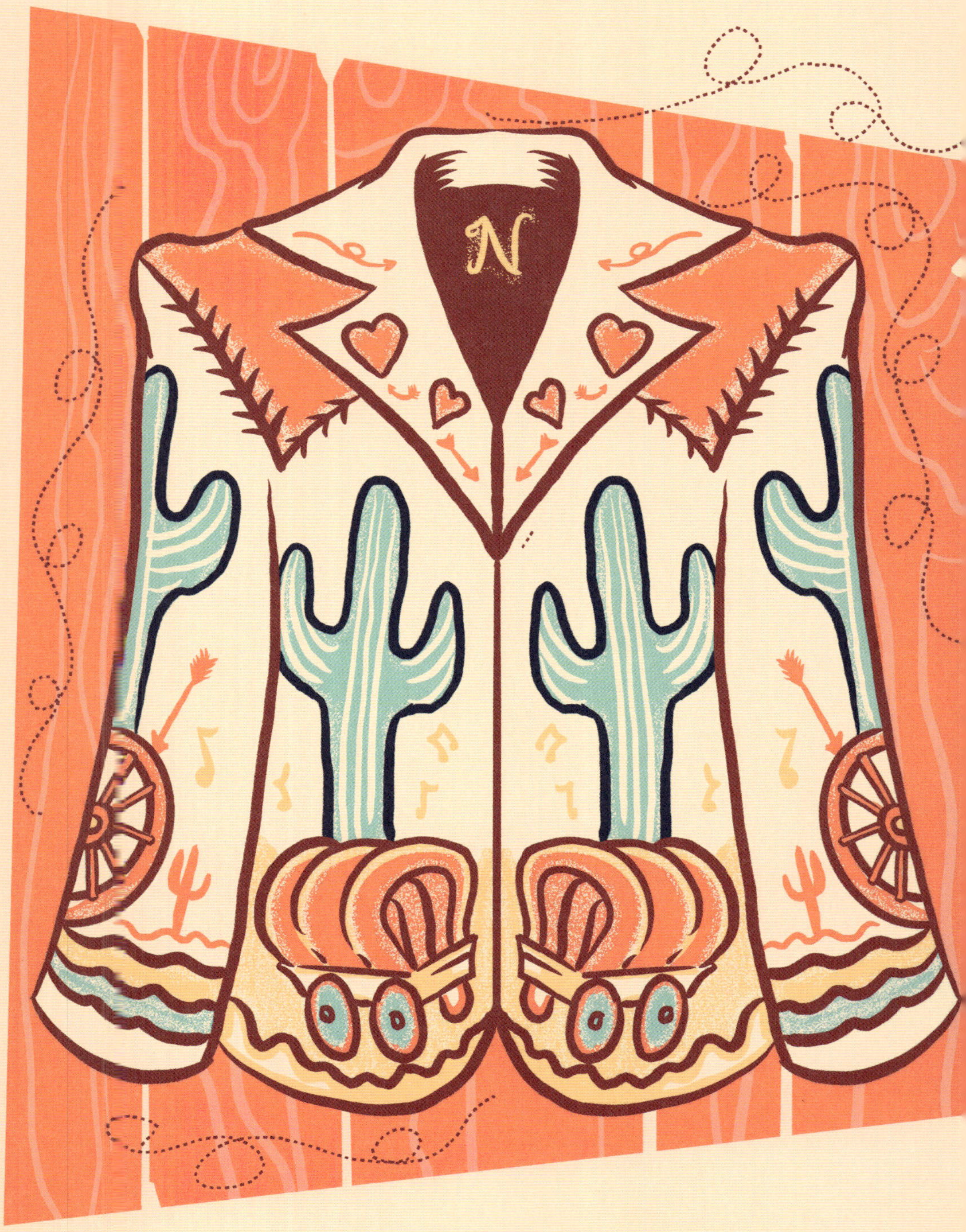
N

into the Country Music Hall of Fame in 2006 and has amassed a whopping 60 chart-topping singles: more than any other artist from any genre.

With hits like "Check Yes or No," "Amarillo By Morning," "Run," "Carrying Your Love with Me," and "Give It Away," George Strait's impact on country music is undeniable. As impressive as his career is his longtime marriage to his wife, Norma. The couple eloped to Mexico in December 1971 and remain happily married to this day.

S

STYLE

Country music fashion has always been iconic, but like the music itself, it has evolved with each decade. For many artists, their style is an extension of their music and often becomes a part of their personal identity.

In the 1930s and 1940s, country fashion was heavily influenced by Western culture. Think singing cowboys with wide-brimmed Stetsons, shirts with piping, and pearl snaps and neckties, a look popularized by Gene Autry and Roy Rogers. Meanwhile, Patsy Montana embodied the quintessential cowgirl look of the era.

The Nudie suit took off in the 1950s, thanks to Lefty Frizzell. Designed by Nudie Cohn, these suits were flashy and eye-catching, covered in fringe, rhinestones, appliqués, and intricate stitching. For decades Porter Wagoner, Glen Campbell, and Hank Williams all made statements with their Nudie suits, while artists like Kitty Wells popularized modest gingham dresses.

The rise of the Nashville Sound brought a more polished style to country music in the 1960s. Male artists often opted for sleeker, less flashy suits with ties. Patsy Cline ditched her signature cowgirl dresses for more sophisticated outfits, and June Carter Cash was frequently seen in A-line skirts and feminine dresses adorned with lace or ruffles.

"No matter the decade, classic country music style has remained true to its roots."

SEE ALSO:

CAMPBELL, GLEN

CLINE, PATSY

COWBOY BOOTS

HAT ACTS

NINETIES COUNTRY

SIGNATURE STYLE

TWAIN, SHANIA

WAGONER, PORTER

By the 1970s and 1980s, the bolder the look, the better. Denim was a staple, and rhinestones were everywhere. The 1980 film *Urban Cowboy* fueled a surge in the popularity of Western wear and George Strait looked as if he'd stepped straight off the big screen. Women's fashion embraced statement shoulder pads and bold designs. Master tailor Manuel Cuevas, who worked for Cohn in the 1960s and 1970s, moved his business to Nashville in 1988 and began to design custom Western-style jackets and suits for the likes of Dwight Yoakam, Marty Stuart, and Johnny Cash.

The 1990s brought a more casual yet still traditional vibe to country music fashion, with Garth Brooks and others rocking jeans, big belt buckles, boldly printed button-up shirts, and cowboy hats. Shania Twain stood out with her head-turning looks, from crop tops and leopard print to high-waisted jeans.

Today's country stars don't seem to follow one set trend: instead, they're creating their own signature styles. No matter the decade, classic country music style has remained true to its roots, with cowboy hats, boots, fringe, pearl snaps, plaid shirts, denim, and leather remaining timeless staples.

SWIFT, TAYLOR

In the summer of 2006, a song called "Tim McGraw" slowly began to take over the country radio airwaves. The title of the song instantly turned heads, and its heartfelt storyline was impossible to forget. This was the start of what would become a wildly successful career for a young artist named Taylor Swift.

Inspired by female powerhouses Faith Hill and Shania Twain, Swift brought a breath of fresh air to country music during a time when male artists dominated the genre. With songs about young love, high school, and heartbreak, Swift changed the game, creating an entirely new lane with her deeply personal lyrics and signature storytelling.

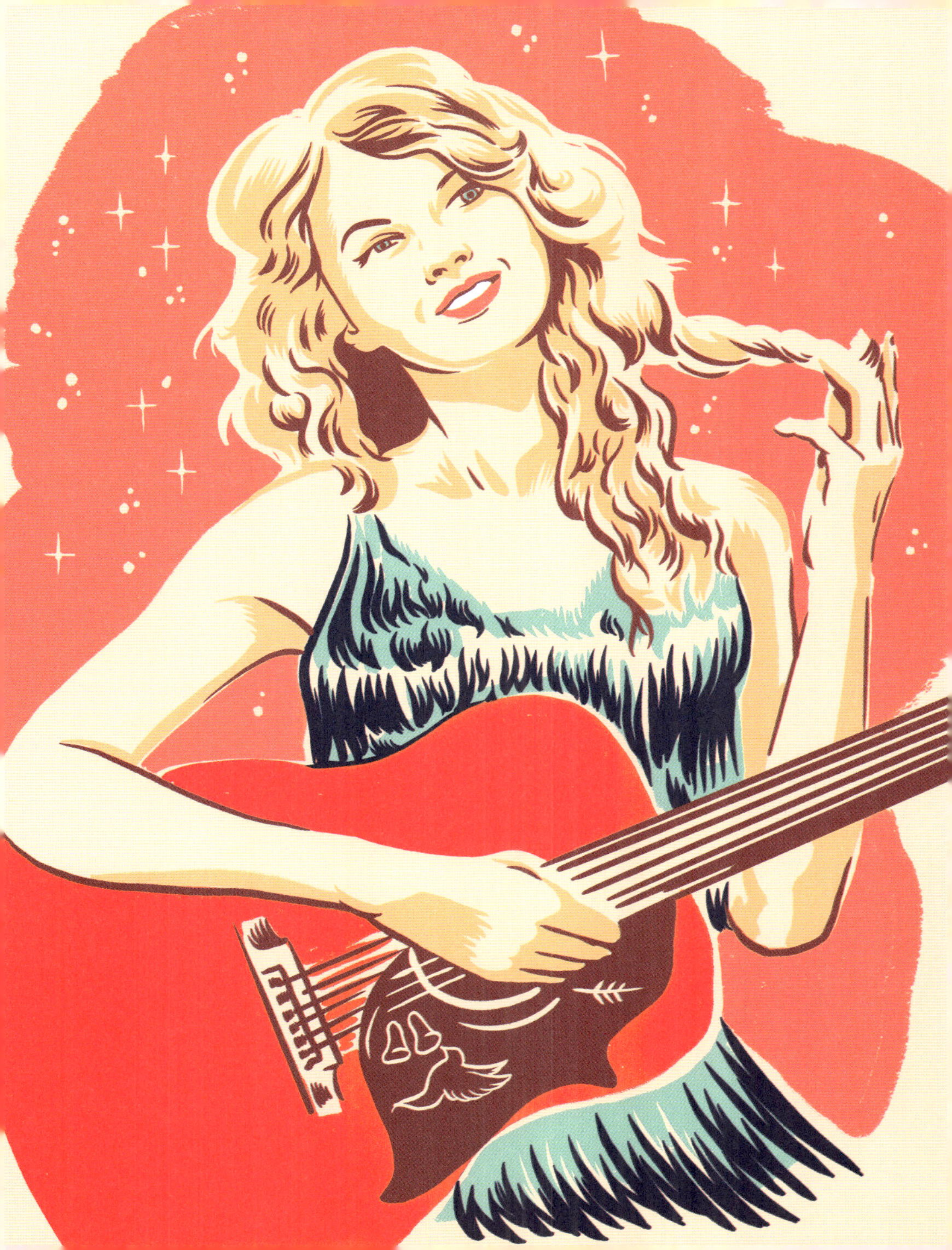

T

"While she has long since moved beyond country music, her impact on the genre is lasting and impossible to forget."

SEE ALSO:
BLUEBIRD CAFE
TWAIN, SHANIA

Swift released four country albums: her eponymous self-titled debut (2006), *Fearless* (2008), *Speak Now* (2010), and *Red* (2012). With *Taylor Swift* in 2006, she became the first female solo artist in country music history to write or co-write every track on a platinum-selling debut. Even more impressively, she wrote *Speak Now* entirely solo.

During her time in country music, Swift shattered records, earned countless accolades, and, in 2009, she became the youngest CMA Entertainer of the Year winner in history. While she experimented with a mix of pop and country on *Red*, her 2014 release 1989 marked her official departure from country music. Though she's ventured into new musical territory, her songwriting has remained front and center. It's no coincidence that Swift was discovered at The Bluebird Cafe, a legendary songwriting venue in Nashville, because it's her self-penned lyrics that has always set her apart.

Her style of music and songwriting opened the door for a new generation of female artists, including Kelsea Ballerini and, most recently, Megan Moroney. Taylor Swift has gone on to become one of the most successful and influential artists in history, and while she has long since moved beyond country music, her impact on the genre is lasting and impossible to forget.

TATTOOS

In country music, storytelling runs deep, and sometimes that extends beyond the songs. Tattoos often give artists another way to share their stories, pay tribute to their roots, honor their faith, or celebrate major milestones in their lives and careers.

Several country stars have meaningful tattoos. Keith Urban has multiple designs, including a phoenix on his left arm. It's a symbol of resilience, representing his journey through tough times and emerging stronger on the other side. Miranda Lambert's most recognizable piece, a pistol

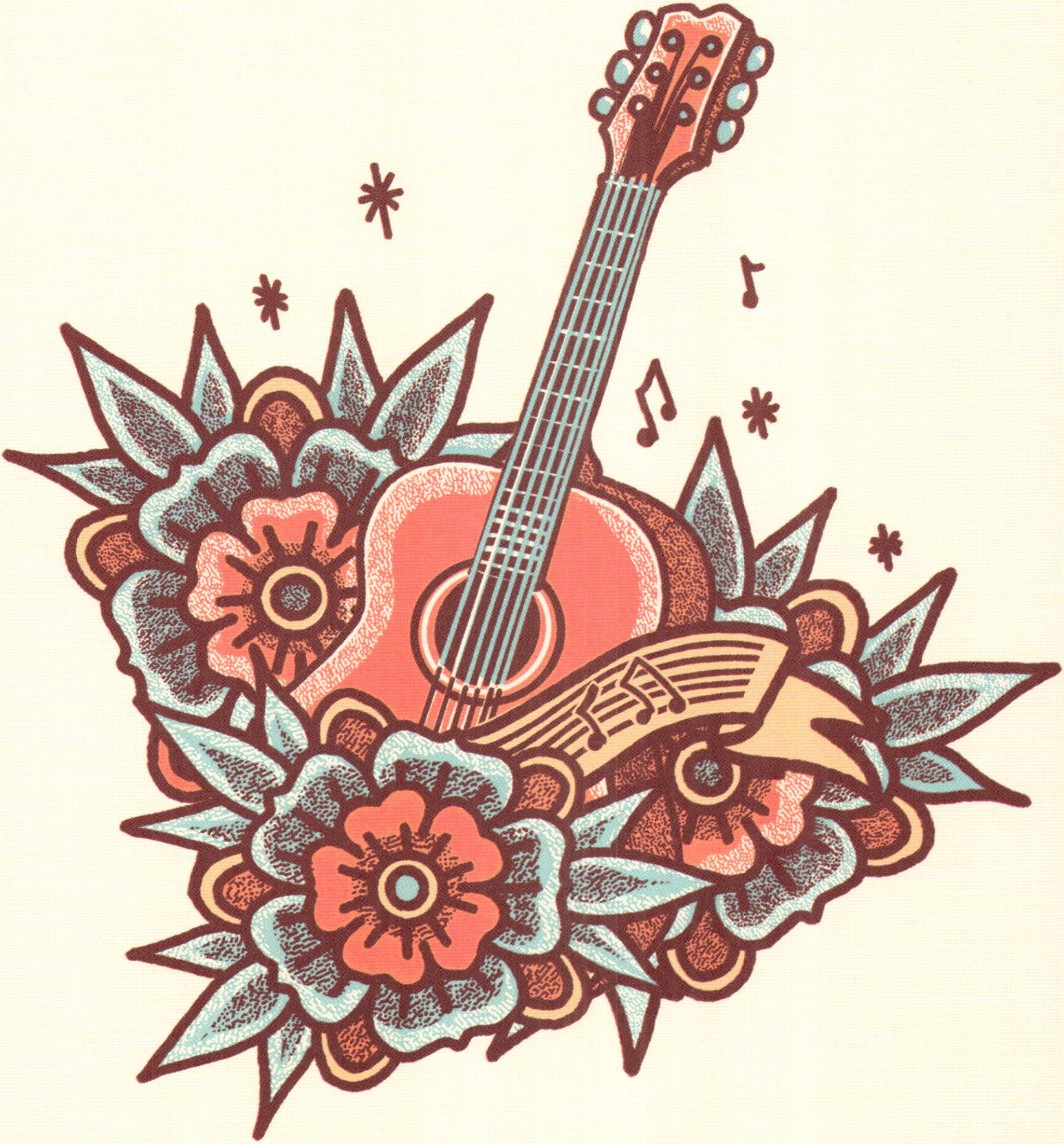

T

"Tattoos give artists another way to share their stories, pay tribute to their roots, honor their faith, or celebrate major milestones."

SEE ALSO:

GRAND OLE OPRY
LAMBERT, MIRANDA
SHELTON, BLAKE
STYLE
URBAN, KEITH

with wings on her forearm, perfectly represents her personality: "an angel and a little pistol." Ashley McBryde, who is covered in tattoos, is especially known for the giant eagle on her chest, a symbol of strength and how far she's come on her musical journey.

Carly Pearce also has several tattoos that reflect her story, including a feather in honor of her late grandfather and matching "show pony" tattoos with her bandmates. But one of her most meaningful designs is her Grand Ole Opry stamp tattoo, which celebrates the moment she fulfilled her childhood dream of becoming an Opry member in August 2021. The unique design was inspired by an unexpected source: a cookie she spotted on tour with a guitar styled like the Opry logo. Combined with her childhood love of stamps, it became the perfect way to mark the accomplishment. To make it even more personal, she added the year of her induction to the tattoo.

Blake Shelton's famous tattoo has a story on the complete opposite end of the spectrum. On his forearm, Shelton sports a design of deer tracks between barbed wire. As he's shared in interviews, he originally sketched the tracks himself, hoping the tattoo artist would get creative with the design. The end result was less than ideal, and it's now often mistaken for ladybugs. Shelton has admitted the tattoo was a mistake, but he continues to wear it with pride.

THE CHICKS

Natalie Maines and sisters Martie Maguire and Emily Strayer make up The Chicks (formerly known as the Dixie Chicks), one of the most successful female groups of all time, who've earned a global fanbase with their signature blend of country, bluegrass, and pop.

Formed in Texas in 1989, the group started out busking on the streets of Dallas and touring the country in an RV. After two original members departed, Maines stepped in as lead singer, and the trio as we know it was formed. Their debut single arrived in 1997, but it was "There's Your Trouble" and the title track of their breakthrough album, *Wide Open Spaces*, that launched them up the charts. In a decade dominated by influential female country artists like Shania Twain and Faith Hill, The Chicks found their own lane with their harmonies and fiddle-and-banjo-driven sound.

Their second album, *Fly* (1999), solidified their superstar status with hits including "Ready to Run," "Cowboy Take Me Away," and the light-hearted murder ballad, "Goodbye Earl." By 2000, they were touring with George Strait and collecting major awards, including Entertainer of the Year from both the CMA and ACM.

In 2002 they returned to their roots, releasing *Home*, a stripped-down bluegrass album. That same year, they found themselves in a public feud with Toby Keith after Maines criticized his patriotic anthem, "Courtesy of the Red, White, and Blue," calling it "ignorant." Then, in March 2003, while on tour in London, Maines told the crowd they were "ashamed that the president of the United States is from Texas," and criticized the impending U.S. invasion of Iraq. Although Maines apologized a few days later, the backlash was brutal, with the group facing radio boycotts, protests, and even death threats.

"One of the most successful female groups of all time, who've earned a global fanbase with their signature blend of country, bluegrass, and pop."

SEE ALSO:

FIDDLE

KEITH, TOBY

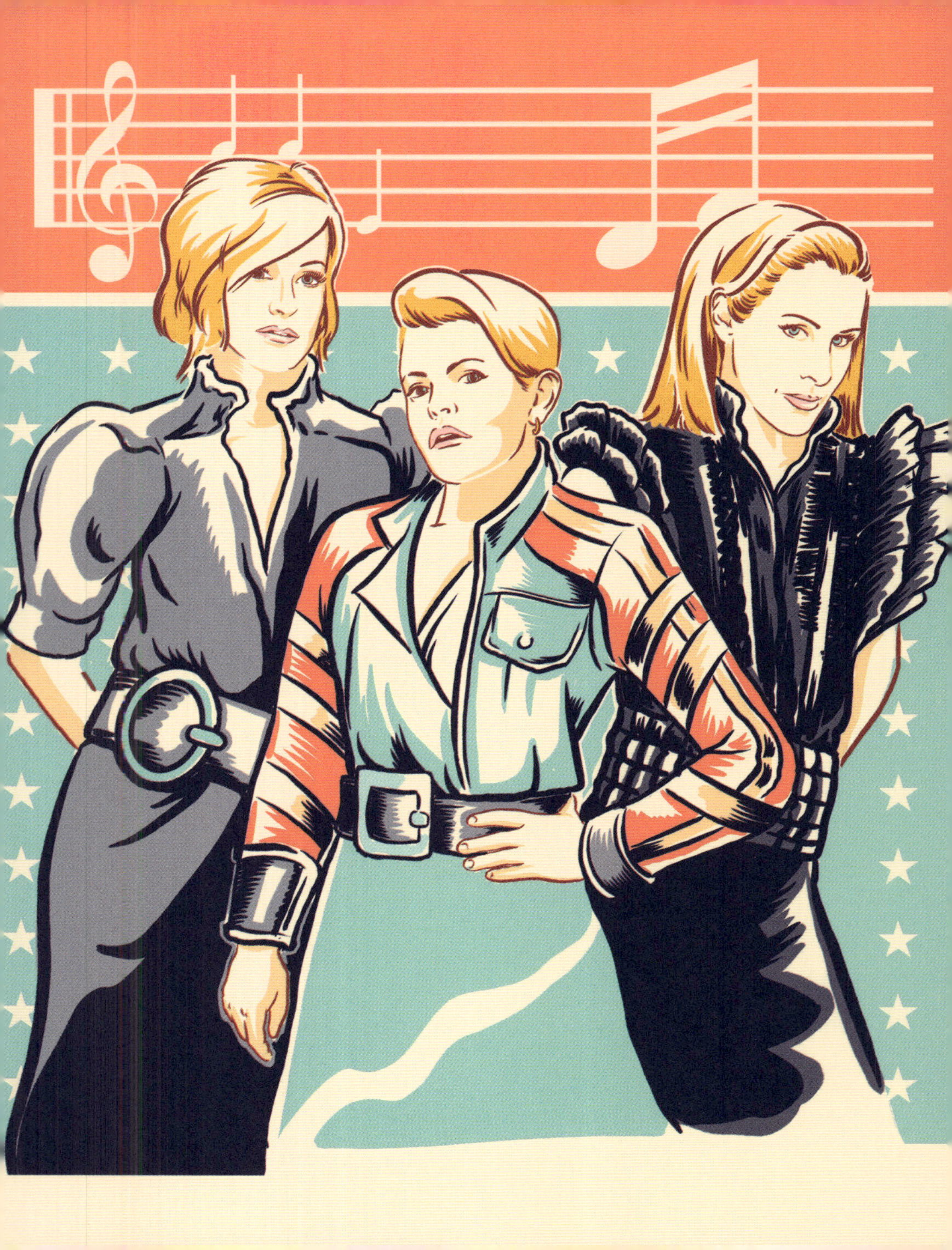

They later addressed the controversy in their 2006 single, "Not Ready to Make Nice," which won three Grammy Awards the following year but didn't receive the same recognition at country music award shows. Afterward, the group stepped back from the spotlight, performing only on a handful of occasions during their hiatus. In 2018, they began hinting at new music, and in 2020, they delivered with the release of *Gaslighter*.

T

THE JUDDS

"Little did they know the stunning family harmonies they created around the supper table would one day lead them to become one of country music's most iconic duos."

SEE ALSO:

COUNTRY MUSIC HALL OF FAME AND MUSEUM

FAMILY TIES

NINETIES COUNTRY

Mother-daughter duo Naomi Judd and Wynonna Judd made their official debut as The Judds in 1983, but they had been singing together long before that. Little did they know the stunning family harmonies they created around the supper table would one day lead them to become one of country music's most iconic duos and earn them a place among the legends in the Country Music Hall of Fame.

Their story began when Naomi (born Diana Ellen Judd) gave birth to Wynonna (born Christina Claire Ciminella) in 1964. They moved often during Wynonna and her sister Ashley's early years, spending much of their time in Kentucky. Living on welfare with no television or phone, they entertained themselves by singing and listening to the *Grand Ole Opry* on the radio. Sensing they had something special, the pair headed to Nashville to chase a record deal, reinventing themselves along the way by changing their names to Naomi and Wynonna.

With a cheap tape recorder, they made a demo, and Naomi began shopping it around Nashville. Their big break came in 1982 while Naomi was working as a nurse. She had a chance run-in with producer Brent Maher and gave him their tape. Maher liked what he heard and helped them record a more polished version, which reached RCA/Curb Records. The label invited them in for a live audition, and they landed a deal on the spot. Before long, their debut single was on the radio.

With their sassy, soulful songs, The Judds began to dominate the airwaves, leading the resurgence of traditional country with their blend of Appalachian folk, bluegrass, and country sounds. "Mama He's Crazy" was their first number one, followed by hits like "Girls Night Out," "Love Is Alive," and "Grandpa (Tell Me 'Bout the Good Ole Days)."

In 1990, Naomi announced plans to retire from touring due to her hepatitis C diagnosis. The Judds launched a 124-date farewell tour with a pay-per-view special, and

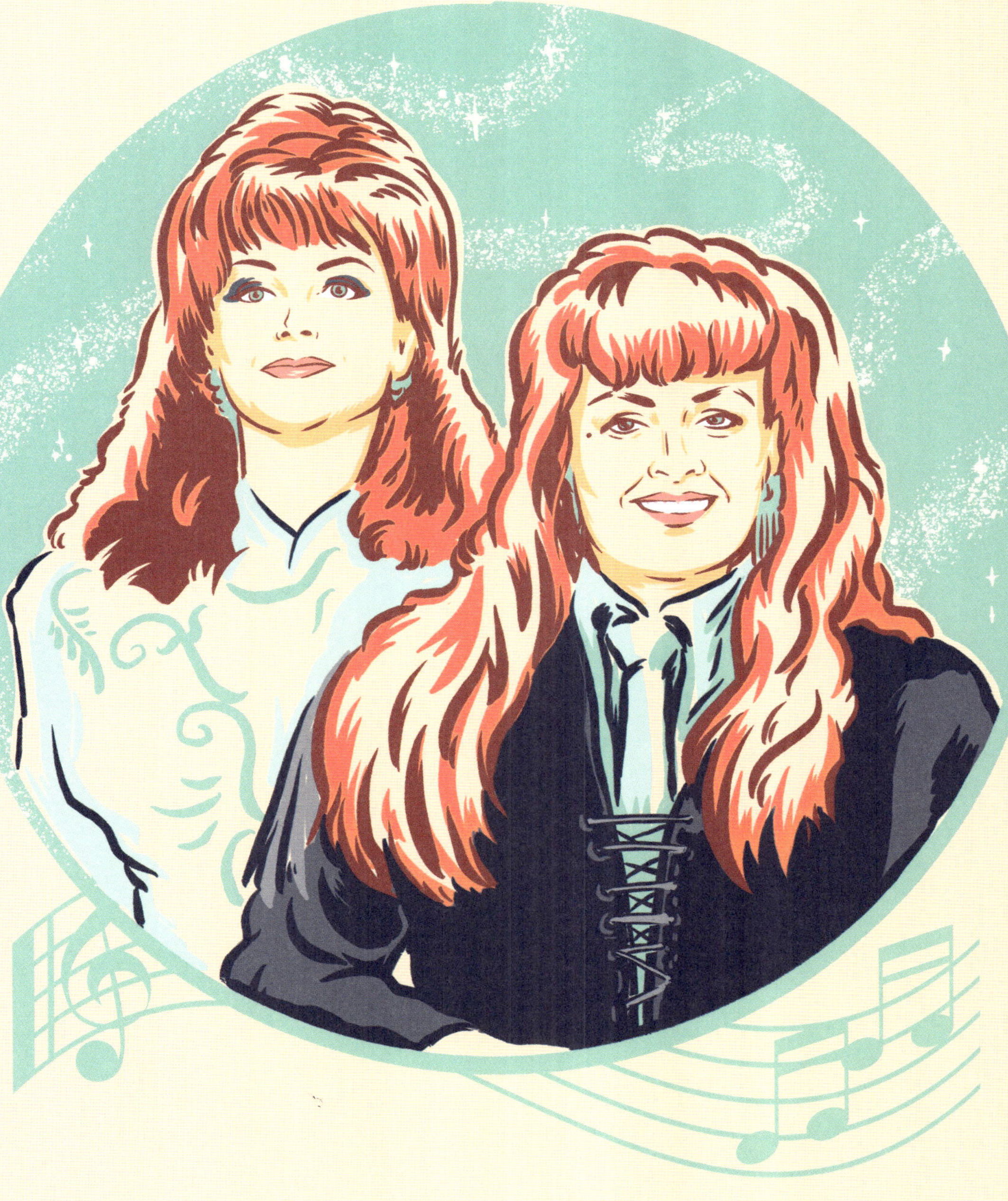

Wynonna went on to become a superstar in her own right. The Judds reunited several times, including the Super Bowl XXVIII halftime show in 1994, a 2000 tour, and a 2022 CMT Music Awards performance of "Love Can Build a Bridge." Tragically, Naomi passed away on April 30, 2022, the day before their Hall of Fame induction. Naomi and Wynonna had a strained relationship, but music kept them together. Their differences, in personality and artistry, are what made The Judds so unforgettable.

THREE CHORDS AND THE TRUTH

"Three chords and the truth is more than just a saying: it's the heart of country music."

SEE ALSO:

SONGWRITERS

As country music continues to evolve, there's always debate about what counts as "real" country. For me, it all comes back to what legendary songwriter and Country Music Hall of Famer Harlan Howard once said: country music is "three chords and the truth." I can't think of a better way to describe a genre built on simple melodies and honest lyrics.

In Howard's quote, "three chords" refers to the simple guitar chords that form the backbone of many country songs, while "the truth" speaks to lyrics about real-life experiences: love, heartbreak, hardship, loss, hard work, life's simple pleasures, and everything in between.

Countless legendary songs, from Dolly Parton's "Jolene" and Willie Nelson's "Blue Eyes Crying in the Rain," to Alan Jackson's "Livin' on Love," follow this simple formula. What sets country music apart from other genres is that, even as production styles have changed over time, storytelling remains at its core. Massive crossover hits from artists like Morgan Wallen, when stripped down and performed acoustically, reveal the same truth: the story at the center of the song is what makes it country.

"Three chords and the truth" is more than just a saying: it's the heart of country music. It continues to guide songwriters and shape the genre today, reminding us that at its core, country music is built on honest stories about real life.

T

TOUR BUS

When you spend hundreds of days a year on the road, it helps to bring a sense of home with you. Many country artists have outfitted their tour buses to feel like a home away from home, creating a sense of normalcy while traveling across the country. Tour buses provide not only a way to get from city to city, but also a place to sleep, unwind, and even write songs (because what else is there to do while driving across the country?).

A true road warrior, Willie Nelson has owned several iterations of his Honeysuckle Rose tour bus since the 1980s. His first bus, the original Honeysuckle Rose, was totaled in 1990. With each new bus, he adds a number to the name: Honeysuckle Rose II, III, and so on, and each is customized with a Western painting on the exterior. Nelson loves his bus so much that it's rumored he sometimes sleeps on it when he's at home on his Texas ranch.

Kenny Chesney shared his love for his tour bus, a white Silver Eagle he dubbed "Moby," in his 2014 song, "If This Bus Could Talk." The track tells the story of his career through the bus, from opening for Patty Loveless in 1993 and playing county fairs, to a 2004 Virginia Beach show he had to cancel due to a hurricane. "Oh, the stories he could tell, if this bus could talk," he sings. Though Moby is no longer Chesney's main bus, it still travels with him on tour and has logged over a million miles (1.5 million km).

From 2008 to 2022, Dolly Parton traveled nearly 360,000 miles (580,000km) around the US in her tour bus, which she lovingly coined her Gypsy Wagon. Now, fans have a

"Tour buses provide not only a way to get from city to city, but also a place to sleep, unwind, and even write songs."

SEE ALSO:

CHESNEY, KENNY
DOLLYWOOD
NELSON, WILLIE
PARTON, DOLLY

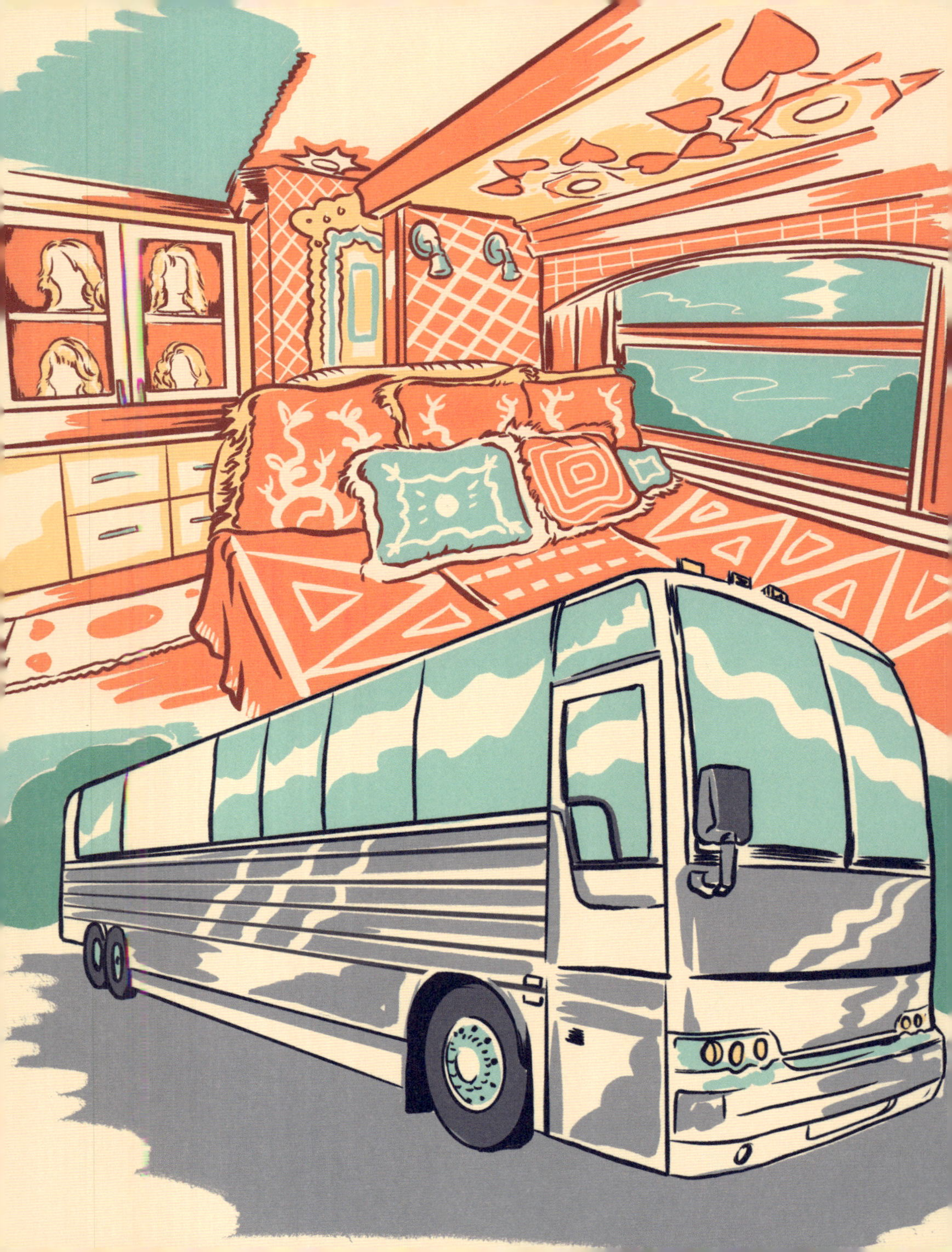

once-in-a-lifetime chance to stay in her iconic bus at Dollywood's DreamMore Resort and Spa. The Prevost motor coach features many customizations, including three bunks instead of six to make room for her wardrobe and a custom wig cabinet.

In today's social media age, fans have the opportunity to peek inside many artists' tour buses with stars like Jason Aldean, Kane Brown, and Kelsea Ballerini opening the doors to their homes on wheels on TikTok and Instagram.

TOUR PRANKS

In country music, it's become a tradition for tourmates to prank each other while on the road. While this most often occurs on the final night of a tour, it can happen at any moment. The pranks are all in good fun, helping to build camaraderie among the artists and their crews.

Some pranks are more light-hearted, like when Luke Combs bought Jordan Davis bags of dirt in honor of his song "Buy Dirt" and dumped a big bag by his microphone on stage. Or when Taylor Swift and her band pulled one over on Keith Urban, rushing the stage during "Kiss a Girl" dressed as the iconic rock band KISS. And then there was Megan Moroney, who bought a tiny John Deere tractor and surprised Kenny Chesney by dressing like him and riding the mini tractor while he performed "She Thinks My Tractor's Sexy."

Some artists have become known pranksters, and Brooks & Dunn are prime examples. In 1994, the iconic duo pranked Faith Hill by placing a headless eel in her bed while on tour in Canada. Faith got her revenge when they returned to the U.S., alerting customs about missing jewelry, leaving Kix Brooks convinced he was about to be strip-searched. In 1996, they took it up a notch by renting a hot air balloon and "kidnapping" then-tour-opener Jo Dee Messina from her bus and giving her a ride, even though she was terrified of heights.

"Most pranks hit the internet within minutes, letting everyone enjoy the hilarity of a good old-fashioned tour prank."

SEE ALSO:

BROOKS & DUNN

HILL, FAITH

PAISLEY, BRAD

SHELTON, BLAKE

T

If there were an award for the best tour prankster in country music, it would go to Brad Paisley. Artists know that when they sign on to tour with him, they have to keep their guard up. He's pulled pranks like hijacking video screens to play quirky clips mid-performance and sending his crew onstage in crazy costumes. Once, he even snuck raw chicken onto Blake Shelton's bus inside an air freshener, leaving the bus smelling rancid days later. Some of his tourmates have managed to get him back. In 2008, Jewel arranged for police to meet his plane in Nashville. Officers handcuffed him as he denied doing anything wrong. Paisley later admitted the prank was "as good as it gets."

Before social media, fans rarely saw these pranks unless they were at the show when it happened. Now, thanks to smartphones, most pranks hit the internet within minutes, letting everyone enjoy the hilarity of a good old-fashioned tour prank.

TRAVIS, RANDY

Randy Travis is often credited with saving country music. When he emerged on the scene in the mid-1980s, the genre was facing an identity crisis. With his signature baritone voice and songs that resonated with both traditional and modern fans, Travis helped bring country music back to its roots. He went on to build a timeless catalog that includes 23 number one singles and 21 top tens.

Born Randy Bruce Traywick in May 1959, he grew up in rural North Carolina where his father introduced him to the music of legends like Hank Williams, Ernest Tubb, and George Jones. A high-school dropout and self-described "juvenile delinquent," Travis eventually turned his life around as he began to take music more seriously. He moved to Nashville and worked as a cook at the Nashville Palace while chasing a record deal. For five years, labels rejected him for being "too country." Then, in late 1984, a Warner Bros. executive discovered him performing at the Palace.

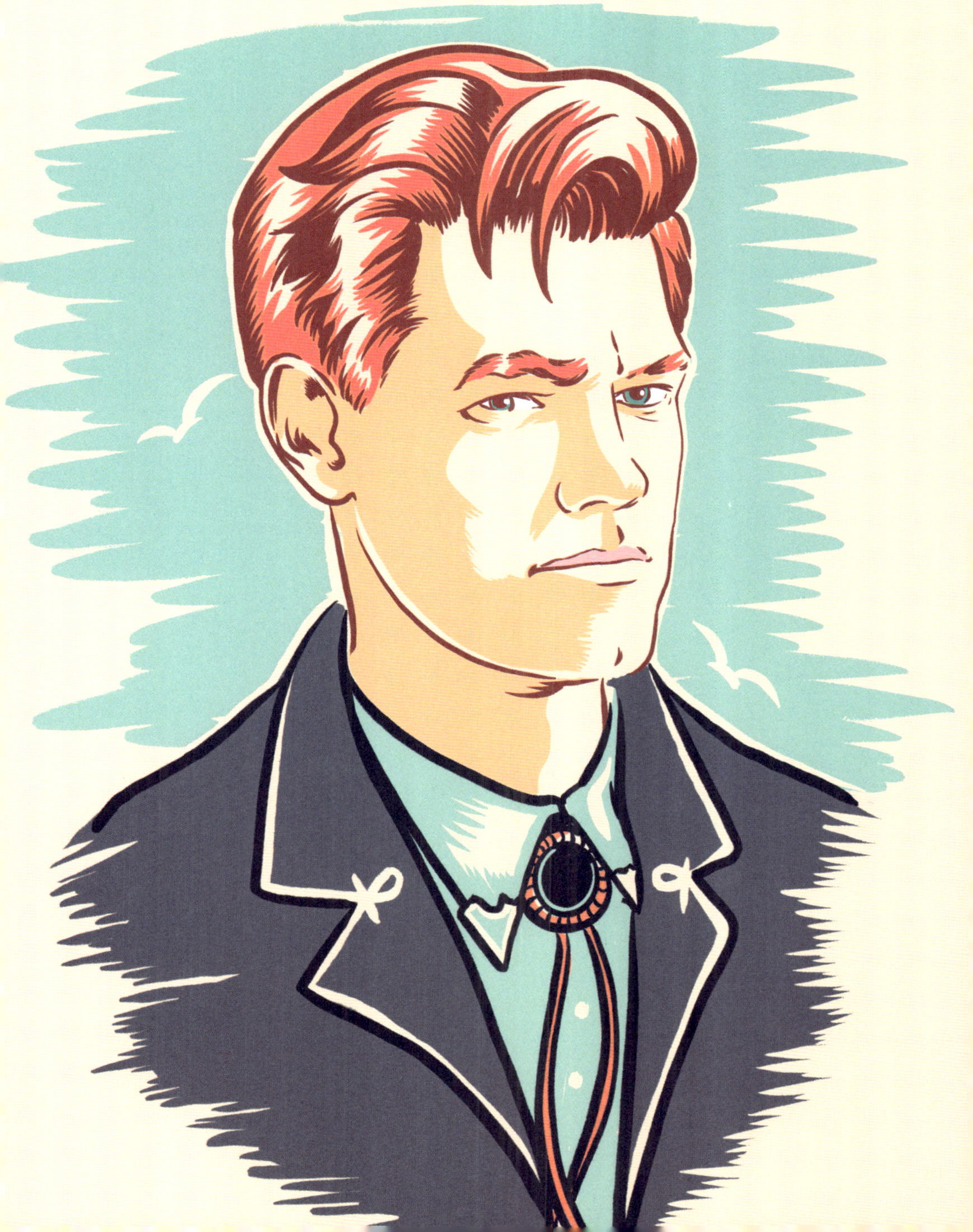

T

"With his signature baritone voice and songs that resonated with both traditional and modern fans, Travis helped bring country music back to its roots."

SEE ALSO:

BARITONE

COUNTRY MUSIC HALL OF FAME AND MUSEUM

FILM & TV

GRAND OLE OPRY

His debut album, *Storms of Life*, was released in June 1986 and produced four major hits, including "On the Other Hand" and "Diggin' Up Bones." The album reshaped the genre and remains one of country music's most influential records. It led to his Grand Ole Opry induction and earned Album of the Year at the 1986 ACM Awards.

His chart success continued with iconic songs like "Forever and Ever, Amen," "I Told You So," and "Deeper Than the Holler" in the late 1980s, followed by more fan favorites throughout the 1990s and into the early 2000s, including "Three Wooden Crosses." An appearance on the television series *Matlock* sparked Randy's interest in acting, leading to roles in 20 feature films and several guest spots on TV shows.

In 2013, Randy suffered a near-fatal stroke and was given less than a one percent chance of survival. He later developed aphasia, which affected his ability to speak and sing. He had to relearn how to walk and now often uses a wheelchair. He made a comeback appearance in 2016 when he sang "Amazing Grace" during his induction into the Country Music Hall of Fame.

Randy Travis has faced more than his share of challenges and through every setback, he has always found a way to carry on.

TWAIN, SHANIA

Shania Twain's story is a true rags-to-riches tale. Born Eilleen Regina Edwards in Timmins, Ontario, Canada, she grew up in poverty with her mother, stepfather, and four siblings. Money was tight, food was sometimes hard to come by, and she and her mother often faced abuse from her stepfather. She began performing in local bars at the age of eight and by the time she was ten, she was writing her own songs as an escape from her turbulent home life.

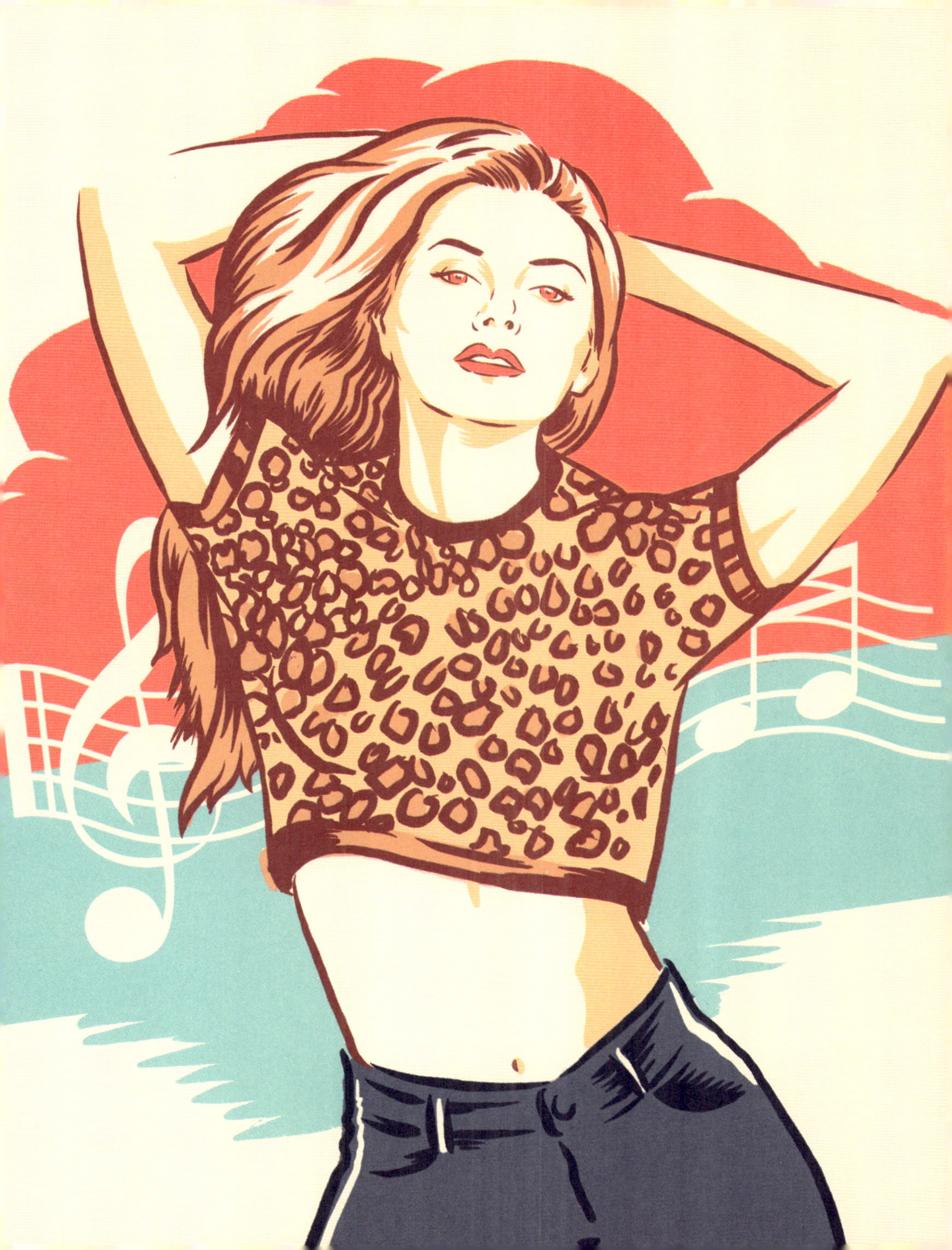

T

"Twain created country-pop as we know it, blazing a trail and opening doors for future generations of female artists."

SEE ALSO:

SWIFT, TAYLOR

In 1987, tragedy struck when her parents were killed in a car accident. At 22, Twain became the caregiver for her three younger siblings. She supported the family by singing at a resort, where a Nashville music executive happened to see her perform. That encounter led to a demo, a record deal, and the start of one of the most successful careers in country music history.

Twain adopted her stage name at her record label's request, choosing "Shania" from an indigenous Ojibwa name, and "Twain" from her stepfather's last name. Her self-titled debut album arrived in 1993 but failed to leave a major mark on the charts. Everything changed when rock producer Robert "Mutt" Lange entered the picture. Impressed by Twain's voice, he offered to work with her. Before long, they were making more than just music together. The pair fell in love and tied the knot in late 1993.

With Lange at the helm, Twain's next project, *The Woman in Me*, proved to be a massive success. Eight of the 12 tracks appeared on Billboard's Country Singles chart, including four number one singles. The Grammy-winning album spent 29 weeks at number one and became the best-selling country album of 1995.

Her third album, *Come on Over*, shattered records to become the best-selling country album of all time, producing 12 hit singles, including "You're Still the One," "Man! I Feel Like a Woman!," and "That Don't Impress Me Much." She followed with *Up!* in 2002 before taking a nearly 15-year break from recording. During that time, she endured a highly public divorce from Lange in 2010 and a debilitating Lyme disease diagnosis that changed her voice. At one point, she thought she'd never sing again, but she returned in 2017 with fifth album *Now*, Las Vegas residencies, and world tours.

Twain created country-pop as we know it, blazing a trail and opening doors for future generations of female artists.

TWITTY, CONWAY

T

Conway Twitty is one of country music's most successful artists, with 55 number one singles overall and 40 on the Billboard country chart. A multifaceted artist, songwriter, and entertainer, his career spanned five decades. Born Harold Lloyd Jenkins in Friars Point, Mississippi in 1933, he received his first guitar at the age of four. After moving to Arkansas when he was ten, Twitty had already written his first song and formed a band. A faithful listener of the *Grand Ole Opry*, he dreamed of performing there one day.

A talented baseball player, Twitty was offered a contract with the Philadelphia Phillies but was drafted into the US Army before he could accept. After he was discharged, he discovered Elvis Presley and his life changed forever as he launched his music career in Memphis playing rock 'n' roll. After a few label changes, his massive hit "It's Only Make Believe" propelled him to teen idol status. He appeared in a handful of movies and inspired the Broadway show *Bye Bye Birdie*. He chose his now-famous stage name after spotting "Conway, Arkansas" and "Twitty, Texas" on a road map and blending the two.

Despite his success in rock 'n' roll, his heart belonged to country music. His transition to country proved to be difficult at first because many disc jockeys were skeptical of his intentions, but he proved himself with hits like "Next in Line" and "Hello Darlin'," which would ultimately become his signature songs.

Known for his sex appeal and steamy lyrics, Twitty built a strong (primarily female) fan base. Some of his songs were controversial due to their suggestive subject matter, but that didn't slow his success. His concerts were strictly business: Twitty rarely spoke on stage, letting the music speak for itself. He also enjoyed a wildly successful string

"Despite his success in rock 'n' roll, his heart belonged to country music."

SEE ALSO:

COUNTRY MUSIC HALL OF FAME AND MUSEUM

DUETS

GRAND OLE OPRY

LYNN, LORETTA

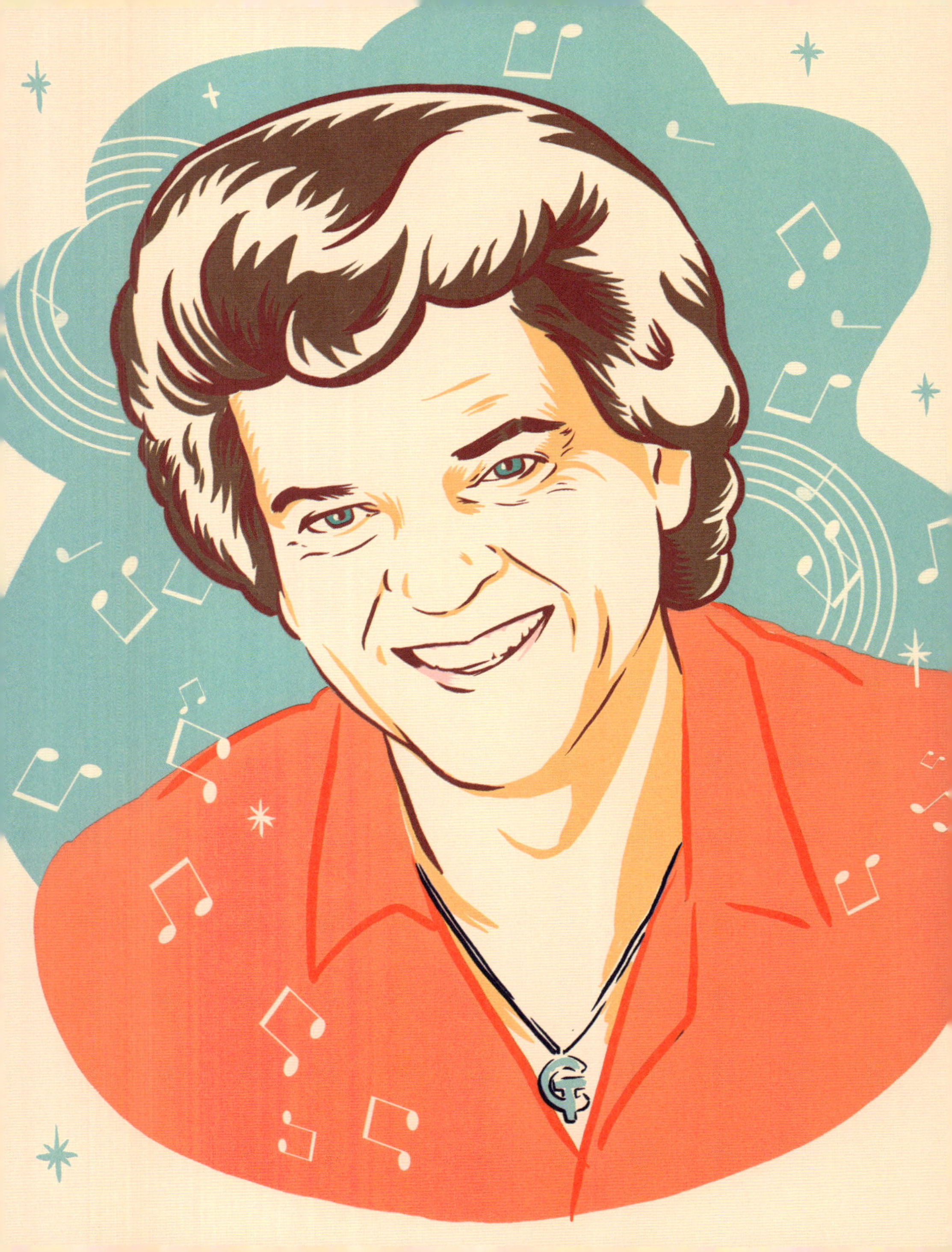

of chart-topping duets with fellow country icon Loretta Lynn, forming one of the genre's most iconic pairings.

Taking a page from Elvis Presley's book, he built Twitty City in Hendersonville, Tennessee, a tourist destination similar to Graceland. The property eventually got caught in an estate battle and was later sold. Twitty passed away suddenly in 1993 at the age of 59. At the time, no country artist had more number ones and, while he never became an official Opry member, he was inducted into the Country Music Hall of Fame in 1999.

UNDERWOOD, CARRIE

"Her career came full circle in 2025 when she returned to American Idol *as a judge, two decades after winning the competition that launched her career."*

SEE ALSO:

FILM & TV
GRAND OLE OPRY
PAISLEY, BRAD

Dynamic vocalist Carrie Underwood was born in 1983 in Checotah, a small town in Oklahoma with a population of just 4,000. She and her two sisters lived a simple life; her father was a paper mill operator and her mother, a schoolteacher. She started singing in church and around her hometown, and at the age of 14 was offered a record deal in Nashville. This ultimately fell through due to a change in management, but as Underwood once said, "Everything has a way of working out." Several years later, she would audition for *American Idol* and her life would change forever.

For her audition, the 21-year-old delivered a stunning cover of Bonnie Raitt's "I Can't Make You Love Me," marking the beginning of her groundbreaking career. She was crowned the winner of *American Idol* in 2005 and quickly became country music's hottest new star.

Propelled by megahits like "Jesus, Take the Wheel" and "Before He Cheats," Underwood's debut album, *Some Hearts*, became the best-selling debut country album of all time; and that was only the beginning. Chart-topping hits like "All-American Girl" and "Last Name" followed and, in 2008, Underwood was inducted into the Grand Ole Opry by fellow Oklahoma native Garth Brooks. Over the course of her career, she's sold 85 million records and landed 29 singles at the top of the charts, 14 of which she co-wrote.

Despite describing herself as "awkward" and "shy," Underwood commands the stage with undeniable confidence. She's a three-time ACM Entertainer of the Year and although the CMA Entertainer of the Year trophy has somehow eluded her, there's no doubt she deserves it.

A woman of many talents, Underwood has also explored acting, launched her own activewear brand, authored a

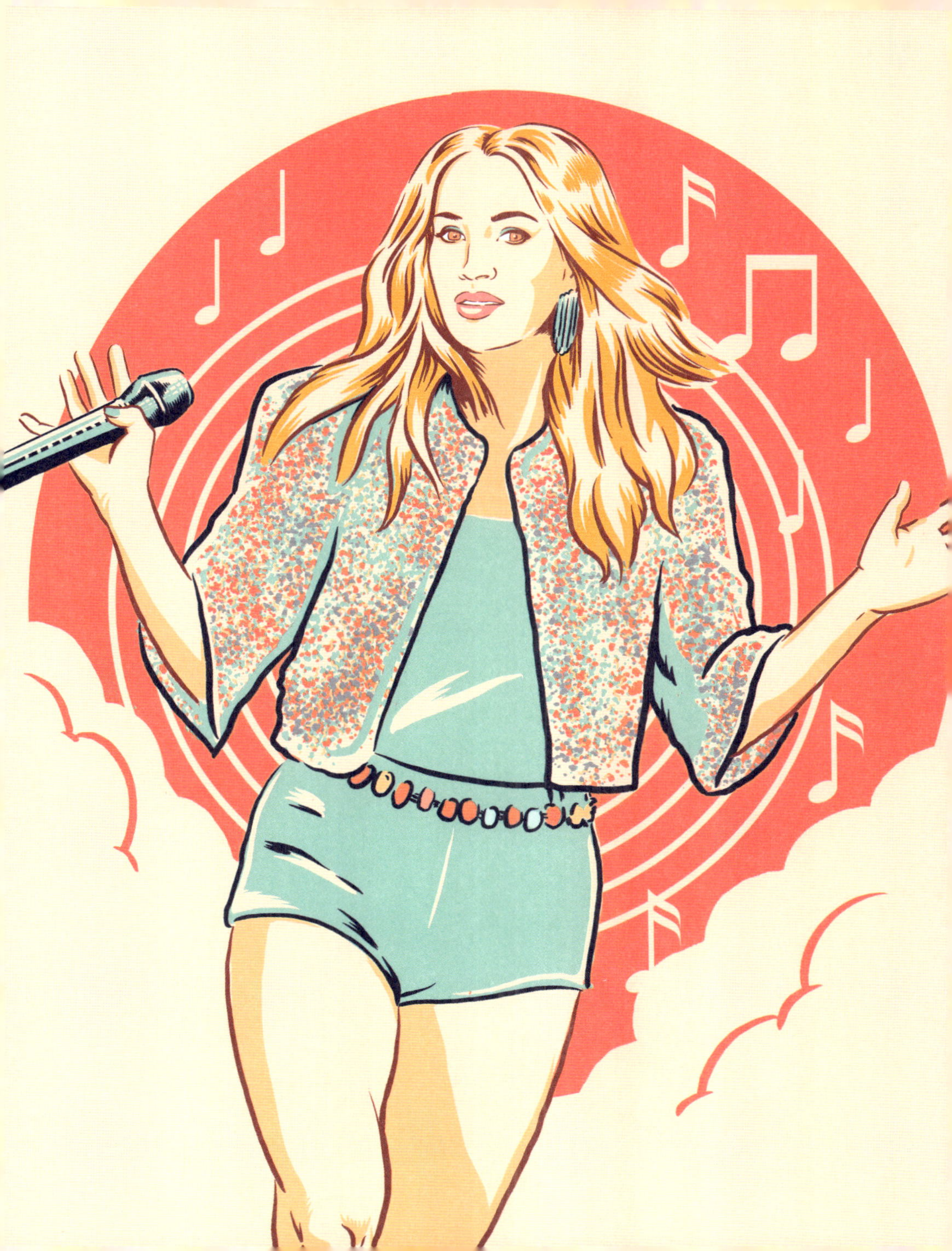

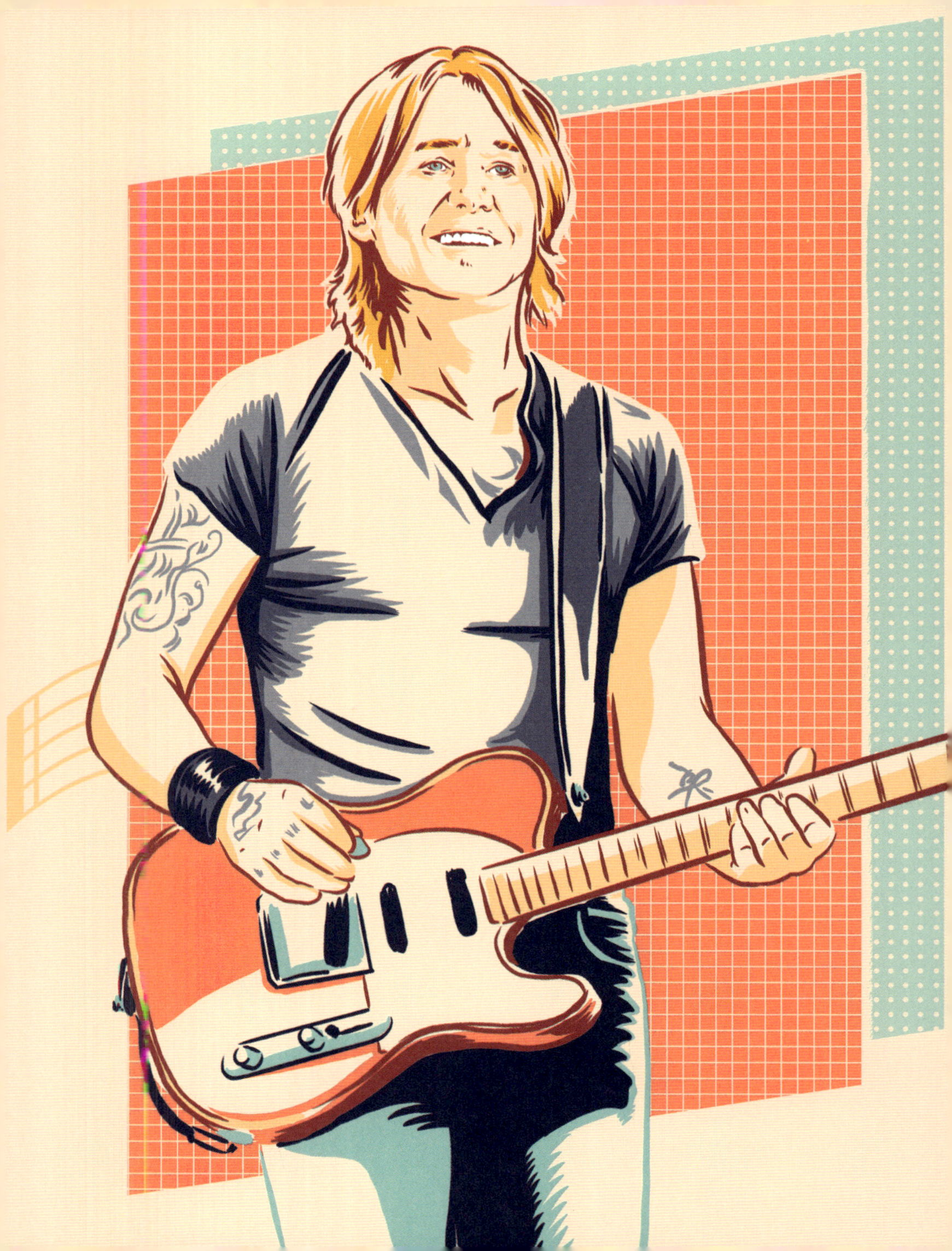

best-selling book, and channeled her passion for health and fitness through her app, fit52. She enjoyed a wildly successful multi-year Las Vegas residency and starred in the opening of NBC's *Sunday Night Football* for more than a decade. She co-hosted the CMA Awards for 12 years, 11 alongside Brad Paisley, and one with Reba McEntire and Dolly Parton.

Her career came full circle in 2025 when she returned to *American Idol* as a judge, two decades after winning the competition that launched her career. Although she's won over 100 major awards and has become an international superstar, Carrie Underwood remains humble and has proven to be a force in every aspect of her career.

URBAN, KEITH

Born in New Zealand and raised in Australia, Urban's love for country music began with his father, who filled the family home with the smooth sounds of Don Williams. Urban has called Williams "the sound of my entire childhood" and one of his biggest musical influences. The country star can pinpoint the exact moment his musical path was set: seeing Johnny Cash live with his family at just five years old.

A natural talent, Urban quickly became a standout in Australia, performing at talent shows and landing steady guitar gigs as a teenager. At 15, he dropped out of school to tour the country and, by 1991, had released his self-titled debut album in his home country. In 1992, Urban moved to the US where he worked as a road guitarist on various tours. He later formed the band The Ranch, releasing one album in 1997 and charting two singles before the group disbanded the following year.

Returning to his solo career, Urban launched his American debut in 1999, and country radio embraced him instantly. His sound—blending country, pop, and rock with fiddle, banjo, and his signature guitar riffs—was a bit progressive for the time, but it worked. The early 2000s brought a

"Even if the awards and chart-topping hits disappeared tomorrow, he'd still be out there making music, simply because he loves it."

SEE ALSO:

GRAND OLE OPRY

remarkable run of success, beginning with the top 20 hit "It's a Love Thing" and sparking a decades-long string of chart-toppers.

Over the years, he's collaborated with artists across genres, from Eric Church and Carrie Underwood to John Mayer and P!nk. A gifted vocalist, songwriter, and musician, Urban is also known for his guitar work. A multiple ACM and CMA Entertainer of the Year, Urban's live shows are among the best in the business, with no two ever the same. Watching him perform is mesmerizing: he doesn't just play, he puts his whole body into the music. His connection with the crowd makes it clear he genuinely wants to be there.

A member of the Grand Ole Opry and winner of multiple Grammys, Urban is an international ambassador for country music, playing sold-out shows and topping charts across the globe. For me, the best thing about Keith Urban is knowing that even if the awards and chart-topping hits disappeared tomorrow, he'd still be out there making music, simply because he loves it.

WAGONER, PORTER

When you think of Porter Wagoner, the first thing that comes to mind is his flashy rhinestone Nudie suits, but there was much more to this country music icon than his stage wear. He was also a talented singer, songwriter, TV personality, producer, and businessman. Wagoner grew up idolizing Grand Ole Opry stars Bill Monroe and Roy Acuff. Little did he know he'd one day follow in their footsteps and be inducted into the Country Music Hall of Fame.

Born in 1927, he was raised on a farm in West Plains, Missouri. A seventh-grade dropout, he began performing with his band, the Blue Ridge Boys, in his early twenties. His big break came at a butcher shop where he cut meat and sang for customers. That led to a radio gig and a record deal in 1952.

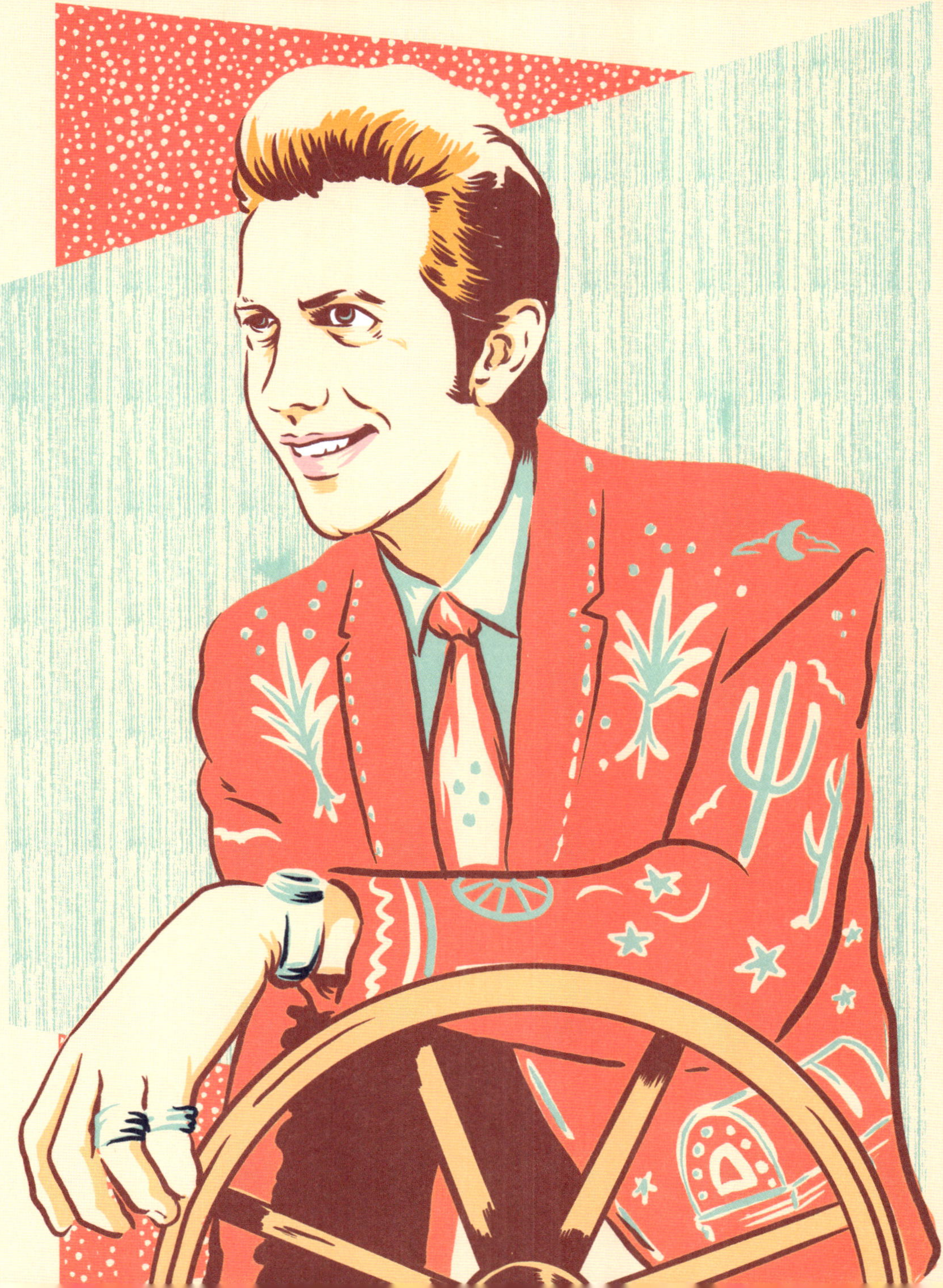

W

"At its peak, The Porter Wagoner Show *aired in an impressive 100 markets."*

SEE ALSO:

ACUFF, ROY

COUNTRY MUSIC HALL OF FAME AND MUSEUM

DUETS

FILM & TV

GRAND OLE OPRY

PARTON, DOLLY

His career started slowly due to poor record sales, but in 1954 he scored his first hit with "Company's Comin'." The chart-topping "A Satisfied Mind" followed the next year, and his first TV stint came on ABC's *Ozark Jubilee*, filmed in Springfield, Missouri. It was short-lived, as Wagoner negotiated out of his contract to join the Grand Ole Opry and move to Nashville.

From there, his career took off. He was tapped to host a music show sponsored by the Chattanooga Medicine Company. *The Porter Wagoner Show* debuted in 1960 and ran for over two decades, featuring performances by Wagoner, regulars like Jeannie Seely and Mel Tillis, and guests such as George Jones and June Carter Cash. At its peak, the musical variety show aired in an impressive 100 markets.

The show is best known for helping launch Dolly Parton's career. She and Porter formed a successful musical partnership that spanned several years and their duets, like "Please Don't Stop Loving Me" and "Making Plans," became iconic. Things took a turn in 1974 when Parton decided to leave the show. Their split led to a legal battle, but over time they managed to settle their differences privately and eventually reconciled. Following the passing of his hero Roy Acuff, Wagoner stepped into the unofficial role of Grand Ole Opry ambassador, proudly performing on its iconic stage right up until his death in 2007.

W

WALLEN, MORGAN

There's no denying that Morgan Wallen is one of the biggest, if not the biggest, modern country stars. He dominates the charts, sells out massive stadium tours, and shapes the current sound of country music with his blend of country, pop, rock, and hip-hop. Although he's occasionally found himself wrapped up in controversy, his impact on the genre is undeniable.

Wallen's childhood in Sneedville, Tennessee—a small town just outside Knoxville where he was born in 1993—revolved around two things: sports and music, much like Kenny Chesney, who grew up in the same area and graduated from the same high school. He began singing in his father's church at just three years old, started playing baseball at four, and, by age seven, was taking violin and piano lessons.

Baseball became his main focus in high school and, by his junior year, he was already being scouted by colleges. An elbow injury sidelined that dream, however, and he turned back to music as a way to cope. He taught himself guitar and began writing songs at 18, not knowing he would soon become one of country music's biggest stars. At 20, his mother signed him up to audition for *The Voice*. Although his stint on the show was brief, it was enough to catch the attention of Big Loud Records, who signed him in 2016.

His debut single, "The Way I Talk," introduced him to the country world, but the real turning point came with "Whiskey Glasses" in 2018. Momentum skyrocketed with his sophomore project, *Dangerous: The Double Album*, solidifying his place at the top of the genre. Albums *One Thing at a Time* and *I'm the Problem* followed, and the hits keep rolling in.

"If there's a record to be broken, Morgan Wallen will likely break it, if he hasn't already."

SEE ALSO:

CHESNEY, KENNY

LOWER BROADWAY

PHILANTHROPY

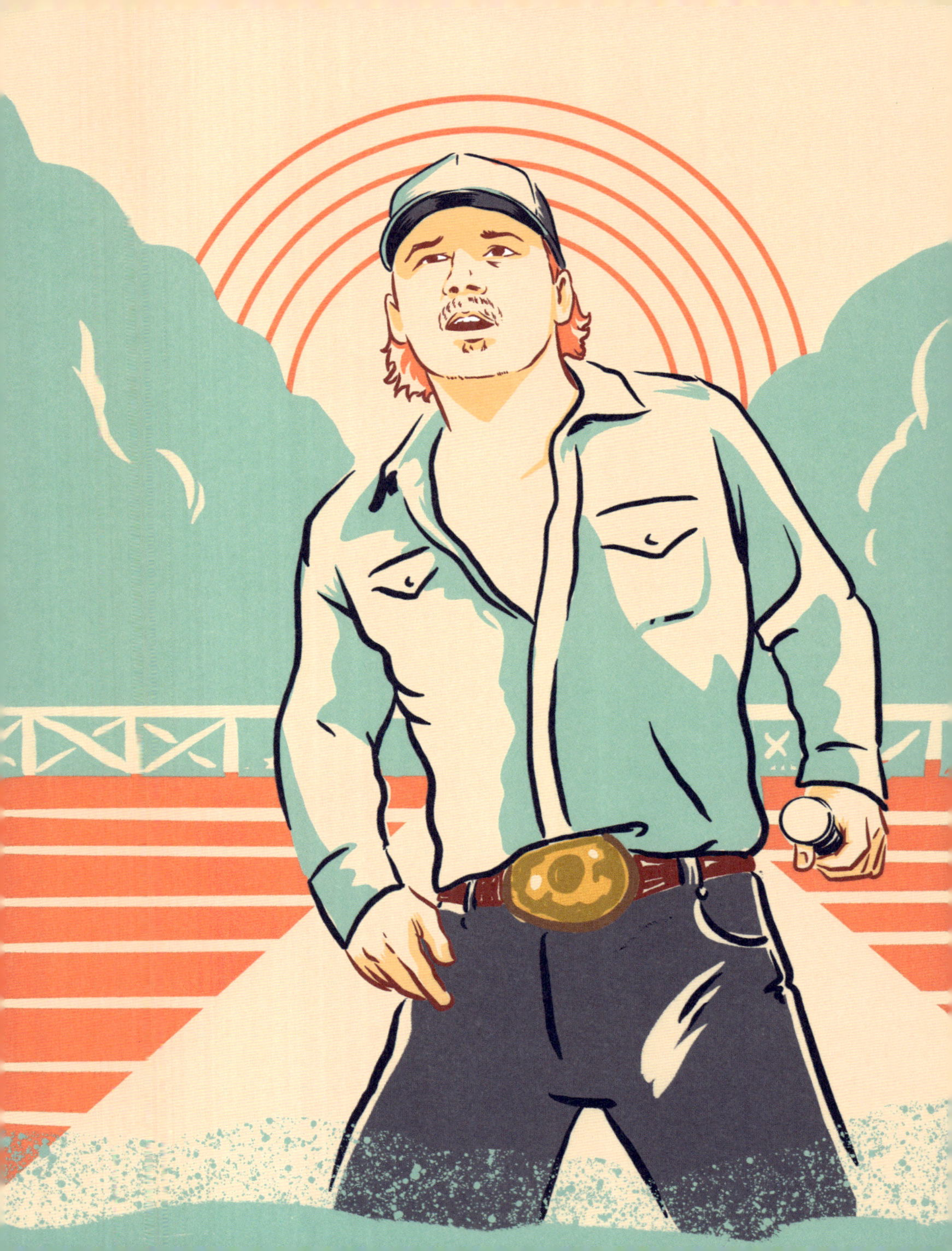

Wallen has proven to be a force on the road, with a dedicated fan base that helps him consistently sell out stadiums. He also gives back, donating a portion of all ticket sales to the Morgan Wallen Foundation. Beyond music, he has expanded his reach by partnering with Eric Church to purchase the Field & Stream brand and opening Morgan Wallen's This Bar & Tennessee Kitchen near Lower Broadway in Nashville.

A somewhat mysterious figure, Wallen rarely does interviews and keeps his social media focused solely on music. Maybe that's part of his allure; he rarely gives fans a peek behind the curtain. But one thing is certain, if there's a record to be broken, Morgan Wallen will likely break it, if he hasn't already.

W

WHITLEY, KEITH

"Whitley's haunting baritone vocals had a special way of conveying emotion, transporting listeners into the stories he told through his songs."

SEE ALSO:

BROOKS, GARTH

COUNTRY MUSIC HALL OF FAME AND MUSEUM

WALLEN, MORGAN

Born in 1954, Keith Whitley was instrumental in the traditionalist movement of the 1980s, keeping classic country sounds alive as others pushed the genre's boundaries. Although he released just three albums during his short life, his influence on the genre remains strong today.

Drawn to music early on, Whitley was considered a bluegrass prodigy. As a teenager he connected with future legend Ricky Skaggs, and they would go on to perform in various bluegrass bands together for several years. He launched his solo career in 1984 after moving to Nashville and signing with RCA Records. His debut EP was said to have been "too country" for its time, but success soon followed with his 1985 album *L.A. to Miami*, featuring songs like "Miami, My Amy" and "Ten Feet Away."

His true breakthrough came in 1988 with *Don't Close Your Eyes*, an album he co-produced after scrapping the original version. It produced a trio of number one singles with the album's title track as well as the now iconic ballads "When You Say Nothing at All" and "I'm No Stranger to the Rain." Whitley's personal life began to flourish around the same time his career began to take off—he married fellow country star Lorrie Morgan in 1986 and they welcomed a son the following year.

Whitley had long struggled with alcoholism and, at the height of his burgeoning career, sadly succumbed. He died from acute alcohol poisoning at his Tennessee home on May 9, 1989, aged just 34. His death shocked the country music world and black ribbons lined Music Row in his honor.

Whitley's haunting baritone vocals had a special way of conveying emotion, transporting listeners into the stories he told through his songs. His traditional sound has influenced generations of country stars, including Garth Brooks, Chris Young, and Morgan Wallen. His timeless songs remain staples, often covered by today's biggest

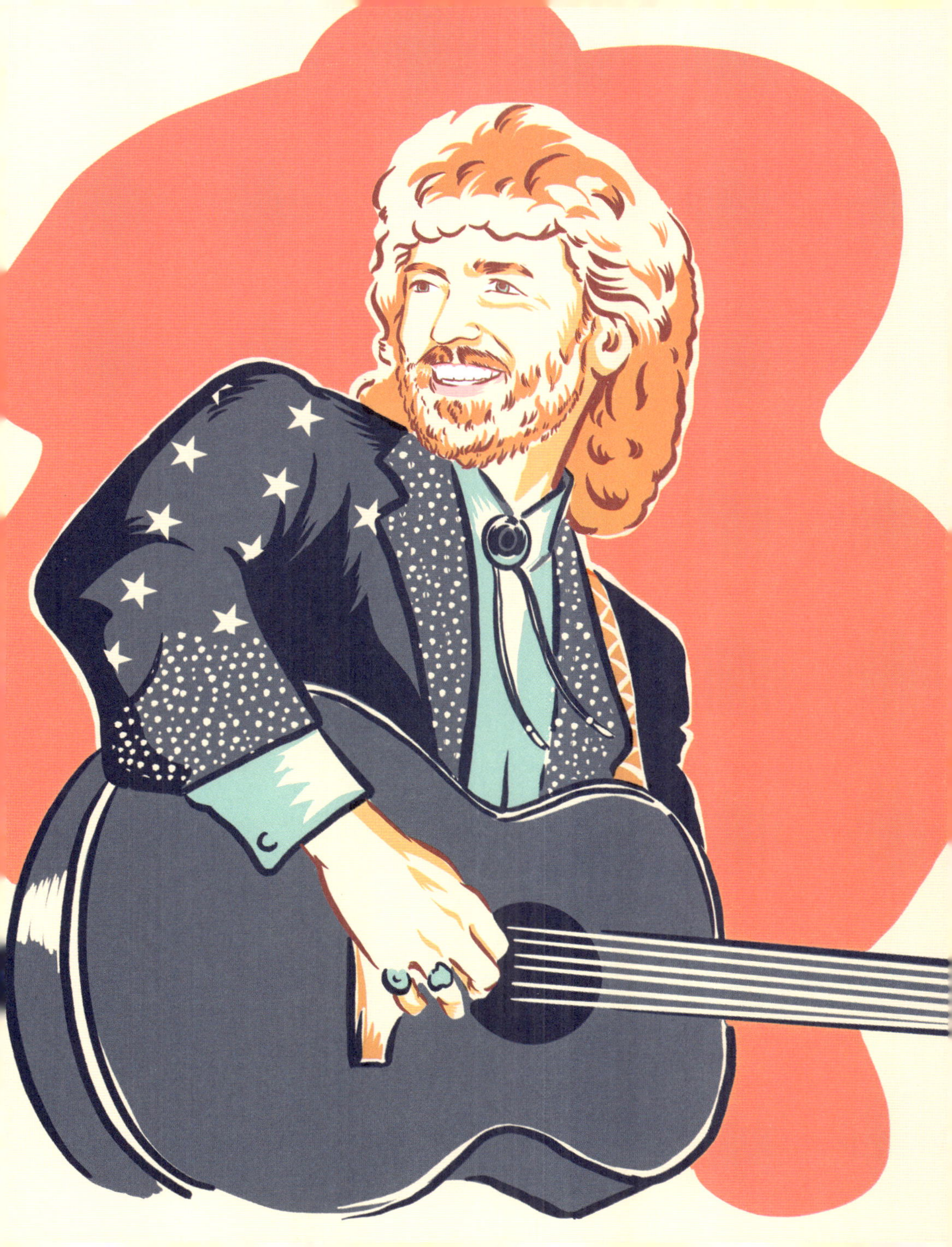

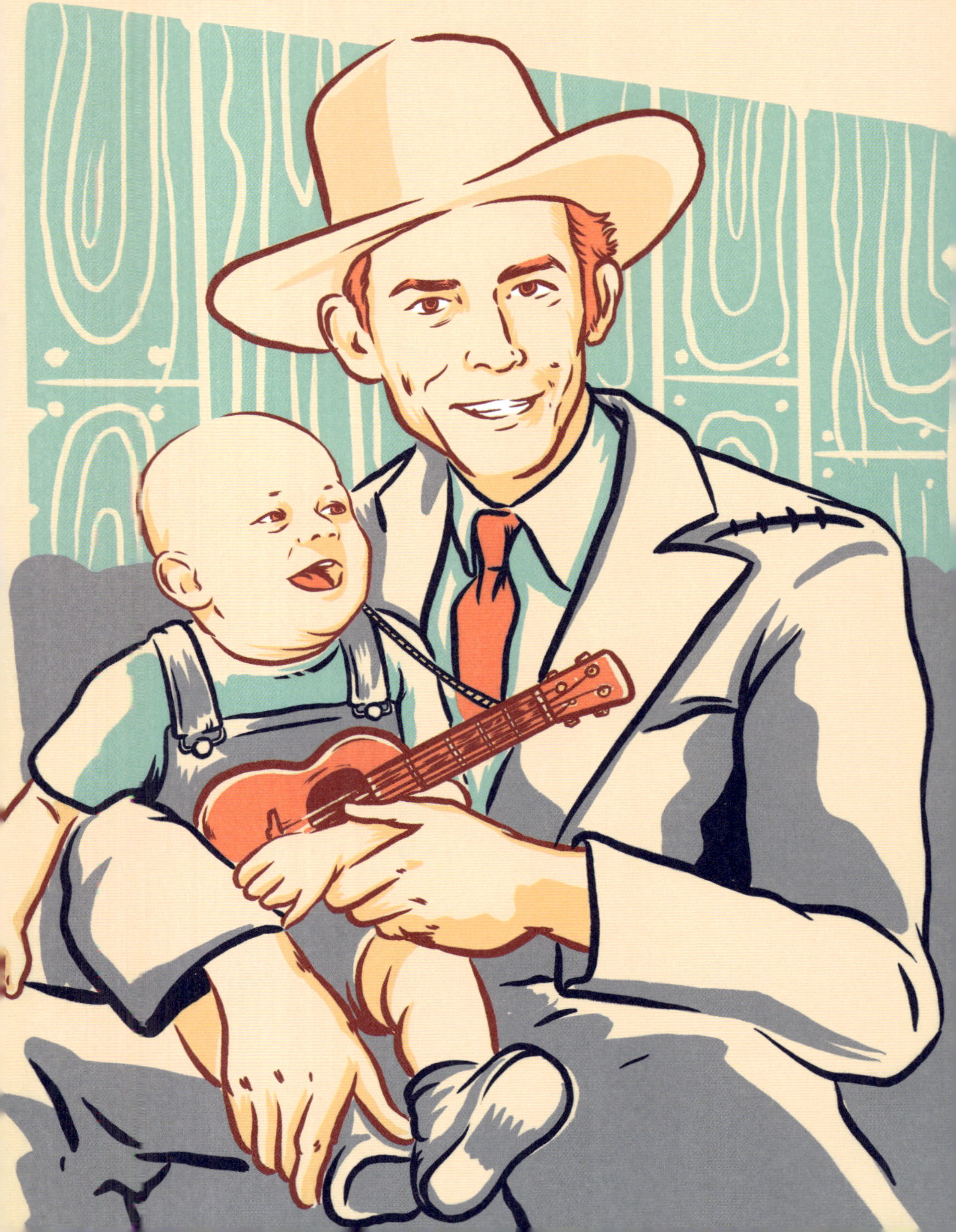

stars as well as newcomers on shows like *The Voice* and *American Idol*. In 2022, Lorrie Morgan was present as Whitley was posthumously inducted into the Country Music Hall of Fame, cementing his well-deserved place in country music history.

WILLIAMS FAMILY

The Williams family is about as close to country music royalty as it gets, with a lineage that includes Hank Williams, Hank Williams Jr., and his children, who have carried the "Family Tradition" forward.

Hailed as "country music's first superstar," Hank Williams was a true pioneer. Launching his career in the 1930s in Alabama, by the late 1940s he'd signed a record deal, joined the Grand Ole Opry, and built a catalog of hits including "I'm So Lonesome I Could Cry," "Your Cheatin' Heart," and "Honky Tonk Blues." By the early 1950s Williams was a major star, but his battle with alcoholism led to missed shows, his firing from the Opry, and ultimately a tragic ending. He died at just 29, leaving behind two children: Hank Williams Jr., with Audrey Williams, and Jett Williams, whose mother, Bobbie Jett, had a brief relationship with Hank before his death.

Hank Jr. was only three when his father died, and his mother quickly encouraged him to follow in his dad's footsteps. By age eight he was performing, and he made his Opry debut aged just 11. As a teen, he released an album of his father's songs but soon grew to despise living in his dad's shadow. After a near-fatal mountain-climbing fall in 1975 left him with extensive injuries, he relearned how to talk and sing. Soon, he found his true voice with a rowdy country-rock sound and built a wildly successful career with songs like "Born to Boogie," "All My Rowdy Friends Are Coming Over Tonight," and "A Country Boy Can Survive." His nickname, "Bocephus," was given to him by his father before his death.

"The Williams family is about as close to country music royalty as it gets."

SEE ALSO:

FAMILY TIES

GRAND OLE OPRY

W

Jett Williams would later record music of her own and now co-manages the Hank Williams estate with her half-brother, Hank Jr. Several of Hank Jr.'s children have followed in the family's musical footsteps, including his first son, known professionally as Hank III, daughters Hilary and Holly, and son Sam Williams. In 2025, Sam honored his grandfather's legacy with "Honkytonkin'," sampling ten seconds of Hank Williams's 1948 hit "Honky Tonkin'." The song, which Hank Jr. also re-recorded and turned into a chart-topping hit in 1982, showcased how the "Family Tradition" continues across generations.

"WILL THE CIRCLE BE UNBROKEN"

"If country music had a theme song, 'Will the Circle Be Unbroken' would be it."

If country music had a theme song, "Will the Circle Be Unbroken" would be it. The song has a long-standing history, dating back to the 1930s with the "First Family of Country Music," the Carter Family. The band was made up of husband and wife A.P. Carter and Sara Dougherty Carter, along with Sara's cousin, Maybelle Addington Carter. They were discovered at the 1927 Bristol Sessions and went on to play an instrumental role in country, bluegrass, Southern gospel, and folk music.

A.P. Carter adapted the lyrics from an old hymn into a song once known as "Can the Circle Be Unbroken." The lyrics tell the story of a mother's death and offer a prayer for a reunion with her and other loved ones "in the sky," referring to Heaven. The Carter Family's recording of "Can the Circle Be Unbroken" became the best-selling record of 1935. The song has been passed down through the Carter family and sung by every generation since.

Other artists have recorded their own versions of the song, including the Nitty Gritty Dirt Band with special guests Mother Maybelle Carter, Jimmy Martin, and Roy Acuff, as well as George Jones, Randy Travis, and many more.

SEE ALSO:

BRISTOL SESSIONS

COUNTRY MUSIC HALL OF FAME AND MUSEUM

GRAND OLE OPRY

W

Over the years, the song has taken on new meaning. Many interpret the "circle" as country music itself, a nod to the icons who forged the path and today's artists who carry on the tradition. Metaphorically, the "circle" has also become a reference to the iconic circle of wood at the center of the Grand Ole Opry stage.

"Will the Circle Be Unbroken" was the last song performed at the Opry at the Ryman before it moved to the Grand Ole Opry House, and the first song played when the Opry reopened after the devastating 2010 flooding. An all-star Opry cast performed the classic hymn to celebrate the Opry's 100th anniversary in 2025. Additionally, the song is performed at every Country Music Hall of Fame Medallion Ceremony, welcoming the newest members, and its title is displayed proudly in the Hall's rotunda, highlighting its importance to the genre.

WILSON, LAINEY

Lainey Wilson is a Grammy, CMA, and ACM Award winner, a proud member of the Grand Ole Opry, and one of modern country music's most celebrated stars. Despite what some may think, her success didn't happen overnight. It took years of hard work and dedication to get to where she is today, and she faced countless rejections along the way.

"Wilson's journey has been nothing short of amazing. The best part? She's only just getting started."

SEE ALSO:

GRAND OLE OPRY

SIGNATURE STYLE

Born in Baskin, Louisiana—with a population of about 200—in 1992, Wilson had dreams that stretched far beyond her tiny town. At 19 years old, Wilson left Baskin in her rearview and headed to Nashville, determined to turn her dreams into reality. She spent three years living in a small camper trailer outside a family friend's studio, where she learned to write songs and faced some of the toughest times of her life.

With hopes to catch her big break, Wilson auditioned for shows like *American Idol* and *The Voice*; however, she never made it past the initial rounds. She says the rejections lit a fire under her to keep going, so she never gave up.

Nearly a decade after moving to Nashville, Wilson earned her first platinum-certified song with "Things A Man Oughta Know," a testament to her unwavering dedication to her craft. From there, Wilson was on a fast track to superstardom. She landed multiple number one singles with songs like "Heart Like a Truck" and "Watermelon Moonshine," and her stint on the show *Yellowstone* further fueled her success.

Fans are drawn to Wilson's down-to-earth personality and kind spirit. She certainly hasn't forgotten where she came from or who helped her get there, and in an industry that often changes people, that's a refreshing thing to see. Wilson's journey has been nothing short of amazing. The best part? She's only just getting started, and fans have a front row seat to the story of a legend in the making.

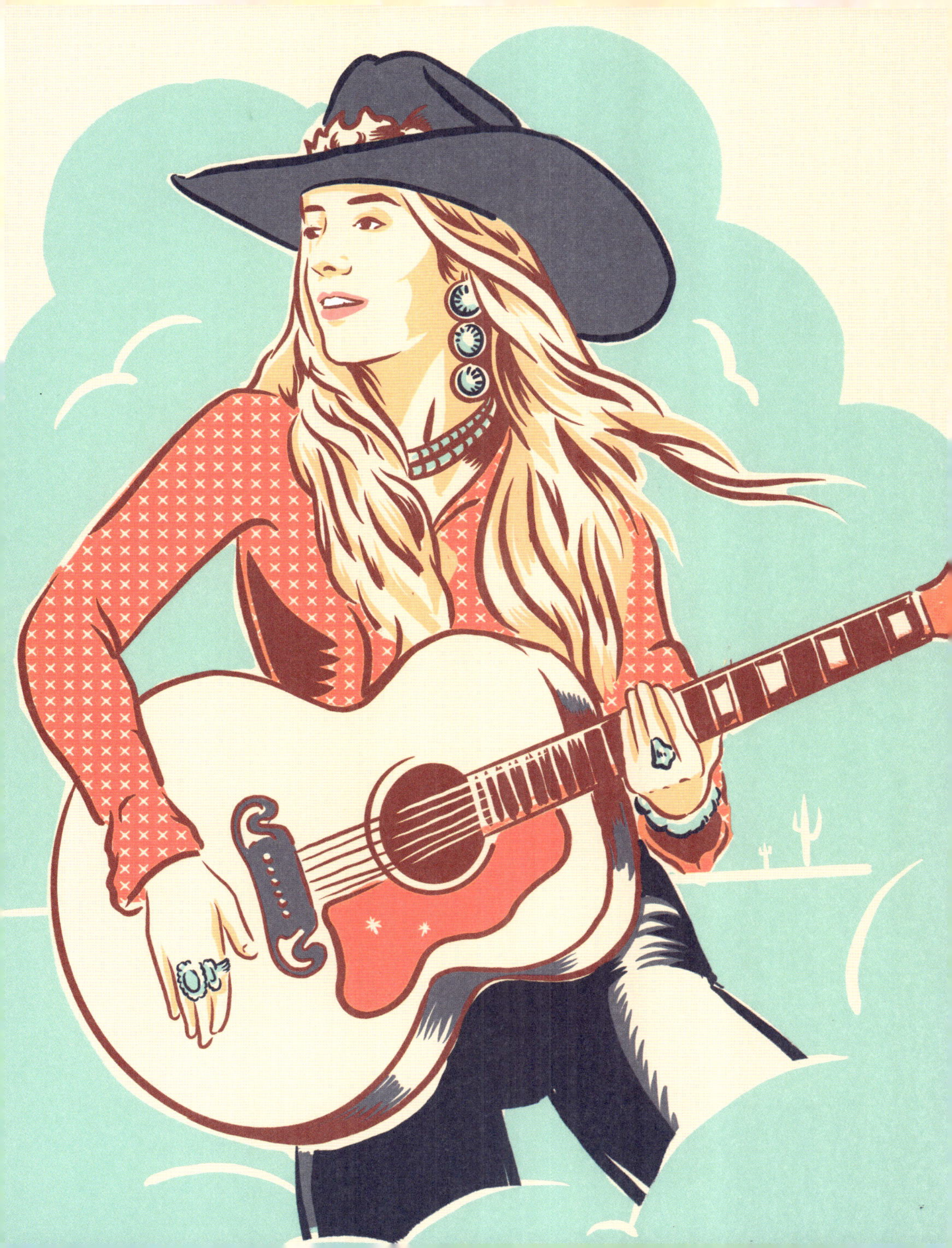

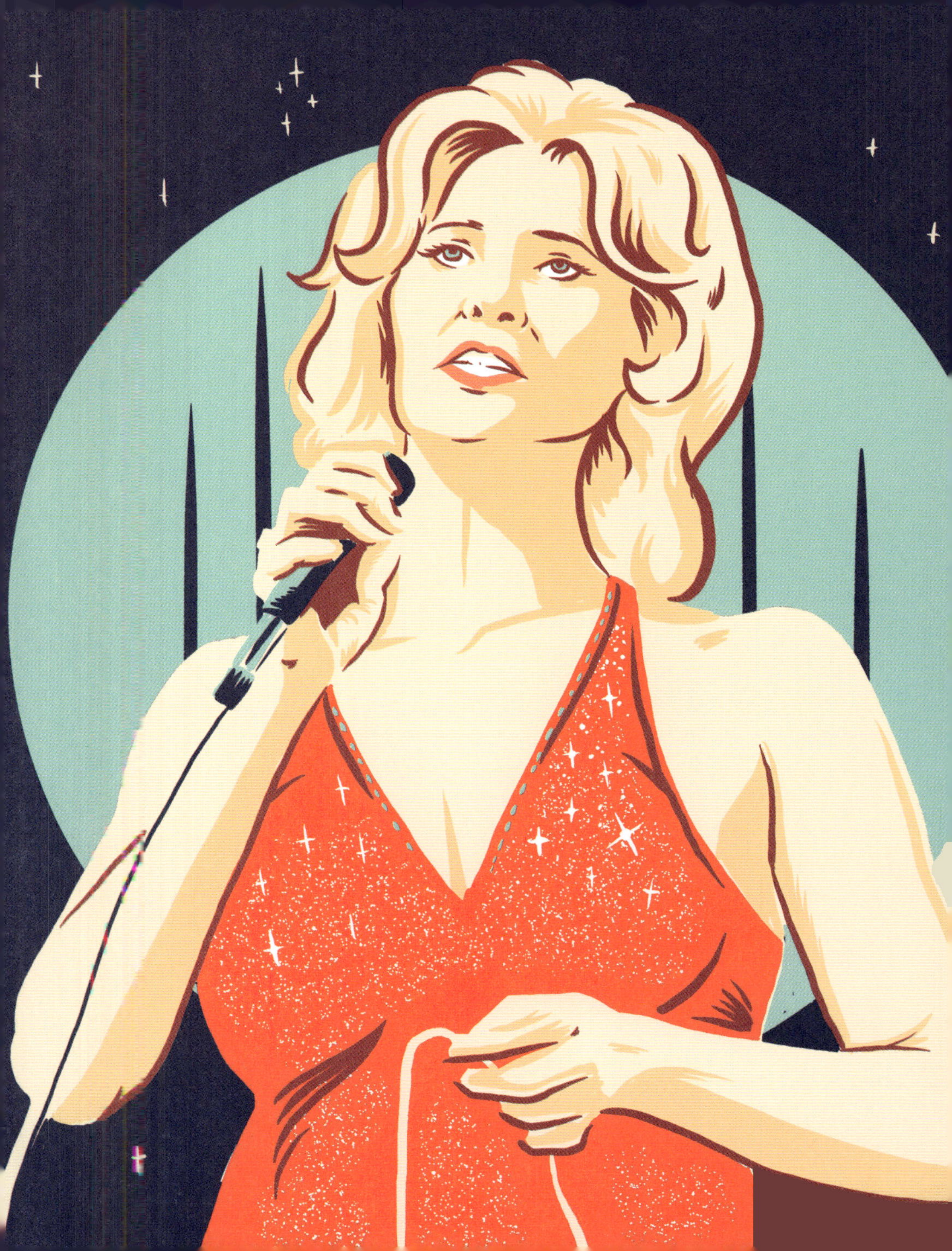

WYNETTE, TAMMY

W

Known as "The First Lady of Country Music," Tammy Wynette was a trailblazer who paved the way for female singer-songwriters for decades. Born Virginia Wynette Pugh in 1942, she grew up on a cotton farm in Mississippi. Her father, who died before she turned one, had musical aspirations himself and hoped that his daughter would someday chase the dreams he didn't have a chance to pursue.

She was a teenage bride, tying the knot with her high-school boyfriend Euple Byrd before graduation. They had two children and constantly struggled to make ends meet. Wynette enrolled in beauty school, determined to leave poverty behind. Wynette and Byrd divorced in 1965 after welcoming a third child. As a single mother of three, she worked as a beautician in Birmingham, Alabama, and landed a side gig singing on a local TV show.

That same year, she began making trips to Nashville, chasing a dream that didn't come easy. After countless rejections, she finally met producer Billy Sherrill at Epic Records. He saw what others had missed. He signed her, changed her name to Tammy, and together they created history with songs like her career-defining anthem, "Stand By Your Man."

Her life offstage was as storied as her music. Wynette married five times, but her relationship with fellow legend George Jones captured the world's attention. They wed in February 1969, and their daughter Georgette arrived following year. Fans became infatuated with their relationship, which was often quite tumultuous. The couple recorded several duets, both during and after their marriage, including the chart-topping singles "We're Gonna Hold On" and "Golden Ring."

Wynette died in April 1998 due to a blood clot. Her funeral took place at Nashville's Ryman Auditorium and was broadcast live for fans around the world, and Dolly Parton, Loretta Lynn, and Randy Travis were among

"Her voice conveyed emotion in every note, leaving listeners hanging on to every word."

SEE ALSO:

COUNTRY MUSIC HALL OF FAME AND MUSEUM

JONES, GEORGE

those who sang at the service. Shortly after her passing, Wynette was posthumously elected as a member of the Country Music Hall of Fame.

Wynette showcased vulnerability through her music like no female country artist had ever shown before. Her lyrics touched on everything from love and heartbreak to broken homes and divorce. Her voice conveyed emotion in every note, leaving listeners hanging on to every word. Tammy Wynette walked so artists like Reba McEntire, Carrie Underwood, and Miranda Lambert could run.

YEARWOOD, TRISHA

"Trisha Yearwood once said music feels more like a calling than a choice."

SEE ALSO:

BELMONT UNIVERSITY
BROOKS, GARTH
GRAND OLE OPRY

A powerful vocalist, Trisha Yearwood once said music feels more like a calling than a choice. You can hear that in her voice and feel it when she sings: she was born for this.

Born in 1964 and raised in Monticello, Georgia, Yearwood moved to Nashville right after high school and studied music business at Belmont University. On weekends, she sang at a local bowling alley until she landed a job recording demos, which proved to be more profitable and flexible.

With no backup plan, Yearwood worked hard to become a solo artist and an internship at Mary Tyler Moore's Nashville label opened doors. By 1991, she had a record deal and was on the radio with "She's in Love with the Boy." The song shot to number one, making history as the first debut single by a female country artist to top the charts in 27 years. Her self-titled debut album proved to be a success and hits like "Wrong Side of Memphis," "Walkaway Joe," and "The Song Remembers When" followed. Her version of "How Do I Live," featured on the *Con Air* soundtrack, reached number two on the Billboard Country Chart.

Yearwood's career soared in the 1990s with wins at the Grammys, CMAs, and ACMs. She was inducted into the Grand Ole Opry in 1999. In the early 2000s, she continued

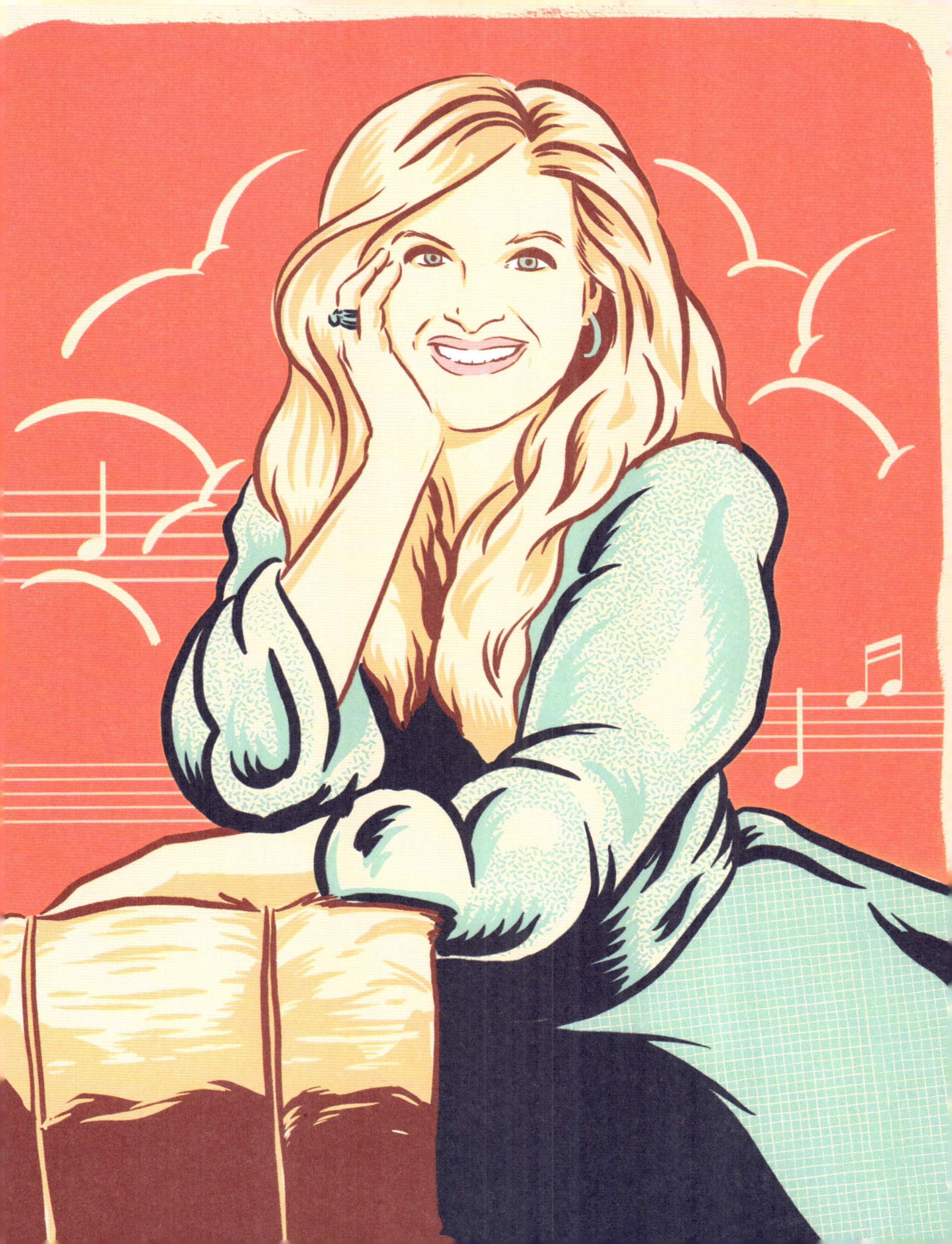

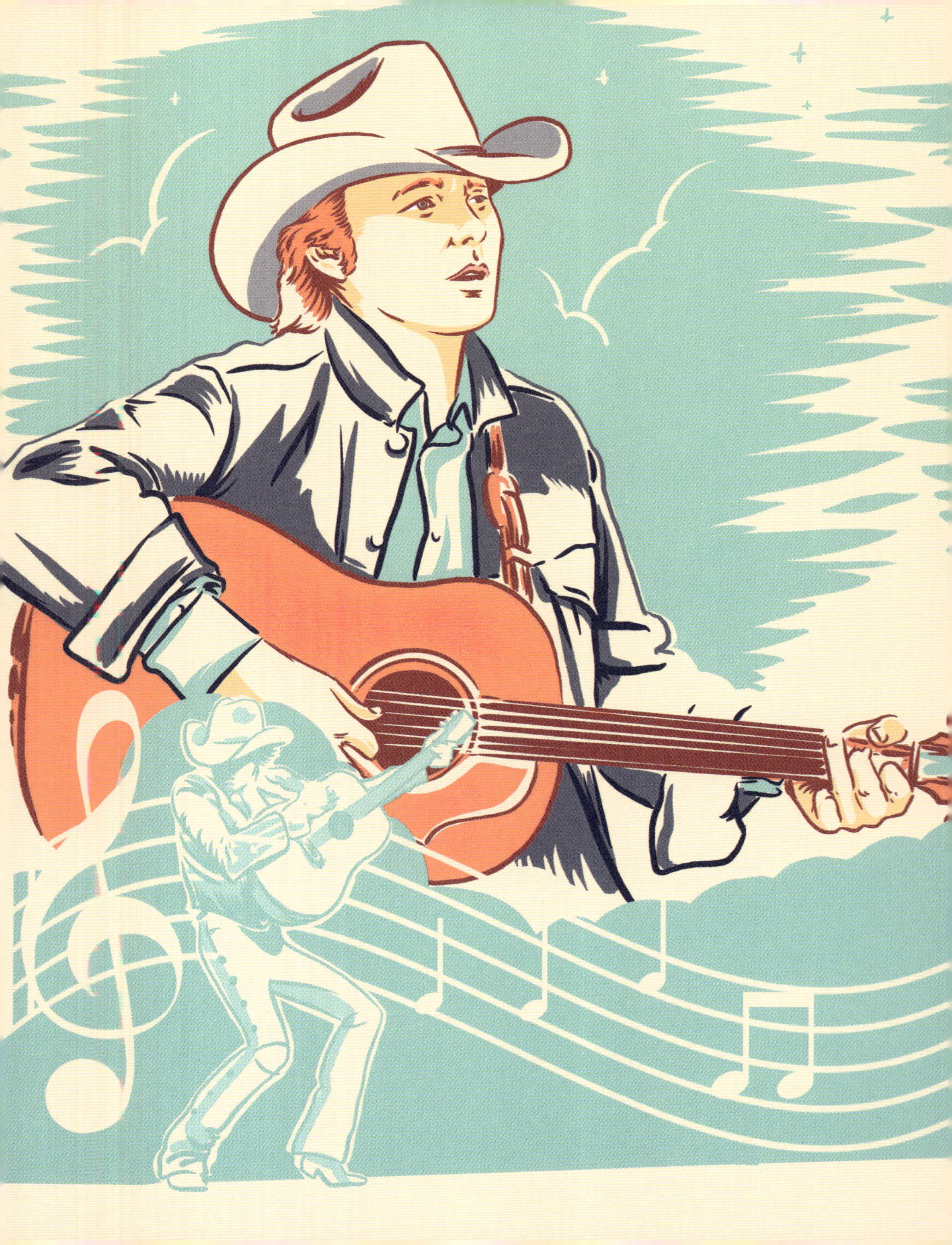

Y

releasing music, including the underrated "Georgia Rain," a soaring tale of young love that remains one of her best recordings. A woman of many talents, Yearwood also found success in the kitchen. Her Emmy-winning *Trisha's Southern Kitchen* ran for 17 seasons on Food Network. She's also published four best-selling cookbooks, sharing her beloved Southern recipes with fans across the world.

Early in her career, Yearwood formed a friendship with Garth Brooks. They sang background vocals on each other's debut albums, and he promised that if he ever made it big, he'd take her on tour. He kept that promise and more. In 1997, they recorded the duet "In Another's Eyes" and won a Grammy together the following year. Though they were both in relationships with other people at the time, they eventually found their way to each other. By 2005, they were married, and they've been inseparable ever since.

Yearwood continues to push herself as an artist, and in 2025 she released an album she fully co-wrote and co-produced for the first time, proving her country music story isn't over yet.

YOAKAM, DWIGHT

Dwight Yoakam's talents and contributions to country music are often underappreciated. A multitalented entertainer, the Kentucky native is known for blending (in his words) "country, rock, hillbilly, and bluegrass," and he reigned over the charts in the late 1980s and early 1990s.

Yoakam was born on October 23, 1956 in Kentucky, where he was introduced to country icons Johnny Cash and Hank Williams through his mother's record collection, and top 40 hitmakers like The Band via the radio. In high school, he played in various bands, experimenting with sounds ranging from country to rock 'n' roll.

After a short stint in college, Yoakam relocated to Nashville in 1977, ready to pursue a music career. He

Y

quickly learned, however, that Nashville's pop-country wave wasn't for him. Pivoting, he moved to Los Angeles and soon found success with what he called "hillbilly" music, becoming a founding father of the L.A. Cowpunk Scene, influenced by rockabilly and punk.

Following the release of an independent EP in 1984, Yoakam landed a record deal and released his debut album, *Guitars, Cadillacs, Etc., Etc.*, in 1986. That record produced his first top ten singles, including "Honky Tonk Man," a Johnny Horton cover, and "Guitars, Cadillacs," often cited as his signature song.

Yoakam rose to fame around the same time as Randy Travis, though their styles were vastly different. Yoakam was praised for his interpretation of the Bakersfield Sound, made famous by his heroes Buck Owens and Merle Haggard, while Travis led the charge for neo-traditional country. In 1988, Yoakam scored his first number one hit with "Streets of Bakersfield," a cover of Owens' classic, recorded alongside Owens himself. Continuing to bring new audiences to the genre with his distinctive voice, Yoakam went on to release hits like "Ain't That Lonely Yet" and "A Thousand Miles from Nowhere" in the early 1990s.

Proving his talents stretch beyond the stage, Yoakam has appeared in over 40 feature films, including *Sling Blade* and *Panic Room*. Though he's a two-time Grammy winner with more than 26 million albums sold worldwide, Yoakam has surprisingly never won a CMA Award. He received a Lifetime Achievement Award at the 2024 Americana Music Association Honors and Awards ceremony, and fans are rallying for him to earn his rightful place in the Country Music Hall of Fame.

"A multi-talented entertainer, Yoakam is known for blending country, rock, hillbilly, and bluegrass."

SEE ALSO:

BUCK OWENS' CRYSTAL PALACE

HAGGARD, MERLE

TRAVIS, RANDY

ABOUT THE AUTHOR

Lauren Black is the Editor-in-Chief at *Country Now*, one of the US's biggest sources of news about the country music scene, where she curates the program and has presented live concerts with various special guests. Spotlighted among Country Aircheck's Women of Influence, Black has previously held the role of Country Music Expert Writer for Answers.com and her work has been featured on Forbes.com. She has interviewed some of the industry's most prominent stars, including Reba McEntire, Blake Shelton, Luke Combs, Carrie Underwood, Luke Bryan, Miranda Lambert, Lainey Wilson, and many others. Black is a longtime member of the Country Music Association and the Academy of Country Music. This is her first book.

ABOUT THE ILLUSTRATOR

Travis Knight is an illustrator and artist from Chattanooga, Tennessee. His work is inspired by weathered vintage comics, antique postcards, and low-brow zines. He's a part-time musician who loves to take the short drive up to Nashville to enjoy the vibrant music scene. When not working he can often be found hiking in the Smoky Mountains with his dog Ronald. He has worked on commissions for The Cure, Metallica, Smashing Pumpkins, and more, and is a contributor to the cult horror magazine *Fangoria*.

Acknowledgments

Thank you to Andrew Roff and everyone at Greenfinch for believing in me, and in country music. To Emma Bastow, for managing this project and editing my words. And to Travis Knight, for bringing these stories to life with your beautiful illustrations.

To the artist managers, publicists, and teams who answered my calls and emails, you know who you are, and I'm so grateful. Special thanks to Zach Farnum, Donna Hughes, Ebie McFarland, Katy Robbins, and Jessie Schmidt for sharing your time and insights.

To Shannon Anderson, Erin Lefebvre, Madeleine O'Connell, and Andrew Wendowski: thank you for always being a shoulder to lean on and for your friendship along the way. And to everyone at Red Light Management, thank you for always having my back.

To Kenny Chesney: your music inspired me to chase my dreams, your live shows gave me an escape, and through you I've met fans who became lifelong friends. Your songs have truly been the soundtrack to my life.

And last but never least, Ryan, my amazing husband and best friend, and our two incredibly kind-hearted children. I couldn't have done this without your love and support. Thank you for cheering me on. I love you with all my heart.

To my family, Mom, Dad & Jackie, Bill & Kay, Amy & Paul, thank you for your love and encouragement.